W9-DGM-776

THAT GRAND WHIG, MILTON

THAT GRAND WHIG
MILTON

GEORGE F. SENSABAUGH

Benjamin Blom / *Publisher*

First published by Stanford University Press

Reissued 1967 by Benjamin Blom, Inc. Bx. 10452
by permission of the copyright holders
Library of Congress Catalog Card No. 67-29815

Printed in U.S.A. by
NOBLE OFFSET PRINTERS, INC.
NEW YORK 3, N. Y.

Ad Matrem et Patrem

PREFACE

Scholars in the politically minded twentieth century have given detailed attention to John Milton's positions on individual freedom and the nature of government. In 1934, for example, William Haller, in his *Tracts on Liberty in the Puritan Revolution*, pointed out Milton's relation to the contemporary cry over freedom of conscience; in 1941 Don M. Wolfe, in his *Milton in the Puritan Revolution*, depicted him against the background of political dispute during that time; in 1942 Arthur Barker, in *Milton and the Puritan Dilemma*, traced the development of his thought through the crucial decades of the Long Parliament and the Protectorate; and in 1945 Zera S. Fink, in *The Classical Republicans*, presented him as among those who, in the seventeenth century, found inspiration in the ancient theory of a mixed state. To these volumes may be added many articles and essays, which, taken together, have disclosed Milton's relation to the political and religious crosscurrents of his day or to political principles which allowed Englishmen to cut off the head of their king and to experiment with a Commonwealth government. Such studies have shown, among other things, that Milton grew with his age and that Milton the poet cannot be easily separated from Milton the political philosopher.

But whether Milton, through his polemical tracts, led many Englishmen of the seventeenth century to accept his positions on individual freedom and the nature of government has yet to be ascertained. For a number of years, to be sure, scholars accepted David Masson's assumption that Milton exerted a powerful influence in politics during his own time; but William Riley Parker, in *Milton's Contemporary Reputation*, could find little to support such an assumption, and to date no important testimony has come to light to reverse his conclusion that Milton played a relatively minor role in the stirring drama of the Puritan Rebellion. The legend of Milton the statesman, however, which Masson invoked, still whets curiosity; and if it now seems fairly certain that during his own time Milton failed to achieve the political stature often attributed to him, this hardly precludes the possibility that he might have become, as sometimes suggested, a significant figure later in the seventeenth century, when Whig principles of government triumphed in Englishmen's minds. Effectiveness in political disputes at this time would, in a sense, give him a greater claim to true statesmanship than would influence during the Puritan Rebellion inasmuch as the Commonwealth withered for lack of support, whereas Whig theories of government, ratified in the Revolutionary Settlement and in the Bill of Rights, still lie at the basis of English society and indeed animate free men everywhere in the Western world. This study therefore purposes to trace the impact of Milton's arguments in the battle of ideas which led to the acceptance of the Settlement and the Bill of Rights, to examine sermons, newspapers, broadsides, and tracts for testimony to measure his importance during a period of significant political change.

Titles have been shortened and normalized, and obvious errors in punctuation and spelling silently corrected. Greek words have been frequently transliterated into Latin, unless for some reason it seemed wise to retain the original; but most seventeenth-century usages have been maintained in the quotations. Unsigned tracts or those of doubtful origin have been sometimes assigned to authors in accordance with listings in *The Dictionary of National Biography* or in Donald Wing's *Short-Title Catalogue.*

Thanks should be extended to Godfrey Davies, French R. Fogle, and Virgil K. Whitaker, who read the manuscript and made many useful suggestions, and to John Robert Moore, who generously gave me several late seventeenth-century references to Milton. John Walter Good, William Riley Parker, Dora Neill Raymond, and George W. Whiting have also, through their publications, furnished me with a number of references, some of which have been incorporated into this volume. I am grateful to the editors of *Modern Language Notes* and *Studies in Philology*, to the Trustees of the Henry E. Huntington Library, and to the editorial committee of the recent group of essays entitled *The Seventeenth Century* by Richard Foster Jones and others, published by the Stanford University Press, for permission to use, in part, several articles already in print. And it is only fitting to say that without help from the American Council of Learned Societies and fellowships granted by the John Simon Guggenheim Foundation and the Huntington Library this volume could never have been brought to completion.

G. F. S.

STANFORD UNIVERSITY
STANFORD, CALIFORNIA
January 30, 1952

CONTENTS

Chapter One

A REVOLUTIONARY PROGRAM

JOHN MILTON, during the tumultuous years of the Puritan Rebellion, presented to the people of England through a series of controversial tracts a revolutionary program for man and society. More than midway through this series, he claimed for his program a certain unity of plan inasmuch as, by philosophic design, he had, as needs of the conflict arose, successively turned his attention to religious, domestic, and civil liberty. Few readers of the present age, however, would contend that his tracts as a whole possess an inner unity or reveal an organic growth; perhaps most would agree that specific events inspired even his most philosophical pamphlets and that in consequence his thought changed with the times. Moreover, no one could argue that Milton maintained through his program an elevation of style. Conflict with religious and political enemies spurred him to master a kind of invective that made even the most experienced pamphleteers in an acrimonious age appear, by comparison, but rank amateurs. But such limitations neither prevented Milton from recognizing the issues which stood at the heart of seventeenth-century political conflict nor marred his rhetoric when he sought to resolve them. Indeed, through the whole of his program he repeatedly wrote with a compelling eloquence on liberty of conscience and the power of kings, twin issues upon which both the Puritan Rebellion and the Glorious Revolution turned; and his willingness, at the very moment of his poetical ripening, to doff his singing robes and plunge into a sea of hoarse disputes, as well as his later acceptance of the Latin secretariat under the Commonwealth government, testifies that he wished to become through his tracts a significant political figure, that he dreamed of making the people of England then, and in aftertimes, listen to the voice of reason and convincement and tread to the measure of his thought.

During the Puritan Rebellion, however, Milton neither achieved in the eyes of his countrymen the political stature he so evidently desired nor noticeably influenced their habits of mind.[1] This is not

[1] See William Riley Parker, *Milton's Contemporary Reputation* (Columbus, 1940). For Milton's importance as a revolutionary thinker, see Merritt Y. Hughes, "Milton as a Revolutionary," *English Literary History*, X (1943), 87–116.

to say that his voice went unheard, or that either his enemies or friends remained silent concerning his program for man and society. No less a worthy than Thomas Fuller,[2] for example, noticed *Of Reformation in England*, Milton's initial skirmish in prose with the prelates and with episcopal establishment endorsed by Archbishop Laud; and *The Doctrine and Discipline of Divorce* elicited a full-dress reply shortly after it had dropped from the press.[3] Moreover, John Goodwin's *The Obstructours of Justice*, which contended that Charles I had been justly tried and sentenced to death, leaned heavily upon Milton's *The Tenure of Kings and Magistrates*, a debt to which marginal notes gave recognition;[4] and after the Commonwealth government secured Milton as its Secretary of Foreign Tongues his fame grew apace. *Eikonoklastes*, his official answer to the reputed King's Book, *Eikon Basilike*, attracted attention at home; *Pro Populo Anglicano Defensio*, his reply in the name of the Commonwealth government to the *Defensio Regia* of the international scholar Claudius Salmasius, brought him fame in the Continent—not so great as to make all Europe talk from side to side, as Milton himself claimed, but widespread enough to frighten his enemies and to cause his *Defensio* to be burned at both Paris and Toulouse.[5] In addition to this, notices of *Eikonoklastes* and *Pro Populo Anglicano Defensio*, some of which revealed an admiration and respect for Milton's genuine abilities, appeared in *Mercurius Politicus*, an authorized paper of the Commonwealth government.[6] Such notices, coupled with many others, argue that Milton drew increasing attention as he continued to unfold his program for liberty, though his fame diminished somewhat as the Restoration approached; yet it would be an error to say that he achieved, even during the time of his greatest eminence as Secretary of Foreign Tongues, a position of influence and power in the realm of public opinion commensurate, for example, with that which Oliver Cromwell secured on the field of battle or Henry Vane in the House of Commons.[7] Sober reflection on

[2] *The Holy State* (Cambridge, 1642), Bk. IV, chap. xi, pp. 291-92.

[3] *An Answer to a Book, Intituled, The Doctrine and Discipline of Divorce, Or, A Plea for Ladies and Gentlewomen, and all other Maried Women against Divorce* (London, 1644).

[4] *The Obstructours of Justice* (London, 1649), *passim*.

[5] See J. G. Robertson, "Milton's Fame on the Continent," from *The Proceedings of the British Academy*, III (London, 1908), 2.

[6] J. Milton French, "Milton, Needham, and *Mercurius Politicus*," *Studies in Philology*, XXXIII (1936), 236–52. But see also Elmer A. Beller, "Milton and *Mercurius Politicus*," *The Huntington Library Quarterly*, V (1942), 479–87.

[7] David Masson, in *The Life of John Milton* (London, 1873), III, 434, assumed that Milton, from 1645 onward, exerted influence in the field of pamphleteering comparable to that exercised by Cromwell and Vane in their respective realms of endeavor; but such an assumption cannot be sup-

Milton's political career forces the conclusion that he played a relatively minor role in the march of events during the Puritan Rebellion, that, however much he prodded his enemies or pleased his friends, few disciples within the government, or without, gathered at his feet to hear words of wisdom. His influence upon the minds of men, and hence in affairs of the day, was relatively slender.

But in the Age of Reason disciples flocked to his banner. John Toland, the celebrated deist presumably in the pay of the Whig party, for instance, extolled Milton as a defender of freedom through an extended biography, and before the seventeenth century closed spread Milton's political principles abroad through two editions of his prose tracts, the first collections of this kind to appear. Charles Gildon, in the last year of the century, claimed that Milton was not only an author of "Genius and Learning" but also a "strenuous Defender of the Power and Liberty of the People";[8] and with the ushering in of the new age, radical Whigs like Thomas Birch, Richard Baron, Francis Blackburne, and Thomas Hollis openly proclaimed Milton's political significance, republished his tracts, and worked out his principles through their own party activities and writings.[9] Milton, indeed, became to these men an "Oracle" of political wisdom, worthy to be read and studied by all the young gentlemen of England—a "*great and noble Genius, perhaps the greatest that ever appeared among men*," an author whose works were "*substantial, durable, eternal*" and hence would "*never perish whilst Reason, Truth, and Liberty have a Being in these Nations*."[10] In view of such uninhibited praise it would perhaps not be far from the truth to say that many Whigs in the Age of Reason considered Milton a main source of their strength and shaped their political principles in accordance with those expressed in his program for man and society.

The relatively minor role Milton played in shaping opinion during the Puritan Rebellion and the enthusiasm with which Whigs in the eighteenth century officially embraced him are stories well known and hence need no further recalling. What is not known is how Mil-

ported with evidence. See William Riley Parker, *op. cit., passim.* Even *Areopagitica* fell almost stillborn from the press. See William Haller, *Tracts on Liberty in the Puritan Revolution* (New York, 1934), Vol. I, for an account of Milton's reputation and influence from 1643 to 1647, and *The Huntington Library Quarterly*, XII (1949), 207–12, for "Two Early Allusions to Milton's *Areopagitica*."

[8] *The Lives and Characters Of The English Dramatick Poets* (London, 1699), p. 100.

[9] See John Walter Good, *Studies in the Milton Tradition* (Urbana, Ill., 1915), pp. 174–75.

[10] *Eikonoklastes*, ed. Richard Baron (London, 1756), Preface, pp. iv-v.

ton rose from comparative neglect to his position of eminence, how during the politically convulsed period from the Restoration of Charles II to the ascent of Queen Anne his opinions gained ground and silently won for him many disciples, some of whom stood high in Whig councils. This rise in power and influence in the face of Tory opposition is by far the most fascinating story of all. For during this period England witnessed a Glorious Revolution in political theory as well as in the dynasties of kings. Liberty of conscience, the persistant cry of Puritans and Whigs alike, became widely enough accepted in the last decade of the seventeenth century to support an Act of Toleration and to allow a permanent lapse of the Licensing Act, long a weapon of state for suppressing objectionable views. Moreover, the concept of absolute monarchy by virtue of divine right, the main Tory prop for the tottering House of Stuart, gave way at the Glorious Revolution before the theory of compact, a Whig position which placed William and Mary on the English throne. The Revolutionary Settlement and the Bill of Rights, which secured individual liberties and confirmed the rationality of constitutional government, though achieved by a practical coalition of both Tories and Whigs, nevertheless stood as triumphs of Whig political theory, testaments of Whig victory in the great debates whose issues had been crystallized in the Puritan Rebellion. If Milton contributed to this triumph through his revolutionary program, if Whigs made effective use of his tracts in whole or in part to argue against licensing acts and the divine right of kings, and for toleration, a free press, and the theory of compact, then John Toland and Richard Baron, together with their Whig fraternity in the Age of Reason, quite rightly raised Milton to a position of eminence and recommended him as an oracle to all young gentlemen in England. He in fact contributed so vigorously to the victory of principles which lay at the basis of the Revolutionary Settlement and the Bill of Rights that long before Whigs of the eighteenth century made him an oracle of political wisdom Tories had already with accuracy, if with considerable irony, deemed him "that grand Whig *Milton.*"

II

The story of how Milton contributed to the triumph of Whig views best begins with a glance at the clash of opinion to which he addressed his revolutionary program for man and society. This clash, it must be immediately stated, encompassed so many issues that no attempt can be made to sweep the entire field of conflict. It is sufficient to say for the present that the Puritan Rebellion widely affected English society, that it vigorously invaded the realms of law, economics, religion, and politics. Moreover, the conflict not only covered a broad range of issues; it grew increasingly complex with the passage of time. As friction between Puritan and Anglican in the reign of James I, for instance, eventually flamed into open hostilities between Parliament and Crown, which in turn led to the executions of Archbishop Laud and Charles I, factional quarrels and shifts in allegiance often blurred strict partisan lines. Presbyterians, to cite one example, supported Parliament in the first years of the war; but, after Royalist reverses at Marston Moor and Naseby and the emergence of the New Model Army, they split with the Independents and before the establishment of the Commonwealth government under Oliver Cromwell began to sympathize with the cause of the King. Such shifts among Puritans, coupled with a diversity of opinion expressed on each side, militate against taking any simplified view of the conflict.

It is nevertheless safe to say that the Puritan Rebellion pivoted on the issues of liberty of conscience and the power of kings; and nowhere did the main pro and con arguments concerning these issues emerge more significantly than in the pronouncements of James I, the *Constitutions and Canons Ecclesiasticall* of 1640, the Whitehall debates held by the Council of Officers of the New Model Army, and the official Commonwealth version of the trial of Charles I. These responsible sources not only simplified and sharpened the main arguments concerning these matters at the turn and during the first half of the seventeenth century but also fixed a pattern of dispute which later politicians could easily embroider to fit the needs of *their* day. Here indeed may be found in crystallized form the clash over issues which vexed the entire reign of the Stuarts in England, the debate which Whigs and Tories continued to argue but could not resolve satisfactorily in the public mind until the end of the century. A glance at this basic pattern as it emerged in the Puritan Rebellion, therefore, followed by an analysis of how closely Milton hewed to its lines, should serve to make clear not simply the continuity of the conflict, but the significance of Milton's revolutionary program to the debate of the century as well and hence how it could contribute to the triumph of Whig views. How did this pattern unfold?

James I, shortly before his elevation to the English throne, took a clear stand on the power of kings in *The trew Law of free Monarchies,* a treatise in which he purposed to establish a concept of absolute regal supremacy by reference to divine, natural, and civil law. Turning first to testimony in the divine law, which meant to James I, as to most men of his time, the truth as revealed in Scripture, he retold the Old Testament story of Samuel as evidence that a king ruled by divine right and hence possessed absolute supremacy over his people. He recalled how Samuel, in view of the people's request for a king, had consulted God and then had reported to them what the Lord had disclosed. The sort of king that God revealed to Samuel was an absolute monarch, James I maintained, citing the details of the story; such a king would take his people's vineyards and fields and their servants and children. Yet such a revelation failed to deter the desires of the people to be so ruled and judged or to have a king fight their battles. This relationship between king and subject, James I contended, ought indeed "bee a paterne to all Christian and well founded Monarchies, as beeing founded by God himselfe, who by his Oracle, and out of his owne mouth gaue the law thereof";[11] and he went ahead to say that since the people of Samuel's time had no "leaue to shake off the yoke, which God thorow their importunity" had laid upon them, so people in Christian kingdoms had no such leave either.

The position of James I on the power of kings was thus clear; and to support it further he referred to the story of David and Saul, a tale which became stock-in-trade among Royalist clergymen during the seventeenth century. To James I, David had acted in an exemplary fashion when, in spite of cruel persecutions, he had not presumed, even after he had Saul in his power, "but with great reuerence, to touch the garment of the annoynted of the Lord."[12] To these stories from the Old Testament James I added the testimony of St. Paul, who had bade the Romans to serve Nero for the sake of conscience, despite Nero's record as a bloody tyrant, a "monster to the world," and an "idolatrous persecutor."[13] James I, in fact, found Scripture every-

[11] *The Workes Of The Most High and Mightie Prince, Iames By The Grace of God, King Of Great Britaine, France and Ireland, Defender of the Faith, &c.* (London, 1616), p. 199.

[12] *Idem.*

[13] *Ibid.*, p. 200.

where maintaining his thesis. The kingdoms described in the Old Testament, the commands of the saints, and the injunction of Christ himself to render "to *Cæsar* that which was *Cæsars,* and to God that which was Gods," made it evident to him that monarchy was of divine right, that rulers should possess absolute power, that rebellion against them was, in a sense, rebellion against God Himself. Weaving together his theory derived from the divine law, he concluded that obedience of a people to their lawful king ought to be "as to Gods Lieutenant in earth," that they should obey "his commands in all things, except directly against God, as the commands of Gods Minister, acknowledging him a Iudge set by GOD ouer them, hauing power to iudge them, but to be iudged onely by GOD, whom to onely hee must giue count of his iudgement." Furthermore, the people should fear the king as their judge, love him as their father, and pray for him as their protector, asking for his continuance, if he be good, for his amendment, if he be wicked; and if the king should make unlawful demands, they should eschew and fly his fury without resistance, protesting only "by sobbes and teares to God, according to that sentence vsed in the primitiue Church in the time of the persecution": *Preces, & Lachrymæ sunt arma Ecclesiæ.*[14] Though James I conceded that a people need not obey regal commands which ran directly against God, it is to be noted that he gave them no right to determine such contradictions; and even could they perceive when their king acted unjustly, their resistance could be only passive, in accordance with the example of the primitive Christians. To James I, sound monarchical government stood squarely on the doctrine of divine right in kings and passive obedience in subjects; to him it was a "shamelesse presumption" in any Christian people "to claime to that vnlawfull libertie, which God refused to his owne peculiar and chosen people."

Though Scripture fully revealed to James I the extent of regal authority, he nevertheless supported his theory further by reference to the "fundamentall and ciuill Lawe" and to the laws of nature, as was the custom in seventeenth-century polemics. Civil law he found in the chronicles of Ireland, Scotland, and England, which he claimed revealed the supremacy of the king over Parliament and indeed over the law itself. Parliament, he declared, "is nothing else but the head Court of the king and his vassals," it lying "in the power of no Parlia-

[14] *Ibid.,* pp. 200–201.

ment, to make any kinde of Lawe or Statute, without his Scepter be to it, for giuing it the force of a Law."[15] This principle gleaned from these chronicles, like fundamental laws, such as those governing hoards, for example, made it manifest to James I "that the King is ouer-Lord of the whole land: so is he Master ouer euery person that inhabiteth the same, hauing power ouer the life and death of euery one of them: For although a iust Prince will not take the life of any of his subiects without a cleare law; yet the same lawes whereby he taketh them, are made by himselfe, or his predecessours; and so the power flowes alwaies from him selfe."[16] From such a reading of the chronicles only one conclusion could follow: "the King is aboue the law, as both the author and giuer of strength thereto";[17] but it is only fair to say that James I softened this iron position by claiming that good kings delighted in ruling by law and in making their actions conform to the chief law of the land, the safety of the commonwealth. Nevertheless, James I found in the history of the British Isles civil laws which maintained his theory of regal supremacy; and the laws of nature likewise spoke in his behalf, as two similitudes made clear. By the very nature of things, James I briefly explained, a good father will govern wisely but will suffer no disobedience from his children, and a good head, as the seat of judgment, will exercise "care and foresight of guiding, and preuenting all euill that may come to the body or any part thereof."[18] The self-evident laws of nature, as well as the civil laws of society, simply supported in a different way the theory of regal supremacy so evident in the pages of Scripture. Reason made the theory manifest in civil and natural laws; the divine law itself became known through direct revelation.

Since James I believed that all relevant authority supported the absolute supremacy of the king and that as the Lord's anointed the monarch was responsible not to his people but to God alone, he found no trouble refuting, many years before the Puritan-Anglican conflict broke out in open hostilities, the arguments of all apologists of revolt against the Crown. For example, he recalled and dismissed summarily those who believed it their natural right to free their country from tyrannous kings, who claimed that rebellion against wicked princes was acceptable to God, and who contended that God must favor

[15] *The Workes Of The Most High and Mightie Prince*, p. 202.

[16] *Ibid.*, p. 203.

[17] *Idem.*

[18] *Ibid.*, p. 204.

such uprisings in view of so many successful revolts. He recalled, too, those who maintained that at the time of coronation a king made a compact with his people, a pact of mutual responsibility which relieved the people of their oath if the king failed to keep his part of the agreement, though he knew that these apologists could not, in view of the immemorial Coronation Oath, sworn by the monarchs of England, be dismissed with a pat answer. Indeed, he spent some time in an attempt to belittle the venerable custom. The Coronation Oath could not be called a compact, he stated; but even if it could, who could judge when the agreement was broken and who, except God, could sentence a king? The truth about monarchies, James I then explained, was that kings came into the possession of their crowns not by compact but by the laws of inheritance. From the very nature of Christian commonwealths in their beginnings, he continued, it should be evident that subjects swore duty and allegiance not simply to the living ruler but to all his lawful heirs and posterity as well. Hence it followed that it was unlawful to displace the hereditary successor to the crown; "For at the very moment of the expiring of the king reigning, the nearest and lawful heire entreth in his place: And so to refuse him, or intrude another, is not to holde out vncomming in, but to expell and put out their righteous King."[19] James I thus saw the theory of compact, with its mutual commitments on both subject and king, as actually unlawful, a potential source of conflict rather than a bond of agreement. The laws of primogeniture, coupled with authority by divine right, as well as the pronouncements of civil and natural law—all appeared to him as direct refutations of the notion that kings ascended their thrones through an agreement with their people and could hence hold their positions only so long as they kept their part of the contract.

The theory of James I on the power of kings received the official sanction of his son, Charles I, and became the announced policy of his government in the *Constitutions and Canons Ecclesiasticall* of 1640. Prepared by the Archbishops of Canterbury and York with the help of their clergy, these canons not only upheld the positions of James I but also indicated in specific detail the privileges of kings and the duties of subjects. The results of attempting to put into practice the principles expressed in these canons need not be told here; suffice it to say that both Archbishop Laud and Charles I acted upon them and

[19] *Ibid.*, p. 209.

soon met death on the scaffold. In the realm of theory they are important inasmuch as they reveal how far the government of Charles I had gone in supporting the doctrine of absolute royal supremacy. The document, indeed, opened with one of the clearest and most straightforward definitions of regal power to appear in the seventeenth century, the very first canon stating unequivocally that "The most High and Sacred order of Kings is of Divine right, being the ordinance of God himself, founded on the prime Laws of nature, and clearly established by expresse texts both of the old and new Testaments." A "supream Power" was given to "this most excellent Order by God himself in the Scriptures," the canon continued, that is, "That Kings should rule and command in their severall dominions all persons of what rank or estate soever, whether Ecclesiasticall or Civill, and that they should restrain and punish with the temporall sword all stubborn and wicked doers."[20] In consequence of this injunction, it became treasonable for any person or persons in the kingdom to set up, maintain, or avow, "under any pretence whatsoever, any independent Coactive power, either Papall or Popular (whether directly or indirectly)" that might challenge royal authority.[21] Moreover, even bearing defensive arms against the king appeared as resistance against the powers ordained by God and hence punishable, in the words of St. Paul, with eternal damnation. The official announcement of the government of Charles I through the *Constitutions and Canons Ecclesiasticall* of 1640 thus accorded the king absolute power over the lives and consciences of his subjects. Furthermore, subjects owed the king "Tribute, and Custome, and Aide, and Subsidie, and all manner of necessary support and supply," since such duties had been ordained by the "Law of God, Nature, and Nations, for the publicke defence, care and protection of them"; but it was only "part of the Kingly office to support his subjects in the property and freedom of their estates."[22] The Archbishops of Canterbury and York in this way translated the theory of divine right into practical duties and rights—duties which demanded much from the subject and rights which claimed more for the king. In view of such doctrine, Charles I quite accurately announced as he went to his death that subject and king were "clean" different things.

[20] *Constitutions and Canons Ecclesiasticall* (London, 1640), sig. [B4v].
[21] *Ibid.*, sig. C.
[22] *Ibid.*, sig. Cv.

The theory of absolute regal supremacy by divine right as expressed in *The trew Law of free Monarchies* and in the *Constitutions and Canons Ecclesiasticall* could give only one answer to the issue of freedom of conscience. As supreme arbiter in all matters religious as well as civil, the king possessed the right to bend all subjects to his will, or to declare an indulgence. James I, at any rate, apparently took this position, though he presented less clearly his notions on liberty of conscience than those on the theory of divine right. In his opening address to Parliament in 1603, for example, he announced that he had been ever "free from persecution," or from "thralling" his "Subjects in matters of Conscience";[23] yet such assurances, as he took over his duties as monarch of England, hardly squared with his later practice, as witnesses both in Holland and in America loudly testified before his reign came to a close. Moreover, in his *Basilikon Doron*, a book of kingly advice addressed to Prince Henry, his son, he revealed a definite hostility toward those who, for the sake of conscience, had not bent to his will. Take heed of the Puritans, he advised Prince Henry; they are the pests of the commonwealth, "whom no deserts can oblige, neither oaths or promises binde, breathing nothing but sedition and calumnies, aspiring without measure, railing without reason, and making their owne imaginations (without any warrant of the word) the square of their conscience."[24] Such men, he continued, could not be endured if peace were desired in the realm. In theory, then, James I apparently stood against liberty of conscience; but in practice he persecuted nonconformists or granted them indulgence in accordance with political expedience. Both persecution and indulgence became in his hands instruments of state policy for securing order and peace.

The *Constitutions and Canons Ecclesiasticall* officially announced sentiments on liberty of conscience very much like those expressed by James I. The design of Canon III, for example, was to prevent the growth of popery, and the aim of Canon V was to suppress faction, including "All Anabaptists, Brownists, Separatists, Familists, or other Sect or Sects." Such canons intimated that Anglicans alone possessed legal status in the community; and their avowed purpose was to make every citizen an Anglican and every Anglican a citizen in the hope

[23] *The Workes Of The Most High and Mightie Prince*, pp. 490–93.

[24] *Ibid.*, pp. 160–61.

that such uniformity would bring order and peace to the State. The Church indeed, at least theoretically, became at the hands of the clergy little more than an adjunct to the State, an instrument of cohesion in civil society, though the Archbishops of Canterbury and York would of course have denied this logical extension. Nevertheless, the cry of *No Bishop, no King*, which animated many Anglicans during the first part of the seventeenth century, might have been more accurately phrased, *No King, no Bishop*. The State had in theory encompassed the Church and the king stood supreme over both.

The pronouncements of James I and the proclaimed policy of his son concerning liberty of conscience found direct answers in the Whitehall debates.[25] Begun on December 14, 1648, by the Council of Officers of the New Model Army and continued to the very eve of the trial of Charles I, these debates were addressed to the specific question, "Whether the magistrate have, or ought to have, any compulsive and restrictive power in matters of religion?" This question, so pointedly aimed at Stuart theory and policy, took John Lilburne and other officers, together with John Goodwin, through many carefully phrased statements, replies, and rebuttals touching on the nature of sovereignty and the purpose of government; and as might be expected, they differed sharply on many details. But some agreed that the good of the individual and hence of society depended upon removing the power of the state from the realm of religion and upon granting liberty of conscience. It is true that they could not free their minds of a state-supported religion, but liberty of conscience became a cardinal tenet in their final Agreement, Article IX of which summarized their meeting of minds on this matter. This article stated that the Christian religion should be "held forth and recommended as the public profession" of England, and "That to the public profession so held forth, none be compelled by penalties or otherwise; but only may be endeavoured to be won by sound doctrine, and the example of good conversation." Furthermore, it declared "That such as profess faith in God by Jesus Christ, however differing in judgment from the doctrine, worship, or discipline publicly held forth as aforesaid, shall not be restrained from, but shall be protected in, the profession of their faith and exercise of religion according to their consciences, in any place except such as shall be set apart for the public worship . . . so

[25] See A. S. P. Woodhouse, *Puritanism and Liberty* (London, 1938), pp. 125–69, for the text of these debates.

as they abuse not this liberty to the civil injury of others, or to actual disturbance of the public peace on their parts."[26] The Council of Officers could not, however, "necessarily extend to popery or prelacy" the liberty of worship they freely granted to others, since both Catholics and Angelicans, to their way of thinking, would, if in power, curtail freedom of conscience and persecute those considered unorthodox. For the good of the state, then, toleration could hardly be extended to those who opposed toleration; but all other Christians could profess faith and exercise religion according to conscience. Such a view, which conceived of Church and State operating in separate spheres and recognized sectaries as citizens of the community, directly opposed the announced theories and policies of James and Charles I.

If the Agreement of the Council of Officers concerning liberty of conscience contrasts sharply with the official policy of the House of Stuart, the speeches of John Bradshawe, who presided at the trial of Charles I, show a difference as clear on the power of kings. On the very first day of the trial, January 20, 1649, Charles I asked by what authority he had been brought before the High Court of Justice, and to the question he posed on that day, he heard John Bradshawe answer, "in the name of the People of *England*," by whose sufferance the king had been elected to office.[27] Such an answer brought a reply from Charles I that the Crown of England was not then nor ever had been elective. It was "Hereditary," he claimed, and had been so for nigh one thousand years. Moreover, as the trial continued he repeatedly maintained that as king he could not be "tryed by any Superiour Jurisdiction on Earth," a Stuart argument to which John Bradshawe just as repeatedly replied that he was being called to account by "the supream Authority of the Commons of *England* assembled in Parliament."

On the last day of the proceedings, January 27, 1649, Bradshawe reviewed the whole case, answering in detail the claims of Charles I. The King, he admitted, had spoken very well of that precious thing called peace; what a pity he had not studied the peace of the kingdom as well as he had spoken of it at the trial! But actions, Bradshawe contended, must "expound intentions," and the King's actions had been "clean contrary" to what he had claimed. Moreover, Bradshawe

[26] Woodhouse, *op. cit.*, pp. 361–62, n. 26.

[27] *King Charls His Tryal: Or A perfect Narrative of the whole Proceedings of the High Court of Iustice In The Tryal of the King in Westminster Hall* (London, 1649), p. 6.

continued, the King had "let fall such Language" as if he had "been no waies Subject to the Law" and had acted as if the law had not been his "Superiour." At this point he admonished Charles I for not ruling by law, though he conceded that the King had said that he had. The main question, Bradshawe went on, was who expounded the law: the King and his party, or the courts of justice? It was not lawful, he declared, for the King to set his single judgment and that of his adherents against the highest court of justice. Furthermore, who made the law—the King, or the King and the High Court of Justice, that is, the Parliament of England? To Bradshawe it was clear that Parliament was the sole maker of law, and that superior to the law itself, as the ultimate "Parent or Author" thereof, stood the "People of England."[28] He held as entirely "erronious" the principle that the King was the sole *legis lator*, or that, in accordance with the Stuart theory of divine right, a sovereign could not be judged by his people.

Such a position needed the support of authority. Consequently, Bradshawe turned to the ancient and venerable lawyer, Henry de Bracton, whose *De Legibus* carried considerable weight in the seventeenth century. In Book I, chapter viii, of *De Legibus* Bracton had said that the king was under God only, that in his kingdom he possessed no peer: *Parem autem non habet in regno suo.*[29] Now, Bradshawe explained, this statement should be interpreted to mean that the king had no peer in the sense that he was *major singulis* but *minor universis*—that is to say, above every individual but under the whole body politic. Since Royalists had employed this very passage to prove the supremacy of regal authority, Bradshawe invoked other statements from *De Legibus*, particularly the oft-used phrase from Book II, chapter xvi, which claimed that God and the law were superior to the king, as well as his barons and counts, who as his peers could put a curb upon him "if the king be without a bridle, that is without law."[30] In addition to Bracton's work, Bradshawe turned to the chronicles of England and Scotland to substantiate his position of Parliamentary

[28] *King Charls His Tryal*, pp. 31–32.

[29] *Ibid.*, p. 32. For the original passage in Bracton, see *Henrici De Bracton De Legibus Et Consuetudinibus Angliæ* (ed. Sir Travers Twiss, London, 1878), I, 38.

[30] *Ibid.*, pp. 32–33. For the context of this passage, see Sir Travers Twiss, *op. cit.*, I, 269. This much-mooted passage, which appears to contradict some of Bracton's other pronouncements, has been explained as one of the many *"addiciones"* to *De Legibus*, that is, one of the doubtful passages added later by another hand. See George E. Woodbine, *Bracton De Legibus Et Consuetudinibus Angliae* (New Haven, 1922), II, 110. See also David Ogg, *England in the Reign of Charles II* (Oxford, 1934), II, 452 and note, for a discussion of how Bracton was employed in seventeenth-century political controversy and of the difficulties in interpreting him.

supremacy. Here, in contrast to the findings of James I, he discovered in the oaths of coronation a theory of compact. He admitted, to be sure, that kings of England ascended their thrones by the laws of heredity; yet he stressed that in a just cause the people might refuse them the crown. For, he continued, "there is a contract and a bargaine made betweene the King and his People," a contract with reciprocal duties and rights; and if this "one tye," this "one bond" holding people and king together should be broken, then "farewell Soveraignty."[31] Such was Bradshawe's answer to the Anglican doctrine of hereditary succession, and such was his justification of the trial of Charles I. Whatever irregularities and illegalities may have attended the trial itself, he cannot be accused of misunderstanding the fundamental issues at stake. In his claim that the law was superior to the king and not the king to the law, and in his challenge to hereditary succession with the theory of compact, he struck at the core of seventeenth-century conflict. His answers to Charles I rang through political controversies during the next fifty years.

Responsible sources thus clearly evidenced a fundamental division of mind over liberty of conscience and the power of kings. On the one side stood those who believed in church uniformity and in divine right; on the other, those who contended for freedom of worship and for the theory of compact. The main pro and con arguments embedded in this basic pattern of conflict not only met squarely the issues of the Puritan Rebellion but also guided political disputes to the ascent of Queen Anne. Indeed, in the pronouncements of James I, the *Constitutions and Canons Ecclesiasticall*, the Agreement of the Council of Officers, and the speeches of Bradshawe appeared the debate of the century, the controversy which remained unresolved until Englishmen accepted the principles underlying the Revolutionary Settlement and the Bill of Rights. If Milton followed this basic pattern, he therefore spoke to the debate of the century; and if he clothed the main arguments of his day in eloquent language, men in aftertimes would be likely to remember and use what he said.

III

Both as a private citizen and as a public official Milton spent a good deal of time and some of his best efforts attempting to resolve in the

[31] *King Charls His Tryal*, p. 39.

minds of his countrymen questions concerning liberty of conscience and the power of kings. No need exists to present all that he said on these issues, or to point out how his thought grew as he developed his program for man and society.[32] It will be sufficient to examine his chief arguments, whether they appear early or late, and to note how closely they followed the basic pattern of dispute that emerged during the Puritan Rebellion. Such a procedure should clarify at once the significance of Milton's revolutionary program to the debate of the century.

In his very first pamphlet, *Of Reformation in England*, Milton addressed himself to the burning question of religious persecution and liberty of conscience. He deplored that "freeborn" Englishmen and "good Christians" had been compelled through Stuart policy to forsake their dearest homeland to seek freedom on the "wide Ocean" and in "the savage deserts of *America*" because their "conscience could not assent to things which the Bishops thought *indifferent*."[33] But he did more than deplore such persecution. He argued, in *The Reason of Church-Government Urg'd Against Prelaty*, that Church and State should be separate, that only when ecclesiastical power and civil power moved in different realms could conscience be free—a position which he developed in greatest detail in two late pamphlets, *A Treatise of Civil Power* and *Considerations Touching the Likliest Means to Remove Hirelings out of the Church*. Milton never tired repeating this argument, for he believed it fundamental to the achievement of freedom of conscience; he even went beyond Article IX of the Agreement, rejecting state religion in any form and emphasizing the Pauline concept of Christian liberty, which freed man from Old Testament ceremonial and canon law. Even his divorce tracts may be considered pleas for such liberty; but *Areopagitica*, aimed primarily at the Licensing Act of 1643, called out his best arguments for freedom of conscience in relation to a theory of state.

In the first part of *Areopagitica*, Milton played on the prejudices

[32] For books concerning such, see particularly Arthur Barker, *Milton and the Puritan Dilemma* (Toronto, 1942), and Don M. Wolfe, *Milton in the Puritan Revolution* (New York, 1941). For accounts of lesser importance, see Jesse F. Mack, "The Evolution of Milton's Political Thinking," *The Sewanee Review*, XXX (1922), 193–205; W. G. Tarrant, "Milton and Religious Freedom," in *The Place of Jesus in Modern Religion and other Essays* (London, 1909), 101–28; William Willis, *John Milton: Political Thinker & Statesman* (London, 1909); and Arthur Lloyd Windsor, *Ethica: Or, Characteristics of Men, Manners, and Books* (London, 1860).

[33] *The Works of John Milton* (Columbia Edition, New York), Vol. III, Part 1, pp. 49–50. All subsequent references to Milton's works will be from this edition, unless otherwise noted.

of the English people by associating the enactors of the Licensing Act with the perpetrators of the Spanish Inquisition. To a nation which shuddered each November 5 at the memory of the Gunpowder Plot, such an association would be an effective argument against the Act itself. Milton next contended that the Act could not accomplish its primary objective of improving the moral life of the nation and hence was worse than useless. From these negative positions, Milton then moved into his strongest and most eloquent argument: the positive good which liberty of conscience could achieve in the State. He assumed in this part of his argument that the attainment of truth was desirable and hence the pursuit of it a definite good. Well then, Milton declared, "Truth is compar'd in Scripture to a streaming fountain; if her waters flow not in a perpetuall progression, they sick'n into a muddy pool of conformity and tradition."[34] This comparison made it possible for him to contend that sects and schisms, like waters perpetually flowing, actually contribute to the recognition of truth. In view of this, he continued, no complaints should be made of divisions in Church and State; indeed, the real "dividers of unity" are not schismatics but those "who neglect and permit not others to unite those dissever'd peeces which are yet wanting to the body of Truth." Hence, "To be still searching what we know not, by what we know, still closing up truth to truth as we find it (for all her body is *homogeneal*, and proportionall) this is the golden rule in *Theology* as well as in Arithmetick, and makes up the best harmony in a Church; not the forc't and outward union of cold, and neutrall, and inwardly divided minds."[35] Thus to Milton, as to other exponents of liberty of conscience, truth could be found only through the dust and heat of debate, only through its grappling with error in a free and open encounter. For this reason he placed the "liberty to know, to utter, and to argue freely according to conscience, above all liberties";[36] and so confident was he of ultimate victory that he envisioned, through the release of restraints, the reformation of England—a nation rousing herself as if from a sleep, shaking her invincible locks and forging the arms of war, trying all things, seeking all things, studying all things, receptive to the voice of reason and convincement and to truth as revealed by God. No static state for Milton, no cold uniformity through forcing of conscience, no ideal of order and peace alone as

[34] *Ibid.*, IV, 333. [35] *Ibid.*, IV, 339. [36] *Ibid.*, IV, 346.

the main aim of civil society; the sectaries which were "very pests" to James I were to Milton instruments of national good.

Though Milton moved beyond the Agreement of the Council of Officers concerning liberty of conscience, he saw eye to eye with John Bradshawe on the power of kings. In fact, with almost incremental repetition through his tracts on civil liberty he stressed the theory of compact; and *Eikonoklastes*, as Royalists in agony realized, struck at the doctrine of regal supremacy through the body of Charles I. But *The Tenure of Kings and Magistrates* and *Pro Populo Anglicano Defensio* spoke most cogently to the issue at hand.

In this first tract, Milton traced the origin of government to an agreement among free men who had banded together for the purpose of protecting themselves against wrongs and oppressions. To insure proper protection, Milton went on, they chose from among themselves a ruler, one blessed with outstanding integrity and wisdom; but to prevent injustice and arbitrary power they took it upon themselves to frame laws. Hence, "While as the Magistrate was set above the people, so the Law was set above the Magistrate"; and to assure that the law was not misapplied they bound the magistrate with an oath, sometimes with the express warning that if he proved unfaithful to his trust, the "people would be disingag'd" from their part of the bargain. The very origin of government convinced Milton "that the power of Kings and Magistrates is nothing else, but what is only derivative, transferr'd and committed to them in trust from the People, to the Common good of them all, in whom the power yet remaines fundamentally, and cannot be tak'n from them, without a violation of thir natural birthright."[37] But Milton not only upheld the theory of compact; he scorned the Royalist notion that the king inherited his throne by the laws of primogeniture, declaring that to say a king had as good a right to his crown and dignity as any man to his inheritance was "to make the Subject no better then the Kings slave, his chattell, or his possession that may be bought and sould."[38] Now Milton conceded, as John Bradshawe had also, that custom allowed some kings to come to their thrones by inheritance; but to interpret such a custom to mean that a subject could be called to account for his actions whereas a king could not was, to Milton, a manifest injustice. To say indeed that kings were accountable to none but God was "the ouerturning of

[37] *The Works of John Milton*, V, 10.
[38] *Ibid.*, V, 11.

all Law and government" for the reason that such a notion made all covenants, including the Coronation Oath, "meer mockeries," sworn to no purpose. Far from being accountable to God only, kings held their thrones by sufferance of the people, Milton concluded; hence it logically followed that the people might "as oft as they shall judge it for the best, either choose him or reject him, retaine him or depose him though no Tyrant, meerly by the liberty and right of freebórn Men, to be govern'd as seems to them best."[39] Few Puritans dared take the theory of compact further than this.

Pro Populo Anglicano Defensio stated at much greater length the same theme. To the claims of Salmasius in his *Defensio Regia* that Charles I had been unjustly tried and condemned, that the laws of God, of nature, and of civil authority stood on the side of the English monarch and not on the side of the High Court of Justice, Milton replied, in the name of the Commonwealth government, that Salmasius had misinterpreted these laws, that in reality they supported the proceedings of the High Court of Justice. Thus to Salmasius' contention that the king had received his power directly from God, that he had come to his throne by right of inheritance, that he as supreme head stood above law and hence was answerable to none save God only, Milton responded that Charles I had received his power through a pact with the people, that he was their servant and hence ruled by their sufferance, that he was answerable, as indeed were all citizens, to the law since the law stood supreme over all. Even as John Bradshawe had cited Book I, chapter viii, of Bracton's *De Legibus* to maintain his position that the law made the king, not the king the law, so also did Milton;[40] and when Salmasius, like James I, referred to the primitive Christians as models of Christian behavior, because they had refused to offer resistance except with prayers and tears even to tyrannous kings, Milton replied that these Christians under Julian the Apostate had mocked their emperor, had made fun of his beard, and had openly rejoiced at the news of his death. How now! Had Salmasius read aright the behavior of the primitive Christians? Through the whole of *Pro Populo Anglicano Defensio*, Milton turned back upon Salmasius his own authorities, reinterpreted his readings of Scripture and of natural rights, as well as his references to civil laws found in tradition and custom, to argue the justice of the Common-

[39] *Ibid.*, V, 14.
[40] *Ibid.*, VII, 442–43.

wealth cause; he gave his whole soul, and his sight, to maintain against a powerful antagonist the validity of his government's claims.

Through a large part of his revolutionary program Milton thus hewed to the basic pattern of seventeenth-century conflict. No man of his time spoke more eloquently to questions which vexed the entire period, or reasoned more cogently in an attempt to resolve them; but apparently neither he, nor others who loudly chorused against Stuart theory and practice, affected the public mind deeply enough before the Puritan Rebellion or during the years of the Commonwealth for liberty of conscience and the theory of compact to remain very long official policies of the English government. The notion of regal supremacy and the concept of uniformity in worship had become so ingrained in Englishmen's minds through organs of Church and State since the time of Henry VIII that, when Puritanism weakened in the last days of the Protectorate, Anglican doctrines again asserted their power and assured the restoration of Charles II. To this temporary triumph, Royalist pamphleteers no doubt contributed much, as Cromwell's Secretary of State, John Thurloe, acutely observed; and against the rising tide of allegiance to Anglican doctrines, effected by these pamphleteers, Milton, in desperation, raised his voice to warn his countrymen that, should the monarch return, the same fight would have to be fought again, and on the same grounds. Cries of anger against Puritans and paeans for the Royal entourage drowned his agonized utterance, but his prophecy came true. After a short honeymoon between the returned monarch and the people of England, the smouldering conflict over liberty of conscience and the power of kings again flamed, rising to a height of fury in the struggle between Tories and Whigs concerning the succession of James, Duke of York, only to subside for a while and then rise to a climax in the Glorious Revolution. Perhaps the perversity of mankind, so manifest to Milton in Restoration cries for the king, would not have inspired so much of his great poetry could he have known that in this phase of the debate of the century some basic doctrines of the Puritan Rebellion, modified by Whig thought, would soon triumph, and that to this victory of Whig theory, ratified in the Settlement and the Bill of Rights, he himself would contribute significantly through his revolutionary program for man and society.

Chapter Two

ROYALIST REACTION

THE RESTORATION of Charles II presaged among poets and politicians alike a return of peace and prosperity; but it failed, as Milton had predicted, to secure stability for a nation long distraught with discord and strife. After the dissolution of the "Rump" and the excluded members in March of 1660, the jockeyings of General Monk from that time until the Convention Parliament in April, and finally the triumphal entrance of the King on May 29, many Royalists, in view of their years of sequestration and exile, returned to their old positions of privilege and power with the understandable desire to secure them through a uniform Church and an absolute Crown. They codified their position under the ministry of Edward Hyde, Earl of Clarendon, and passed laws to consolidate their strength. The Corporation Act of 1661 ejected from town councils and other corporations all who failed to hold Royalist views; the Act of Uniformity in 1662 demanded from the clergy adherence to Anglican rituals and beliefs; the Press Act of the same year re-established censorship over most printed matter; the Conventicle Act of 1664 forbade assemblies of more than four, unless of the established faith; and the Five Mile Act of 1665 increased the stringency of the earlier Uniformity Act and forced on teachers, among other things, an oath of passive obedience. These acts, as well as others, constituted what became known as the Clarendon Code, which embodied the sentiments of a rejuvenated party best described as "Cavalier-Church" from Edward Hyde's administration to the Popish Plot, though the Code itself lost favor during the time of the Cabal and never again captured the allegiance it enjoyed during the first years of the Restoration. Such stringent laws against religious and political freedom legally split the nation into Conformists and Nonconformists, or Church and Dissent; and partially out of this schism, coupled with other divisions on issues both foreign and domestic, sprang, within a couple of decades, the Tory and Whig parties.

This gathering of political forces after the Restoration saw Milton in comparative seclusion,[1] pondering the destiny of man in *Paradise*

[1] *The Intelligencer* for Monday, April 25, 1664 (No. 33, p. 266) printed a dispatch from

Lost, Paradise Regained, and *Samson Agonistes.* On the eve of the return of the King he had, it is true, attempted to stem the tide of Royalist feeling in *Brief Notes Upon a Late Sermon* and in *The Readie and Easie Way to Establish a Free Commonwealth.* Furthermore, a short time before these last frantic efforts he had reasserted his main positions on Church and State in *A Treatise of Civil Power in Ecclesiastical Causes* and in *Considerations Touching the Likeliest Means to Remove Hirelings out of the Church.* But with the Restoration he went into hiding, escaped punishment through the Act of Oblivion, and retired, after a short time in custody, to a life of poetry and friends, consciously removing himself from the march of political events. Echoes of his revolutionary program sounded when the Reverend Thomas Tomkyns scanned *Paradise Lost* for seditious lines,[2] when the Licenser of the Press excised from his *The History of Britain* a passage on the Long Parliament and the Westminster Assembly of Divines,[3] and when Sir Peter Wentworth, a member of the Council of State under the Commonwealth government, left a bequest of one hundred pounds to "Mr. John Milton, who wrote against Salmasius."[4] But only twice did Milton rise up to address himself to current affairs: once in answer to "a Scurrilous Libel" by "some little scribling Quack," which apparently he never published; and once in contribution to the controversy over the Catholics, which he entitled *Of True Religion.* These pamphlets, coupled with a translation into English of a *Declaration* concerning the election of John Sobieski as King of Poland and Brabazon Aylmer's unsuccessful attempt to publish, in the very year of Milton's death, his *Letters of State* (unauthorized editions appeared two years later in 1676), constitute Milton's contributions to the political life of his country during the Royalist reaction and the reign of the Clarendon Code;[5] but they apparently had

Newbury for April 20, which told of a riot of Nonconformists in that town. "The Ring-leader of them was One *Milton*, who was apprehended." Moreover, *The Calendar of State Papers, Domestic*, for September 24, 1664, reported that several persons, one of them a Milton, had given excuses for not coming to church more than once on Sunday. In view of Milton's retirement, however, these citations could hardly be to the poet.

2 See Bernard A. Wright, "Milton's 'Treason'," *The Times* [London] *Literary Supplement*, June 20, 1929, p. 494, for an explanation of why treason might be read into certain lines of *Paradise Lost.*

3 Whether the Licenser or Milton himself excised the passage is still a question. See Dora Neill Raymond, *Oliver's Secretary* (New York, 1932), p. 325, note 5 for chapter xxi. See also note 6.

4 See Raymond, *op. cit.*, p. 286. Sir Peter Wentworth had been an ardent Republican member of the Council of State under the Commonwealth government. See further, p. 326, note 4 to chapter xxii.

5 William Hayley, an eighteenth-century biographer of Milton, spoke of Milton's publishing in 1661 a work by Sir Walter Raleigh containing political maxims applicable to the times. See

little effect.[6] The same cannot be said, however, of his revolutionary program completed before he went into retirement. Parts of it presumably became a source of Nonconformist polemics, and hence a thorn in the side of the Cavalier-Church party.

I

Milton's contribution to Nonconformist polemics during the Royalist reaction from the Restoration to the Popish Plot may best be appraised against the background of conflicting theories of government between the Cavalier-Church party and the Dissent. Both sides, of course, expressed many different shades of opinion, and allegiance often shifted with shifting events. Moreover, some Nonconformists supported the King. Old William Prynne, for example, despite the exclusion of his Presbyterian brethren by the Act of Uniformity in 1662, nevertheless argued repeatedly for the most extreme notions of regal supremacy. Furthermore, the tenderness Charles II expressed for Puritan consciences in his Declaration of Breda before the Restoration, his expedient attempt at comprehension in his Declaration on Ecclesiastical Affairs in 1660, and his Declaration of Indulgence in 1672 obscured strict party lines. But the cleavage between the two main contending factions was nevertheless fundamental. The Cavalier-Church party, despite Charles II's avowals of toleration and his actual dependence upon Parliament, claimed for the King absolute authority by virtue of divine right and argued for conformity in the Church; Nonconformists, on the other hand, from their illegal conventicles and more often from prison, declared for toleration and for a strict limitation of regal power.

George Morley, the Bishop of Worcester, preached the Coronation sermon for Charles II on April 23, 1661, and in so doing sounded an official note which the Cavalier-Church party harped on with infinite variations for the next twenty years. Casting a critical eye on political theories which had animated the Puritan Rebellion, he assured his congregation that "when the *Soveraignty* over the *whole*,

Raymond, *op. cit.*, p. 323, note 1 to chapter xix. I have been unable to verify this statement. But in 1692 appeared Raleigh's *The Arts of Empire, And Mysteries of State Discabineted,* together with Milton's prefatory "To the Reader," as both had been published in 1658 as *The Cabinet-Council,* which Milton edited at that time.

[6] *The Calendar of State Papers, Domestic* (1675–76, p. 89), records an anonymous letter, which says: "J. Milton has said more for it in two elegant sheets of true religion, heresy and schism than all the pr[elates] can refute in 7 years . . ." It is doubtful, however, that this pamphlet aroused any great interest.

which *ought* to be vested in *one*, is usurped and shared, and exercised by *many*," as may be observed "grossly and visibly" in a "*popular State* or a Democracy," factions and divisions break out in the state since the many, "whether they be more, or fewer, do alwayes under a *pretence* of *Law* and *Liberty* assume unto themselves an Illegal, Arbitrary and tyrannical power."[7] Government by the many, he declared later in his sermon, actually runs contrary to the laws of nature and of God. For what could be more unnatural than for one body politic to have more heads than one, what more confusing than to leave undistinguished the head from the body, the governor from those governed? Yet such unnatural conditions exist in a commonwealth, he maintained, where magistrates are considered "*servants* and vassals unto the people, as being created by them, and accomptable to them, and consequently alwayes in danger and fear of them."[8] Furthermore, he continued, even "as *Monarchy* is more *natural* and more according to *Divine Institution*, and consequently a *better* form of government then *any other*; so of *Monarchies*, that which is by *Succession* is much *more natural* and much *more* according to Divine *Institution*, then *any other* kind of *Monarchy*." In conclusion, he argued that, since "*Monarchy* is from *God*," "whatsoever is Destructive to Monarchy, or Inconsistent with Monarchy, is *not from God*, because Gods Ordinances cannot destroy or clash one against another."[9] With this piece of logic Bishop Morley left his congregation to ponder the iniquities of Puritan political theory and the rightness—nay, divinity—of the principles which supported the throne of Charles II.

George Morley expressed indeed the sentiments of the Cavalier-Church party. In a swelling chorus, pamphleteers and clergymen alike presented the same claims for the throne and likewise refuted Puritan theory. Edward Bagshaw, for example, published in the year of the Restoration *The Rights Of The Crown Of England*, in which he contended, as an apprentice of the Common Law, "*That the Soveraigne Power belonging to the Crown of* England, *is, according to the Law of the Land, given to the King by God, not by the People.*"[10] Claiming that this position had now triumphed over Puritan views,

[7] *A Sermon Preached at the Magnificent Coronation Of The Most High and Mighty King Charles the IId* (London, 1661), p. 12.

[8] *Ibid.*, p. 16.

[9] *Ibid.*, pp. 33–34; 59.

[10] *The Rights Of The Crown Of England, As it is established by Law* (London, 1660), pp. 3–4, and *passim*. This document was begun, the dedication to the King informs us, during the reign of Charles I.

Anglican divines, during the next decade or so, often dressed it up in figurative language, as witness John Lake in *A Sermon Preached At Whitehal Upon The 29th day of May*. The king, John Lake declared, has "No Sovereign Authority of the People above him." Quite to the contrary, he continued, a king is set upon a hill by God, with no one to watch him, no one to reduce him to order by arms, no one to draw distinctions between the king's person and his regal capacity. And as for that "unhallowed Divinity" which claimed that the king was "*Singulis Major, Universis Minor*, Greater then each, less then all," as well as other errors of the Puritan Rebellion, John Lake rejoiced that with the Restoration such no longer obtained. He rejoiced further that the return of Charles II had made such "umbrages" vanish, had made "*Royal Majesty*" look like its real self again, had, even as the little hills did obeisance to the Mountain of the Lord, taught people to "submit to *the King, as supreame*; to pay the lowest homage to Him, as to the Highest Power upon Earth."[11]

Such sentiments fell easily from Cavalier-Church party lips; but perhaps they found fullest development in Samuel Parker's *A Discourse of Ecclesiastical Politie*, which, as later analysis will show, aroused considerable comment. An early frequenter of Milton's house after the return of the King, Parker soon moved away from any liberal views he might have found there to become, within ten years after the Restoration, an exponent of the most conservative Royalist doctrines and eventually a bishop in the Anglican Church. With his return to orthodoxy he published his views at great length in his *Discourse*, in which he argued, mainly, that it was "absolutely necessary to the Peace and Government of the World, that the Supreme Magistrate of every Common-wealth should be vested with a Power to govern and conduct the Conscience of Subjects in Affairs of Religion."[12] Such arguments, of course, revealed nothing new; they merely restated the theories of James I and the policies found in the *Constitutions and Canons Ecclesiasticall* of 1640. But they served a new purpose in that they supported the Clarendon Code and allowed the Cavalier-Church party to claim that government based on them would bring, as Puritan or Nonconformist doctrines would not, peace and prosperity to the State. To clinch its case, the party could always point to the chaos of the Puritan Rebellion, the result, its members con-

[11] *A Sermon Preached At Whitehal* (Savoy, 1670), pp. 36–37.
[12] *A Discourse of Ecclesiastical Politie* (London, 1670), p. 10.

tended, of toleration and false theories of government—that time when every house had been filled with strifes and contentions, when the very foundations of society had been torn down and destroyed.[13] They therefore enjoined people to contrast such chaos with the order England enjoyed under kings. Memories of bloodshed and strife and fear of civil disorders perhaps did more for the Cavalier-Church party than arguments for religious conformity or for divine right; but its members quite rightly stressed the theoretical basis of their activities and policies, a rejection of which would undermine the Clarendon Code and hence their positions of power. Men like John Lake and Samuel Parker, as well as hosts of others, realized that in the long run their case stood or fell on the acceptance or rejection of the doctrines they so fervently preached.

Nonconformists also realized this truth and in consequence, even before the Act of Uniformity drove them out of the church, began a concerted attack against conformity in religion and the concept of regal supremacy. Anabaptists, the sect James I hated most, led the way. In view of troubles in London during the first year of the Restoration, Anabaptists thought it politic to state their positions plainly so that they would not be reproached for irresponsible rebellions. They agreed with most political theorists of the age that magistracy was an ordinance of God, set up for the protection and praise of the good and for the punishment of evil doers; they even went so far as to say that it was desirable for men to obey kings. But they made it clear that kings were to be obeyed only in those commands "*which do not intrench upon, or rise up in opposition to the commands of God*"; and for those commands they went to neither the established church nor the king but to Scripture and conscience.[14] If James I had said very much the same thing, only to follow such a declaration with a statement that the king nevertheless was supreme, Anabaptists could not so twist their logic. Rather, they disclosed that the king should be supreme in civil affairs only: render unto Caesar the things which are Caesar's, but unto God the things which are God's; and with this reference to Scripture, which they interpreted to mean that Church and State should be separate, they not only challenged the theory of absolute regal authority by divine right but also inferred that only through such a separation of powers could people

[13] *A Discourse of Toleration* (London, 1668), p. 24.
[14] *The Humble Apology Of Some commonly called Anabaptists* (London, 1660), p. 17.

secure "quiet and peaceable enjoyment" of religious and civil liberties.[15] With such sentiments, Congregationalists agreed. In a resolution representing one hundred twenty of their churches, they unanimously affirmed the necessity of civil magistrates and of obedience to them for the encouragement of good men and the punishment of evil; they went on record, furthermore, that the civil magistrate should, in some cases, "take care" of men from whom issued blasphemy and error. Yet they maintained that *"in such differences about the Doctrines of the Gospel, or waies of the worship of God as may befal men exercising a good conscience, manifesting it in their conversation, and holding the foundation, not disturbing others in their waies, or worship, that differ from them; there is no warrant for the Magistrate under the Gospel to abridge them of their liberty."*[16]

Neither Congregationalists nor Anabaptists, however, pressed liberty of conscience and hence the limitation of regal authority as often or as effectively as Quakers, who through the Restoration kept up a constant barrage against the rationale of the Clarendon Code, an effort which earned for themselves the undying enmity of the Cavalier-Church party. All that they said and did cannot be told here; suffice it to recall that their words and deeds shook not only religious but also civil authority through the reign of Charles II. It would be impossible, moreover, to summarize in a few sentences the gist of their positions on liberty of conscience and the power of kings. Something of what they meant, however, came from the hand of William Penn, one of their most famous and most articulate writers. In *The Great Case Of Liberty of Conscience Once more Briefly Debated & Defended*, Penn declared that liberty of conscience meant not simply freedom of mind to believe or to disbelieve this or that doctrine; rather, it meant freedom to act in visible ways upon beliefs so firmly held that failure to act for fear of any mortal man would constitute sin and incur divine wrath. Yet Penn wanted it clearly understood that such liberty should not be interpreted to mean activity destructive to government and to the laws of the land, "but so far only, as it may refer to religious Matters, and a Life to come, and consequently wholly independent of the secular affairs of this."[17] Furthermore, Penn continued, persecution should be defined not simply as a strict

[15] *Ibid.*, p. 20.
[16] *A Renuntiation And Declaration Of The Ministers of Congregational Churches And Publick Preachers Of the same Judgment* (London, 1661), pp. 7–8.
[17] (1670), p. 11.

requirement to believe thus and so and to incur penalties for not believing according to the requirement, but as any hindrance erected to prevent meetings to perform religious exercises in accordance with faith and persuasion.[18] To William Penn, liberty of conscience was thus a positive right, a right to be secured through the recognition of two separate powers in life, spiritual and temporal, neither of which should encroach on the other. From this it naturally followed that the king, far from being supreme, had no authority whatever in matters of worship and faith.

Nonconformist arguments against Cavalier - Church doctrines, however, could hardly stop at this theoretical point. Even as the Cavalier-Church party had claimed that its theories would bring peace and stability to the state, so Nonconformists argued that only through recognizing the right of individual worship could the nation secure prosperity and the good of all. John Owen, for example, one of the most celebrated Nonconformists of the time, contended that, since it was the duty of every Englishman to choose his religion and that this would naturally result in many different persuasions, to "confine the Peace and Interest of Civil Societies unto any one of them" would be "scarce suitable unto that Prudence which is requisite for the steerage of the present state of things in the World."[19] Moreover, Sir Charles Wolseley flatly claimed that only through toleration could England secure the Protestant religion and a peaceful and flourishing state; conformity indeed not only militated against such but also disobliged the best men in all parties. Not only religion but reason, Wolseley concluded, not only duty but interest, should make princes and states consider the important matter of freedom of conscience.[20]

Nonconformists and the Cavalier-Church party for nearly two decades argued with increasing intensity the problems which the Restoration had been designed to resolve. But just as Puritan arms had failed to maintain liberty of conscience and the supremacy of Commons, so the Clarendon Code could not secure religious conformity and an absolute Crown. Neither side had won the battle for the minds of men. As this battle moved toward the supposed Popish Plot, the Earl of Shaftesbury, destined to become the leader of the Whig party,

[18] *The Great Case Of Liberty of Conscience*, p. 12. H. F. Russell Smith, in *The Theory of Religious Liberty in the Reigns of Charles II and James II* (Cambridge, 1911, p. 59) states that William Penn drew from Milton for his ideas on toleration, but he presented no evidence.

[19] *Indulgence and Toleration Considered* (London, 1667), p. 19.

[20] *Liberty of Conscience, The Magistrates Interest* (London, 1668), *passim*.

arose in the House of Lords to say that the doctrine of divine right was destructive to government and law, that its danger should be recognized so that it would not destroy the English nation. This doctrine, he declared, had been formulated in the *Constitutions and Canons Ecclesiasticall* of 1640, had been preached and maintained by important members of the Anglican Church, and was "the root that produced the *Bill of Test* last *Session*, and some very perplexed Oaths" that were "of the same nature with that." Now Shaftesbury conceded to the Lords that the king should be obeyed for conscience' sake, that divine precepts demanded obedience to lawful governors; but the doctrine of divine right, he went on, in reality overturned all lawful authority, undermined all constitutional government. If this doctrine held truth, he contended, then the Magna Charta was of no force, and laws were but rules among themselves "during the Kings pleasure." "Monarchy, if of Divine Right," he further explained, could not "be bounded or limited by humane Laws," nay, could not even "bind it self" and hence all "Claims of right by the Law, or Constitution of the Government, All the Jurisdiction and Priviledge" of the House of Lords, "All the Rights and Priviledges of the House of Commons, All the Properties and Liberties of the People" would give way, "not onely to the interest, but the will and pleasure of the Crown." Any worthy man holding this doctrine, Shaftesbury shrewdly continued, "must Vote to deliver up all" not simply "when reason of State, and the separate Interest of the Crown require it," but when the "will and pleasure of the King" became known, for such would be to him the "onely rule and measure of Right and Justice." Such an obligation forced Shaftesbury to stress the importance of understanding the implications of political doctrines, of seeing how "fatal" it would be to all if the concept of divine right "should be suffered to spread any further."[21]

In his speech before the Lords, Shaftesbury thus recognized the continuity of seventeenth-century conflict in the unresolved question concerning the power of kings, and at the same time pointed to the dangers of acting in accordance with a theory of regal supremacy by divine right. In so doing, he fell in line with Nonconformist policy, which was to convince men of the iniquity of Cavalier-Church theory, as well as to implant in their minds the rightness of freedom of con-

21 *Two Speeches* (Amsterdam, 1675), pp. 10–11.

science and the necessity of restricting regal authority by separating Church and State. Since Milton, earlier in the conflict, had already spoken with eloquence and force to these very matters, it would have been strange indeed if Nonconformists, in attempting to make their principles prevail, had allowed his revolutionary program to collect dust.

II

Henry Foulis, in *The History of the Wicked Plots and Conspiracies of Our Pretended Saints*, declared in 1662 that the Puritan faction had spread its principles abroad through the press and that the scurrilous works of "*Needham, Goodwin, Milton, Rogers*, and such like *Billingsgate* Authors" were not unknown to any.[22] No one could deny that the dissemination of these principles had brought the Puritans to power during the Commonwealth and the Protectorate; and now, two years after the Restoration, a historian still remembered Milton as one whose works had notably contributed to the Puritan cause. As the conflict continued, clear signs indicate that Nonconformists had not forgotten him either, that they turned to him often for arguments to support their religious and political positions.

The first of such signs appeared in a satirical pamphlet entitled *Cabala, Or An Impartial Account Of The Non-Conformists Private Designs, Actings and Wayes*. Obviously patterned after serious volumes purporting to disclose secrets of state, this pamphlet claimed that it presented a record of the motions, resolutions, and debates of the inner councils of Nonconformists from August 24, 1662, until December 25 of the same year. The main purpose of the pamphlet was to reveal how Nonconformists discussed tactics and mapped grand strategy to further their cause. One set of minutes, for example, recorded how they had decided to pour out supplications to God to make the King change his heart, to pray for councils whose purpose was to advance religion and Puritan principles, and to strengthen the wavering against popery. Such decisions on aims made it necessary to consider means. Consequently, Richard Baxter arose to move, so the minutes continue, that "their soul-saving Works might be immediately reprinted, *viz. Smectymnuus, Lex Rex, Holy Commonwealth, Antica Valieryme*, with most of *Milton* and Mr. *Goodwyn's* Papers,

[22] *The History of the Wicked Plots* (London, 1662), p. 24.

and all the Sermons preached upon publick Fasts and Thanksgiving-dayes, before the long Parliament, and other Parliaments, from the year 1640. to the year 1658. together with Mr. *Cartwrights* writings."[23] In addition to suggesting that this large order be filled, Baxter moved further that they counter the writings of Anglicans with tracts by men of their own group, like John Owen, for example. Toward the end of the pamphlet, the minutes recorded other tactics through which Nonconformists hoped to accomplish their ends. They agreed in a meeting of September 24 to appoint agents whose purpose was to observe all the failings of the state. These agents, in turn, were to report these failings to a sort of central committee, which would be appointed "to improve them and agravate them, as might most conduce to the good old Cause, especially by engaging the people in conscience against the government, and in passion against the Governours, and in contempt against both, and keep this worm upon their hearts, that the cause is Gods."[24] Somewhat later, they agreed, in accordance with a prior order, that some of their pamphleteers—"Mr. *Needham*, Mr. *Ascham*, Mr. *Canne*, Mr. *Walker*"—should be allowed to invent and publish such things as might amuse the people and improve the estate of the Dissent.[25] Thus Nonconformists, according to this satirical account of their secret conventicles, laid definite plans to disrupt the government of Charles II so that they could discredit the party in power and then establish their own way of life. In this campaign, they considered the press one of their most effective weapons; among those to speak their cause through the press, they considered Milton important enough to move that most of his works be republished. The records are silent as to whether Nonconformists actually employed Milton at this time; but even a satirical account holds some measure of truth and indicates, if it fails to demonstrate, that he spoke effectively in their behalf.

A second indication that Nonconformists employed Milton's tracts appeared during the trials of John Twyn, Thomas Brewster, Simon Dover, and Nathan Brooks, the first for printing and dispersing a treasonable book, and the latter three for printing seditious, scandalous, and malicious pamphlets. These trials, some of the first fruits

[23] *Cabala, Or An Impartial Account Of The Non-Conformists Private Designs, Actings and Wayes* (London, 1663), p. 12.

[24] *Ibid.*, p. 29.

[25] *Ibid.*, p. 33.

of the Press Act, aroused a great deal of interest, not only because of the severity of the sentences—John Twyn was hanged, drawn, and quartered—but also because they revealed strong Nonconformist sympathy for a free press. According to *The Newes*, for instance, at least three thousand fanatics attended John Twyn to his last resting place.[26] The book which brought Twyn to his doom was entitled *A Treatise of the Execution of Justice*, and the tracts which brought the others heavy punishment were *The Speeches and Prayers of Some of the Late King's Judges* and *The Phoenix, or Solemn League and Covenant*. These works, according to a contemporary account of the trials, were but three of over three hundred such "*Treasonous, Seditious, Schismatical*, and *Scandalous* Books, Libels, and Papers, Printed since his Majesties Return," all of which had been listed so that they could be readily produced whensoever those in authority should ask that such steps be taken.[27] A partial list of these pamphlets and books apparently came out under the title of *Considerations and Proposals In Order to the Regulation of the Press*,[28] a compilation made by Roger L'Estrange, whose zeal in detecting sedition as it rolled from the press earned him the official position of Surveyor of the Imprimery. Now Milton appeared on L'Estrange's list as a seditious author; and in *Toleration Discuss'd*, which L'Estrange published a few months before the trials, Milton was designated as one of the mainstays of the Nonconformist press.

The list of seditious pamphlets and books that L'Estrange assembled in his *Considerations and Proposals* included nearly all recent publications expressing opinions on religious and political matters not encompassed by Cavalier-Church orthodoxy. Thus under the heading entitled "Instances of Pamphlets containing Treasonous and Seditious POSITIONS," it would be only natural to expect that some of Milton's tracts should appear. Actually, L'Estrange included only one: *The Tenure of Kings and Magistrates*, which illustrated the particular position that "The Power of the King is but Fiduciary; and the Duty of the Subjects but Conditional." L'Estrange, however, was not content to let the matter rest without comment; he described Milton's pamphlet as one "Proving that it is Lawful for any who have the

26 *The Newes* (April 28, 1664), No. 34, p. 273. Twyn is not mentioned by name, but the reference seems to be clearly to him.

27 *An Exact Narrative Of The Tryal and Condemnation Of John Twyn* (London, 1664), sig. A3v.

28 London, 1663.

Power, to call to Account a Tyrant, or wicked King, and after due Conviction to depose, and put him to Death, if the ordinary Magistrate have Neglected, or Deny'd to doe it."[29] This was the very position maintained in *A Treatise of the Execution of Justice*, the printing of which sent Twyn to his death; and for this reason a tradition holds that its sentiments found their origin in Milton's tract.[30] It seems more likely, however, that this book was "an *Arrow* drawn out of a *Presbyterian Quiver* [*Lex Rex*]," as the narrative of the trial of Twyn stated.[31] Nevertheless, it is clear that L'Estrange connected *The Tenure of Kings and Magistrates* with Twyn's defection, and it is probable that because of this connection Milton was unofficially mentioned during the trial as an evil influence on the people of England Chief Justice Hyde, at least, could have been expected to say as much in view of his vigorous opposition to Nonconformist ideas and his unsympathetic condemning of John Twyn to death.

A closer connection between Milton and the Nonconformist press appeared in L'Estrange's *Toleration Discuss'd*, a lengthy pamphlet in which Conformity, Zeal, and Scruple conducted a tedious debate on the pros and cons of the theoretical conflict between the Cavalier-Church party and the Dissent. Conformity, as might be expected, upheld the positions of the Cavalier-Church party; Zeal and Scruple usually argued for liberty of conscience and for a limited regal authority. Through the course of their debate, L'Estrange sometimes let the chips fall without favor; but often he commented editorially, either in the margins or in the text itself, disclosing, as he did so, the intimate connections between Nonconformists of his day and authors of an earlier time. Thus in a discussion of John Goodwin, in which Scruple had expressed an initial hope that Conformity would not deny him "*to be a Reverend Divine*," Conformity stated that he could not be denied this title if men judged him by the doctrines of the Dissent, since Goodwin had expressed their positions when he said that Charles I had been rightly tried and condemned, that never under heaven had a person been more justly sentenced to death. Conform-

29 *Considerations and Proposals In Order to the Regulation of the Press*, p. 19.

30 David Masson (*op. cit.*, VI, 479 ff.) touched on this tradition and quoted a puzzling passage from the *British Chronologist:* "One of the libels was written by Milton to justify the murder of King Charles, and to maintain the lawfulness of subjects taking up arms against their sovereign." Masson, however, was not convinced. Nevertheless, Dora Neill Raymond (*op. cit.*, p. 240) took the tradition to be fact, saying: "Under him [L'Estrange], a poor printer was prosecuted, who, in 1664, published excerpts from *The Tenure of Kings and Magistrates.*"

31 *An Exact Narrative Of The Tryal and Condemnation Of John Twyn*, sig. A2v.

ity then declared that "Mr. *Jenkins*" was of the same opinion, and so were "*Parker, Milton*"; "in fine, the whole Tribe of *Medling Non-Conformists*" were of "the same Leven."[32] And to show that this agreement of minds came not by chance but by design, Conformity called attention to Nonconformist tactics by observing "that whatsoever is first Expos'd and Blown abroad (by the Hirelings of the Faction) from the *Press*, and *Pulpit*, is still Seconded (at least, if the People Relish it) with the Approbation of the *Counsel*: so that the main use of *Sermons*, and *Pamphlets*, is only to dispose the Multitude for *Votes*, and *Ordinances*."[33] From a simple query about John Goodwin, Conformity consciously moved into a discussion of Nonconformist beliefs, a revelation of their sources, and an explanation of how they were disseminated; nor did he stop here. Once the people swallow a principle, he said, "the next news ye hear, is a Vote for putting that Position in Practice."[34]

Roger L'Estrange fervently believed everything he had Conformity say. The main purpose, indeed, of *Toleration Discuss'd* was to expose what he considered were false principles of government and hence to deter people from rebelling against Clarendon's Ministry. Fundamental to this exposé was a revelation of authors responsible for having phrased these principles in a memorable fashion. Thus to Scruple's question, "*Shall the Magistrate make me Act against my Conscience?*" Conformity answered, "Shall the Subject make Him *Tolerate* against *His*?" And as Conformity developed the problem, he declared that some had placed "Soveraignty in the Diffusive Body of the People" and held "it Lawfull for the Subjects to enter into Leagues and Covenants, not only Without the Soveraign's Consent, but Against his Authority," by which false doctrines he placed the names of "*Parker, Goodwin, Rutherford, Milton.*"[35] As the debate continued, Scruple and Zeal spoke less and less and Conformity more and more. What will Nonconformists say if they are asked to reverence the King as the "Supreme Governour"? he asked. Why, "They'll Answer you, NO; *Hee's but the Servant, and Vassal of the People: his Royalty is only a Virtual Emanation from Them; and in Them Radically, as in the first Subject.* (According to *Rutherford, Parker,*

[32] *Toleration Discuss'd* (London, 1663), p. 34.

[33] *Idem.*

[34] *Idem.*

[35] *Ibid.*, p. 71.

Goodwin, Bridges, Milton, and a hundred more)."[36] Moreover, what if they actually resist the king in accordance with their principles, Conformity further inquired, and what if the king is fortunate enough to escape gunshot and is placed in prison, his captors being put to it to find laws or peers to try him? Why, "*Milton's* opinion is that *Every Worthy Man in Parliament, might, for the Publique Good, be thought a Fit Peer, and Iudge of the King,*" a position which a marginal note recognized as having come from page 24 of *The Tenure of Kings and Magistrates.*[37] As the debate drew to a close, discussion turned to the martyrdom of Charles I, the question being, as Scruple phrased it, "Upon Whom the Guilt of the Kings Bloud lyes." Scruple and Zeal disagreed on this matter, but the gist of their discussion made it clear that the factions should bear the blame. Had not one faction particularly "Hunted and Persu'd H'm with Sword, and Fire"? Had it not formerly "Deny'd to Treat with Him, and their now Recanting Ministers Preach't against him, as a Reprobate Incurable; an Enemy to God, and his Church? Marqu'd for Destruction"? This at least was the opinion of Milton in *The Tenure of Kings and Magistrates,* page 32, L'Estrange noted in a marginal reference.[38]

Such comments could mean only one thing. Puritan factions, by the admission of their own advocates, had hounded Charles I to death through sermons and pamphlets, and Nonconformists could do the same to Charles II through the same means. Hence the importance of exposing Nonconformist doctrines and of tracing their origins to authors of an earlier day. Among these authors, in *Toleration Discuss'd,* Milton found a prominent place. If John Evelyn, a few months before Twyn's trial, could record in his diary that Edward Phillips, whom he had secured as a preceptor for his son, had not been at all infected by the principles of his uncle, John Milton, the same could not be said of Nonconformists. According to the Surveyor of the Imprimery, whose opinion on such matters should be of some worth, Nonconformists drew infection directly from Milton and passed it on through sermons and pamphlets to the people of England.

A third indication that Nonconformists drew from Milton in their conflict with the Cavalier-Church party appears in the Samuel Parker–Andrew Marvell controversy over conformity of worship and liberty

[36] *Ibid.,* p. 84.
[37] *Ibid.,* p. 85.
[38] *Ibid.,* pp. 104–5.

of conscience early in the second decade of the Restoration. Marvell had, during the Protectorate, officially helped Milton as Secretary of Foreign Tongues; and both he and Parker, shortly after the return of Charles II, had visited Milton and talked about matters of Church and State. But not long thereafter their paths moved in different directions, Parker, as previously mentioned, eventually becoming an Anglican bishop and an advocate of rigid conformity, Marvell adhering to the principles which later animated the Whig party. The controversy which flowered in 1673 had its roots in the publication of Parker's *A Discourse of Ecclesiastical Politie* some three years earlier, at which time he had argued, as prior analysis has shown, that the civil magistrate possessed absolute power over his subjects, even to the regulation of conscience. Such an unyielding position, so forcefully argued, aroused consternation among Nonconformists—so much so that John Owen attempted to persuade Richard Baxter to make a reply. Baxter, however, declined, whereupon Owen himself answered Parker in *Truth and Innocence Vindicated*, in which he refuted in detail Parker's main position that it was absolutely necessary to the peace and government of the world for the supreme magistrate to be vested with a power to govern the consciences of his subjects; and at the same time he attempted to establish the Nonconformist position, that liberty of conscience is of natural right. Parker replied in 1671 in *A Defence and Continuation of Ecclesiastical Politie* and in 1672 in *A Discourse in Vindication of Bishop John Bramhall and the Clergy of the Church of England*, singling out both Owen and Baxter for particular attack and in so doing jeopardizing the Nonconformist cause. Just when Parker appeared to be master of the field, Andrew Marvell moved into the conflict with his *The Rehearsal Transpros'd*, an attack so witty and learned that Parker became a laughing stock among members of both parties.

Speaking anonymously and calling his opponent Mr. Bayes, a name made ridiculous through the Duke of Buckingham's recent popular farce *The Rehearsal*, Andrew Marvell examined Parker's main positions under headings of *The Unlimited Magistrate*, *The Publick Conscience*, *Moral Grace*, *Debauchery Tolerated*, *Persecution Recommended*, and *Pushpin-Divinity*, during which examination, as well as in prefatory comments, he pointed out Parker's inconsistencies and illogicalities and generally mauled him in a manner reminiscent of Milton's attack upon Salmasius. Marvell's reply was lengthy and no attempt can be made to analyze even a small part of it here; but it is important to see something of its method and tone. To Parker's unfriendliness to the press, for example, Marvell replied: "O *Printing*! how hast thou disturb'd the Peace of Mankind! that Lead, when moulded into Bullets, is not so mortal as when founded into Letters!"[39] To answer Parker's contentions that the king possessed supreme power over conscience, that the Church supported the State, that persecution was justified for the peace of the nation, Marvell pointed to the record of Archbishop Laud after his elevation to Canterbury. "Happy had it been for the King, happy for the Nation, and happy for himself, had he never climbed that Pinacle," Marvell observed.[40] Though at all times friendly to the office of kingship, Marvell nevertheless rendered the Nonconformist cause considerable aid in that he made Parker's claims appear at once both ridiculous and unsound.

The controversy not only aroused a great deal of interest but also brought back memories of an earlier conflict. "Come," cried an unknown pamphleteer, addressing himself to Marvell, "you had all this out of the Answerer of *Salmasius*";[41] and another anonymous author, referring to Milton's recently published *Accidence Commenc't Grammar*, observed that Marvell appeared "to have learned his *Accidence*, but not *Grammar*" and recommended that he see "blind *M*. who teaches School about Morefields."[42] Moreover, Samuel Parker himself, in *A Reproof to the Rehearsal Transprosed*, accused Marvell of drawing from Milton for many specific positions. You know a friend of ours, he said, recalling their earlier visits to Milton, who has vindicated the true meaning of revolt "against a learned Man abroad that indiscreetly and injudiciously enough objected it against the late Rebellion";[43] you should know, too, he might have added with less irony, that you have taken from him arguments for your *Re-*

[39] *The Rehearsal Transpros'd* (London, 1672), p. 6.

[40] *Ibid.*, p. 300.

[41] *S'too him Bayes: Or Some Observations Upon the Humour of Writing Rehearsal's Transpros'd* (Oxford, 1673), p. 130.

[42] *A Common-place-Book Out of the Rehearsal Transpros'd* (London, 1673), pp. 35–36. A seventeenth- or eighteenth-century hand notes in the Huntington Library copy of this book that "It is most probably by Sir R. L'Estrange."

[43] *A Reproof to the Rehearsal Transprosed, in A Discourse to its Authour* (London, 1673), p. 125.

hearsal Transpros'd. At any rate, to Marvell's defense of a free press, Parker replied:

What stiff and stubborn Homilies have you made to make it good that the suppression of a good Libel is *no less than Martyrdom, and if it extend to the whole Impression a kind of Massacre, whereof the Execution ends not in the slaying of an Elemental Life, but strikes at that ethereal and fifth essence, the breath of Reason it self, slays an Immortality rather than a Life?*

"Such fustian bumbast as this," Parker declared, calling attention in a marginal note to *Areopagitica*, page 4, "past for stately wit and sence in that Age of politeness and reformation."[44] As a final recollection, Parker pointed to Marvell's "lump of History," his facetious way of referring to Marvell's use of chronicles to warn magistrates of the dangers of high-handed behavior—a collection of stories, Parker claimed, which would "afford as good Precedents for Rebellion and King-killing, as any we meet with in the writings of *J. M.* in defence of the Rebellion and the Murther of the King."[45]

If *The Rehearsal Transpros'd* reminded Parker of his earlier friendship with both Milton and Marvell and suggested that the younger man had leaned heavily on the blind poet, it drove another author, perhaps Richard Leigh, to reveal that Marvell had pilfered from the whole treasure house of Milton's poetry and prose. In Marvell's account of the civil wars, for example, he saw "nothing but *Iconoclastes* drawn in Little, and *Defensio Populi Anglicania* in Miniature";[46] in Marvell's divesting the King of an "*Unlimited and Uncontroulable Power*," nothing but a concurrence with his "*Dear Friend* Mr. *Milton*";[47] in Marvell's figures of speech concerning "Liberty of Unlicens'd Printing," page 6, "little else than "*Milton's Areopagitica* in shorthand";[48] in Marvell's "Malicious and Disloyal Reflections on the Late Kings Reign," the manner of "*Milton's* Pen, and *Gerbier's* Pencil."[49] Such comparisons, and many others, ranging through a cross section of Milton's poetry and prose, forced Richard Leigh to the conclusion that Marvell had found most of his inspira-

[44] *A Reproof to the Rehearsal Transprosed*, p. 191.

[45] *Ibid.*, p. 212.

[46] *The Transproser Rehears'd: or the Fifth Act of Mr. Bayes's Play* (Oxford, 1673), p. 72. That Richard Leigh was the author of this pamphlet has not been established.

[47] *Ibid.*, p. 110.

[48] *Ibid.*, p. 131.

[49] *Ibid.*, pp. 146–47.

tion in Milton alone. "So black a Poyson has he suckt from the most virulent Pamphlets," Leigh claimed, "as were impossible for any Mountebank but the Author of *Iconoclastes* to swallow, without the Cure of Antidotes. And certainly," he concluded, "if that Libeller has not clubb'd with our Writer (as is with some reason suspected) we may safely say, there are many *Miltons* in this one Man."[50]

But Marvell himself, in *The Rehearsal Transpros'd: The Second Part*, categorically denied any dependence upon Milton. Indeed, he declared that he had anticipated such accusations and therefore had made it a point to "avoid either visiting or sending to him" after he had undertaken the composition of *The Rehearsal Transpros'd*, lest he involve Milton in any way.[51] In a dignified statement, Marvell cleared Milton of any collusion, praised him as "a man of great Learning and Sharpness of wit," and recalled how Parker had visited him in the early years of the Restoration. That Parker should now "insult thus" over Milton's old age, should lay *The Rehearsal Transpros'd* to his charge without taking care to inform himself better, was to Marvell both inhuman and inhospitable—acts that should warn others that Parker was but "a man that creeps into all companies, to jeer, trepan, and betray them."[52] Now this denial was forthright and sincere. Nevertheless it is possible, in view of their close association and community of interests,[53] that Marvell absorbed inadvertently some of Milton's positions. At least, it is clear that likeness between them compelled more than one observer to assume that in his contribution to the Nonconformist cause Marvell owed much to Milton.

A general assumption that Nonconformists both spread abroad Milton's tracts and employed his sentiments to undermine the Cavalier-Church party and to strengthen their own thus persisted through the first decade and a half of the Restoration. Whether they actually did either in accordance with official policy will perhaps never be known. But the very existence of the assumption argues that Milton's principles were gaining adherents and hence becoming a threat to Cavalier-Church domination. Once enough men believed in the iniquity of church conformity and regal supremacy by divine

[50] *Idem.*

[51] *The Rehearsal Transpros'd: The Second Part* (London, 1673), pp. 377–80.

[52] *Idem.*

[53] Years later, Samuel Parker had occasion to recall this association. "Amongst those lewd Revilers," he wrote, "the lewdest was one whose name was *Marvel*. . . . At length, by the interest of *Milton*, to whom he was somewhat agreeable for his ill-natured wit, he was made Under-secretary to *Cromwell's* Secretary" (*Bishop Parker's History of His Own Time* [London, 1727], p. 332).

right and in the virtue of liberty of conscience, and hence a strictly limited monarchy, the Clarendon Code could no longer stand. No one realized this truth more than Roger L'Estrange, who invoked the Press Act and exerted all his powers as Surveyor of the Imprimery to keep such from coming to pass. To him, as well as to others, Milton's principles constituted a genuine threat to the party in power.

III

Opposition to Milton during the domination of the Cavalier-Church party arose in a great shout of derision in the year of the Restoration, only to dwindle away into a steady chant of bitterness and hate. Much of this opposition came as a matter of course and differed little from that which had accompanied his official career; but it is significant that, long after Milton had retired from the arena of combat, his enemies spoke of him as though he were still actively engaged in political conflict. They bitterly assailed his tracts against royalty and read God's justice in his infirmities; they feared mightily the effect of his pen. Such continued bitterness and fear expressed by members of the Cavalier-Church party or by those who sympathized with them indicate how effectively his revolutionary program argued the Nonconformist cause. How did such opposition make itself manifest?

The House of Commons of the Convention Parliament recognized the danger of Milton's tracts to the restored Royalist regime by moving, on June 16, 1660, that the king issue a proclamation against *Eikonoklastes* and *Pro Populo Anglicano Defensio*. An order to the attorney general for drafting such a proclamation was approved at a meeting of the Privy Council on June 27; and on August 13, about two weeks before the Act of Oblivion, the Royal Proclamation itself appeared.[54] The proclamation asked that Milton's two tracts be called in and suppressed, together with John Goodwin's *The Obstructours of Justice*, which, it will be recalled, leaned heavily upon *The Tenure of Kings and Magistrates*. It also charged that chief magistrates, justices of the peace, and vice-chancellors cause these

[54] *A Proclamation For calling in, and suppressing of two Books written by John Milton; the one Intituled, Johannis Miltoni Angli pro Populo Anglicano Defensio, contra Claudii Anonymi aliàs Salmasii, Defensionem Regiam; and the other in answer to a Book Intituled, The Pourtraicture of his Sacred Majesty in his Solitude and Sufferings. And also a third Book Intituled, The Obstructors of Justice, written by John Goodwin* (London, 1660).

three books to be delivered to sheriffs for public burning by the common hangman, and forbade that any man "presume to Print, Vend, Sell, or Disperse any the aforesaid Books" upon pain of the king's heavy displeasure and of such further punishment as might be inflicted in accordance with the laws of the realm. Such measures were to be taken so that the king's subjects might not be corrupted in their judgments "with such wicked and Traitrous principles" as were "dispersed and scattered throughout the beforementioned Books," the Proclamation made clear — an apprehension which apparently prompted two newspapers, *The Parliamentary Intelligencer* and *Mercurius Publicus*, to give the order prominent notice;[55] and soon a dispatch from London reported that the injunctions had been carried out, that the infamous books of John Goodwin and John Milton had been immolated at the Sessions House in the Old Bailey by the hands of the common hangman.[56] Though Milton himself escaped punishment, "a strange omission" as well as an "odd strain of clemency," as Gilbert Burnet observed,[57] the Convention Parliament saw to it that two of his books went up in flames.

Loyal Cavalier-Church party members of Commons no doubt moved that Charles II officially recognize the danger of Milton's tracts because Milton had, in the months preceding the return of the king, attempted to stem the tide of Royalist feeling by answering, in *Brief Notes Upon a Late Sermon*, Matthew Griffith's open advocacy of the restoration of the House of Stuart, and by addressing himself, in *The Readie and Easie Way to Establish a Free Commonwealth*, to General Monk, who before the election of the Convention Parliament guided the destiny of England through the might of his army. These two tracts had no apparent effect on the course of events; but they elicited full-length replies and casual comments and thus reminded the nation that the blind champion of the Commonwealth still fought in behalf of the Good Old Cause. And they aroused fears that his rhetoric, both newly minted and of old coinage, would sway the minds of men and make them march to the measure of his thought.[58]

The Censure of the Rota, which appeared about a month before

[55] See William Riley Parker, *op. cit.*, pp. 103–4, for a clarification of these notices.

[56] *Mercurius Publicus* (Thursday, September 6, to Thursday, September 13, 1660), No. 37, p. 578.

[57] *Burnet's History of My Own Time* (ed. Osmund Airy, Oxford, 1897), I, 283.

[58] For an analysis of Milton's methods, see Wilber Elwyn Gilman, "Milton's Rhetoric: Studies in his Defense of Liberty," in *The University of Missouri Studies*, Vol. XIV (1939), No. 3.

the Convention Parliament assembled, expressed such fears. This pamphlet, an obvious satire which ridiculed not only Milton but also the Rota (a debating society which discussed "airie modells" of government), purported to record a discussion of *The Readie and Easie Way*, as well as the conclusions that august society supposedly reached. Discussion, in the main, revealed opposition to Milton's methods and principles. One member wondered why Milton had not given up writing, since he had scribbled his eyes out to little or no purpose; another resented Milton's attack upon Charles I—a "dirty out-rage," he called it; still another, in reference to Milton's views on marriage and divorce, gave him the dubious "honour to be Styld the Founder of a Sect."[59] Such comments make it evident that members of the Rota had turned their attention not simply to the latest of Milton's tracts but also to a large portion of his revolutionary program, part of which had been effective enough to command a definite following; and as they assembled their bill of particulars against him they agreed that his power lay in his eloquence—an eloquence which might be "thrown away under a Monarchy" but which was "of admirable use in a Popular Government, where Orators carry all the Rabble before them."[60] Indeed, toward the end of the debate, a "Worthy Knight" arose to summarize, in a sense, opinion so far expressed. He declared, among many things, that Milton's work was "all windy foppery from the beginning to the end, written to the eleuation of that Rabble and meant to cheat the Ignorant," that Milton always fought with the "flat" of his hand, like a rhetorician, never with the "Logicall fist."[61] The author of *The Censure of the Rota* thus rightly recognized the power of Milton's eloquence; he saw, furthermore, and apparently feared the effects of Milton's arguments on the people of England. Despite his satirical intent, he expressed an apprehension which never left the Cavalier-Church party: that many of his fellow countrymen would fall under the power of Milton's persuasion.

Such a fear found its fullest expression in George Starkey's *The Dignity of Kingship Asserted*,[62] which appeared almost concurrently

[59] *The Censure of the Rota Upon Mr Miltons Book, Entituled, The Ready and Easie way to Establish A Free Common-wealth* (London, 1660), p. 12.

[60] *Ibid.*, p. 8.

[61] *Ibid.*, p. 13.

[62] *The Dignity of Kingship Asserted: In Answer to Mr. Milton's Ready and Easie way to establish a Free Common-wealth* (London, 1660). William Riley Parker, in his facsimile edition of this book ([New York: Columbia University Press, 1943], Introduction), argues convincingly that G. S., the author, was George Starkey.

with *The Censure of the Rota.* In the "Epistle Dedicatory," addressed to Charles II himself, Starkey revealed why he had written his book. In *The Readie and Easie Way* Milton had endeavored "*to divert those that at present sit at* Helme," he claimed, and "*by* fair pretenses, *and* Sophisticate Arguments, *would easily delude an* inconsiderate Reader *into a* belief, *First,* That the Government of a *Republique* is in it self, incomparably to be preferred before *Kingship,* whether we respect *men* as *men,* or as *Christians. But Secondly, as the Case stands with us, he would strike us into a fear, namely,* That to readmit your Majesty, is unsafe, and hazardable, at the best, and may prove dangerous and ruinous to all."[63] Furthermore, Starkey found Milton's pamphlet "dangerously insnaring, *the fallacy of the* Arguments *being so cunningly hidden, as not to be discerned by any, nor every* Eye"; his language "smooth *and* tempting, *the* Expressions pathetical, *and apt to move the* Affections"; his drift of "desperate consequence, *namely to undoe (if possible) all our* hopes" and to continue, "*nay to settle and fix*" irreparably misery upon England.[64] In short, Starkey made it clear in his dedication that Milton's pamphlet was such a threat to the return of Charles II that he felt compelled to give it an answer.

Starkey approached his task with considerable deference, admitting at the outset Milton's tremendous advantages. Nevertheless, he examined ably, if somewhat pedantically, not only *The Readie and Easie Way* but also arguments found in *Eikonoklastes* and in *Pro Populo Anglicano Defensio.* To Milton's claim that the death of Charles I had brought freedom to England, for example, Starkey replied, Freedom for whom? For the Lords? For the people of England in general? To Milton's contention that the Venetian Republic and Holland should stand as models of good government, Starkey responded that Venice was in reality a monarchy and that furthermore the one standard in Holland was riches.[65] Was this the measure of greatness? But if Starkey found objections to Milton's matter, he had only admiration for his manner: he could never forget that Milton possessed a "*fluent elegant style,*" that Milton had "all the advantages which an *acute wit, ready invention, much reading,* and *copious expression*" could give.[66] For this reason, Starkey believed that Milton

[63] *The Dignity of Kingship Asserted,* sigs. [A8v]-a.
[64] *Ibid.,* sig. a2.
[65] *Ibid.,* pp. 30 ff, 99 ff.
[66] *Ibid.,* pp. 5–6.

was a genuine threat to monarchy in England, a master of rhetoric who through his very powers of persuasion might compel people to look askance at the return of Charles II and with favor upon the dying Commonwealth and the Good Old Cause. Though his immediate fears were unfounded, Starkey took Milton's measure with an accurate eye; the very powers of persuasion in Milton he so genuinely feared later turned many against the kind of monarchy which accompanied the Restoration of the House of Stuart.

Mingled with this recognition of Milton's abilities and the consequent fear of his influence on the minds of men, cries of derision and anger rang out more and more audibly as the Rump and the secluded members dissolved and the Convention Parliament took over the destiny of England. Milton was the "Goos-quill Champion" of the Rump, cried one scurrilous pamphleteer, "an old Heretick both in Religion and Manners, that by his will would shake off his Governours as he doth his Wives, foure in a Fourtnight." Moreover, he went on to call Milton a parasite, a flatterer of tyrannical power, who through his *The Readie and Easie Way* had run himself into briars and would become angry if the nation would not bear him company.[67] To William Collinne, Milton was plainly a fool, deserving to be sent to Bridewell for pretending so much good to his country and not daring to sign his name to his piece—a fool together with John Harrington, both of whom should be laughed at for their "assertions and pretence of maintaining such a rediculous thing as a free State, since in 12 years time we have found by experience, the Nation never was more Quiet, then when governed by a single person."[68] But Roger L'Estrange offered the best of such fare. In *Treason Arraigned*, he accused Milton of writing *Plain English*—a piece, he declared, drawn by no fool but one which "*vomits*" on the ashes of Charles I;[69] in *No Blinde Guides*, written in answer to *Brief Notes Upon a Late Sermon*, he described Milton's "Blasphemous Insolence," which he said invaded the prerogatives of God himself, and mocked at Milton's blindness and his opinions on marriage and divorce;[70] and in *Physician Cure thy Self* he claimed

[67] *The Character of the Rump* (London, 1660), pp. 2–3.

[68] *The Spirit of the Phanatiques Dissected. And The solemne League and Covenant solemnly dicussed in 30 Queries* ([London], 1660), pp. 7–8.

[69] *Treason Arraigned, In Answer to Plain English* (London, 1660), pp. 2–3.

[70] *No Blinde Guides* (London, 1660), pp. 2, 8, 10. See J. Milton French, "'Blind Milton' Ridiculed in 'Poor Robin,' 1664–1674," *Notes & Queries*, CXCVI (1951), 470–71, for a subsequent series of listings of "Blinde Milton" in the satirical almanac, *Poor Robin*.

that a pamphlet entitled *Eye-Salve* presented the same seditious "medicine" that by general report had "strook *Milton* BLIND."[71] Furthermore, as Charles II prepared to sail for England, satirical verse appeared in London, presenting Milton as a poor knave and a wretch;[72] and two days before the King entered Whitehall in triumph, John Heydon, with the prophetic voice of an astrologer, uttered a solemn warning: "If *Milton* beginning to write an Answer to the late Kings Book against Monarchy," he exclaimed, "was at the second word, by the power of God strucken blind: What shall fall upon them that endeavour to destroy his Son; verily they that fight against him, fight against Providence."[73]

Even Milton, equipped as he was with his great powers of rhetoric, could not avail against Providence. The wave of the Restoration swept by, amid mocking laughter for him and shouts of praise for the King, sounds of which still echoed in London streets when, on June 6, Roger L'Estrange moved in for the kill. Let the "*General, the Secluded Members, and the Honest Souldjers, live Long, Happily,* and *Beloved,*" he advised; "and let the *Rest* take their *Fortune.*" And with this introduction he then reviewed Milton's unsuccessful attempts in *The Readie and Easie Way* and in *Brief Notes Upon a Late Sermon* to perpetuate the Rump Parliament and to turn sentiment against the restoration of the King. What Milton's fortune should be for writing thus, L'Estrange failed to divulge; but he implied that Milton deserved punishment.[74] Like his own later Samson, Milton now stood blind among enemies—mocked, derided for a fool, and accounted as one who had justly come by his deserts. But with these cries of derision and vengeance sounded also notes of admiration and fear—admiration for his learning and rhetorical power and fear of his influence on the people of England. Perhaps this is the reason for the motion in the House of Commons on June 16, which resulted in the Royal Proclamation some two months later against *Eikonoklastes* and *Pro Populo Anglicano Defensio.*[75]

[71] *Physician Cure thy Self* (London, 1660), p. 2.

[72] G. S., *Britains Triumph, for her Imparallel'd Deliverance* (London, 1660), p. 15.

[73] *The Idea of Tyranny* (London, 1660), sigs. [N4v–N5], the third part of Heydon's *The Idea of the Law Charactered, From Moses to King Charles* (London, 1660).

[74] *L'Estrange His Apology* (London, 1660), pp. 86, 113, 157. See also William Riley Parker, *Milton's Contemporary Reputation,* p. 102, n. 81, for a discussion of L'Estrange's use of his earlier pamphlets. It is to be noted that L'Estrange sometimes spoke ironically.

[75] Between the motion in Commons and the Royal Proclamation, George Starkey, in *Royal and Other Innocent Bloud Crying Aloud to Heaven for due vengeance* (London, 1660, p. 18), recalled that Milton had deemed Parliament's action against Charles I "Heroick"; and a broadside

Milton stirred Cavalier-Church animosity even after the exciting summer of the Restoration. The ghost of Salmasius returned to answer belatedly, in an *Opus Posthumum,* Milton's *Pro Populo Anglicano Defensio;* Joseph Jane's *Eikon Aklastos,* an early answer to *Eikonoklastes,* reappeared under *Salmasius his Dissection and Confutation of the Diabolical Rebel Milton in his impious Doctrines of Falsehood;* and George Starkey crowed over Milton's defeat by issuing *The Dignity of Kingship Asserted* under a new title, *Monarchy Triumphing Over Traiterous Republicans.* Concurrent with these revived and renewed attacks upon Milton fresh vituperations appeared. David Lloyd, for example, found time to calumniate Milton in his biography of Charles II. While the young king was abroad in exile at Leyden, Lloyd wrote, he made a profound impression upon his professors. Salmasius indeed had been so impressed by the qualities in the murdered king's son that he had been moved to make his defense of Charles I. "A greater, and a better King, was never the subject of a Grammarians Pen, and a nobler Pen was never employed in the defence of a King," Lloyd declared. This observation led Lloyd to comment upon Milton, that "blind Beetle" who would dare deny such a statement, nay, "That mercenary *Milton,*" who had sworn service to the prosperous villainy of the Puritan Rebellion and who had enough "wisedom of the flesh" to justify the lusts of his masters.[76] To David Lloyd, Salmasius and Milton stood in sharp contrast. Salmasius, out of his love for the martyred king's son, wrote his noble vindication of Charles I; Milton, for love of money, justified murder and lust. The epithet, "that mercenary Milton," struck such a congenial note that it became common usage among members of the Cavalier-Church party.[77]

While the Cavalier-Church party scattered such accusations abroad, Milton inspired further comment in the inner councils of state. John Gauden, dissatisfied with his bishopric at Exeter because its revenues were meager, began a celebrated correspondence with Edward

entitled *The Picture of the Good Old Cause drawn to the Life In the Effigies of Master Prais-God Barebone* (London, 1660), included Milton as an example of God's judgment: "Milton *that writ two Books against the Kings, and* Salmasius *his Defence of Kings, struck totally blind, he being not much above* 40. *years old.*"

[76] *Eikon Basilike. Or, The True Pourtraicture of His Sacred Majesty Charls the II In Three Books* (London, 1660), II, 65. About the same time, more scurrilous verse appeared. See, for example, Collonel Baker, *The Blazing-Star, or, Nolls Nose* (London, 1660), p. [i].

[77] It may be that Royalists found this notion in Salmasius' belated reply to Milton. See J. Milton French, "Some Notes on Milton," *Notes & Queries,* CLXXXVIII (1945), 52–55.

Hyde, Earl of Clarendon, to see whether he could better his estate—a tart exchange which touched on matters admittedly of interest to Milton.[78] Gauden obviously had a trump card to play in beginning the correspondence and soon he disclosed it. On the twenty-first of January, 1661, he wrote to Clarendon that he, not Charles I, had been the author of *Eikon Basilike*, the famous "King's Book" which had done so much for the Royalist cause, and that in view of this he had claims on a better position. At first, Clarendon made no reply; but after Gauden pushed his suit by writing to the Duke of York, the chancellor answered, revealing that he had already been informed of Gauden's contribution to the Royalist triumph. "*The particular*" about which Gauden so often wrote, Clarendon said, had been imparted to him under secrecy and he therefore felt that he could not disclose the fact that he possessed such information; and when it ceased to be a secret, he continued, he knew of no one who would "*be glad of it but Mr. Milton.*" Milton, of course, would have gladly shared this information since he had intimated in *Eikonoklastes* that Charles I had not been the author of *Eikon Basilike.* But whether the "particular" of which Clarendon spoke actually referred to John Gauden's claim, or whether Gauden actually wrote the King's Book will perhaps never be known, though it now appears that the Bishop had a large hand in putting the materials for *Eikon Basilike* in order.[79] However true or false the claim may have been, it remained a secret until 1690, when it was released to the public through what became known as the Anglesey Memorandum. Needless to say, Whigs at that time exploited the claim for all it was worth.

As long as Gauden's claim remained a secret, however, the Cavalier-Church party could employ *Eikon Basilike* to strengthen their cause. The sentiments it expressed still appealed to a large body of people and it rapidly became a sort of Royalist bible, to be read and quoted with a reverence just short of that shown for the Scriptures. Cavalier-Church interests therefore demanded a defense of its genuineness, as well as an assault upon its detractors, both of which would cast disfavor upon the Dissent. Thus Richard Perrinchief, in his edition of the works of Charles I, took considerable pains to establish the authenticity of the book and at the same time forwarded reasons

[78] For an account of this correspondence, see Masson, *op. cit.*, VI, 425–35.

[79] For the latest information on the authorship controversy, see Francis F. Madan, *A New Bibliography of the Eikon Basilike of King Charles the First* (Oxford, 1950), pp. 126–63.

for Puritan attacks on it. Indeed, Perrinchief declared, the regicides admitted among themselves that Charles I was the author. John Bradshawe, for example, had asked the printer Royston how so bad a man could write so good a book. Reasons for questioning its integrity, then, were not real but political in that *Eikon Basilike*, as Perrinchief inferred, had achieved a wide circulation and had moved many people into the Royalist fold, and attempts of the Commonwealth government to suppress it had only made people seek after it with more zeal. Suppression failing, the government shifted its tactics and "hired certain mercenary Souls to despoil the *King* of the Credit of being the Author of it." At this point in his story, Perrinchief singled out Milton for especial notice. He called him a "base Scribe, naturally fitted to compose Satyres and invent Reproaches, who made himself notorious by some licentious and infamous Pamphlets, and so approved himself as fit for their service." "This man," he went on, "they encouraged (by translating him from a needy Pedagogue to the office of a Secretary) to write that Scandalous book Εἰκονοκλάστης, (an Invective against the *King's* Meditations and to answer the learned *Salmasius* his Defence of *Charles the First*."[80] But such tactics failed, Perrinchief concluded; examination of the style of *Eikon Basilike* as well as the testimony of those close to the King established the falseness of Puritan claims. And he might have added that for questioning the integrity of *Eikon Basilike* and for writing *Pro Populo Anglicano Defensio* Milton had, as John Taylor observed, been wonderfully punished by being "strucken blind," and "could never since by any art, or skill, either recover his sight, or preserve his Books from being burned by the hands of the common Hang-man."[81] Such punishment further testified to Puritan duplicity and hence to the authenticity of the King's Book. Both God and Charles I stood on the Cavalier-Church side.

Such sentiments expressed the burden of Cavalier-Church opposition to Milton through the remaining years of Royalist reaction to the time of the Popish Plot. The party in power recognized his threat to Royalist principles and the Clarendon Code and hence not only attacked his positions as false and unsound but also attempted to discredit the cause for which he stood by vilifying his character and by

[80] ΒΑΣΙΛΙΚΑ. *The Workes Of King Charles The Martyr* (London, 1662), pp. 94–95. Perrinchief's life of Charles I appeared in 1676 and 1684, and in the *Works* in 1687.

[81] *The Traytors Perspective-glass* (London, 1662), pp. 21–22.

attributing his misfortunes to the justice of God. Even the historian James Heath intimated that Milton had been stricken blind for writing *Eikonoklastes* and *Pro Populo Anglicano Defensio* and flatly stated that the former had been deservedly burned.[82] Robert South, in a sermon preached before the King on the fast day of Charles I in 1663, went beyond Heath's cool historical appraisal to express a hatred for Milton almost unmatched in the Restoration. Attacking the fomenters of the Puritan Rebellion in general, he turned attention specifically toward those who had pleaded conscience for their rebellious actions, who had claimed the support of Scripture as interpreted by their own inner light to carry out the trial and execution of Charles I. He also denounced those as more knowing, but not less wicked, who had insisted not so much upon the warrant of Scripture as upon the dispensations of Providence for their revolt. Milton had spoken roundly to this very matter, Robert South informed Charles II and his Royal congregation—Milton, "their Latin Advocate, who, like the blind Adder, spits his Poison on the King's Person and Cause": *Deum secuti ducem, et impressa passim divina vestigia venerantes, viam haud obscuram, sed illustrem, illius auspiciis commonstratam et patefactam ingressi sumus.*[83] This claim of being led directly by God, South went on to make clear, this plea of conscience, lay at the basis of all Puritan enormities—the imprisonment and murder of Charles I, the breaking of oaths, the persecutions and sequestrations which attended the Rebellion. "O Blessed God," South exclaimed, "to what Heighth can preposterous, audacious Impiety arise!" Now at this very time Nonconformists were crying loudly for liberty of conscience and chafing against the first acts of the Clarendon Code. In view of this, South's implications would be evident. Nonconformist principles were identical with those of a poisonous man and they had furthermore brought misery to England; Nonconformists were therefore poisonous themselves and a threat to the peace of the nation. Through the ancient devices of association and of *argumentum ad hominem*, Robert South thus used Milton to strike against the cause of the Dissent.

[82] *A Brief Chronicle Of the Late Intestine Warr in the Three Kingdoms of England, Scotland & Ireland* (London, 1663), p. 435.

[83] *A Sermon Preach'd before King Charles II, on the Fast (Appointed Jan. 30.) For The Execrable Murder Of His Royal Father* (London, [1708]), pp. 22–23. South's Latin is not identical with Milton's, and has been made to conform, in part, with that in *Pro Populo Anglicano Defensio.*

Nor was he alone in employing such tactics. David Lloyd, in his memoirs of Charles I, recalled the mendacity of the rebels in their attempt to discredit the King's Book by robbing his Majesty of the honor of writing it; and he pointed a finger directly at Milton's *Eikonoklastes*.[84] Moreover, in 1670 Peter du Moulin published a collection of some of his earlier Latin poems, which included some verses "To the Bestial Blackguard John Milton, Parricide and Advocate of Parricide," as well as an account, now for the first time fully revealed, of how he had written the *Regii Sanguinis Clamor*, which had been attributed by Milton to "Morus." Peter du Moulin admitted, to be sure, that some of his lines against Milton were savage and asked that they not be construed "as indicating the private character of the author," since they had sprung from his zeal for the church.[85] But the very fact that he printed these poems at this time, together with an account of how he had fooled Milton by keeping silent as to his authorship of the *Regii Sanguinis Clamor*, indicates his desire to discredit the cause which Milton supported. Furthermore, in 1674 Richard Meggott, Chaplain in Ordinary to Charles II, preached a fiery sermon against the political principles of the regicides and singled out Milton in the Robert South manner. He condemned to hell "that Anti-christian Principle, That it is lawful for the People, upon the ill Managery and Abuse of their Power, by Arms and Force to despose and punish their Princes." Such a principle, indeed, laid an ax to the root of all civil society and destroyed the foundations of all peace and settlement. Fortunately, Meggott continued, the people did not accept this principle nor did the Commons even represent the people. Did the Commons stand for the people of Ireland? No. Did they stand for the people of Scotland? No. For the people of the country, of the city? No. "Were they the Peoples Representatives in Parliament?" "No, so far was it from any of this, that the ablest Writer that was to be had for money, to defend the Villany to the World, being pinched, with the fewness and despicableness of those who were engaged in it, hath nothing to return to it, but that sneaking Blasphemy, That it was the Mysterious Will of the Lord, and so *not many Wise, not many*

[84] *Memoires of the Lives, Actions, Sufferings & Deaths Of Those Noble, Reverend, and Excellent Personages* (London, 1668), p. 221.

[85] *Petri Molinaei P. F.* ΠΑ'ΡΕΡΓΑ. *Poematum Libelli Tres* (Cambridge, 1670). See Masson, *op. cit.*, V, 213 ff. for a discussion of this publication and translations from it, some of which have been used. See John Walter Good, *op. cit.*, pp. 52–53, for Samuel Butler's satirical comments on Milton.

Mighty, not many Noble were *called* to it."[86] Meggott thus not only attacked Milton's defense of the Commons but also carried on the legend that he possessed mercenary motives. It is clear that he, as well as other members of the Cavalier-Church party, thought that their best attack against the Nonconformist cause lay not simply in exploding principles which they believed were false but in vilifying the persons of their political enemies. Such tactics became commonplace on both sides as the conflict unrolled.

Some Cavalier-Church opposition to Milton, however, appeared without vituperation or violent personal abuse. John Warly, for example, examined Milton's *A Treatise of Civil Power* without undue excitement. Warly's main concern was that the age, through factions and the publication of tracts, had exposed the Church to contempt; and his desire was to reassert its ancient authority. In pursuit of this task, he analyzed a number of pamphlets which he considered subversive, one of which was *A Treatise of Civil Power*, whose principal argument had been that a magistrate could not force matters of conscience. Such a position, so dangerous to Church authority, could be come by only through distorting the meaning of Scripture, he maintained; only a "great Agent, for *Libertinism*" could suggest to Parliament, as Milton had done, the "impossibility of the powers interposing in Matters of Religion in some cases." The details of Warly's attack upon Milton's deductions from Scripture need not be listed for the present discussion, but his conclusions possess some significance. He contended that Milton had made little sense by arguing that a magistrate should be obeyed for conscience' sake; for how could a man be obliged to obey him, in accordance with this Biblical injunction, when "some duty is commanded which his Conscience contradicts," which had been the gist of the pamphlet? "To this 'tis enough to say," he concluded, "that the fallacy lyes in the word *Conscience*, which in that place must not signifie each man's *persuasion* or *apprehension* of the Duty, for if it were so, some men would not be obliged to obey their Prince, and their fancies exempt them from subjection."[87] Warly no doubt believed that this analysis had accomplished his task, that he had asserted, according to his stated design, the rights of princes in

[86] *A Sermon Preached before the Right Honourable The Lord Mayor And Aldermen, &c. At Gvild-Hall Chappel, January the 30th 1673/4* (London, [1674]), pp. 33, 45–46.

[87] *The Reasoning Apostate: Or Modern Latitude-Man Consider'd, As he opposeth the Authority Of The King and Church* (London, 1677), pp. 22 ff.

ecclesiastical matters and thus had stopped, as was his hope, "the mouths of a factious Multitude by breaking and diverting the force of their Current." With neither anger nor logic he attempted to turn the people of England away from Nonconformist positions into the orthodox paths of Cavalier-Church thought.

This was also Thomas Lamb's aim in *A Fresh Suit Against Independency*, which claimed that Milton's position on tithes was inimical to the "National Church-Way." The Independents were habitually against tithes as Jewish, Lamb observed, "though the Triers at *Whitehall* were not"; in general, they were against all set maintenance for ministers. As evidence of this position, which ran athwart Anglican policy, Lamb pointed to *Considerations Touching the Likeliest Means to Remove Hirelings out of the Church*, by which title he placed a simple marginal note, "Milton."[88] But Lamb's objections were as gentle as his name; he merely revealed that Milton's tract helped undermine the national church and considered it dangerous enough to call it to public attention.

Such was Cavalier-Church opposition to Milton from the Restoration to the Popish Plot. Some of it showed derision and hate. Some of it expressed fear of his rhetoric and of its effects on men's minds. Some of it vilified his character for the purpose of discrediting the cause he so ably defended. Indeed, in the years immediately preceding the Popish Plot, Milton inspired such anger and fear that Sir Joseph Williamson, the Secretary of State, acted to prevent Daniel Skinner, an enterprising young scholar in possession of two Milton manuscripts, from issuing, either in Amsterdam or in London, Milton's *Letters of State*, which, much to Skinner's annoyance, had appeared without authority in 1676, prefaced by an ironical admixture of praise and blame. Sir Joseph made Skinner feel so uncomfortable over his relation with Milton that, in the exchange of letters which the affair engendered, the young scholar expediently denied any acceptance of Milton's political principles. Nor did the story end here. Milton's sentiments seemed so dangerous to the established government that Isaac Barrow, the Master of Trinity College, Cambridge, threatened Skinner with penalties if he should "publish any writing mischievous to the Church or State."[89] Such events, coupled with Sir

[88] *A Fresh Suit Against Independency: Or the National Church-way Vindicated, The Independent Church-way Condemned* (London, 1677), p. 94.

[89] For the story of Skinner's attempt to publish the *Letters of State* and *De Doctrina Christiana*,

Joseph Williamson's expressed suspicion of Skinner for his association with Milton, to which may be added the assumption that Nonconformists employed Milton's tracts—all argue, not simply that Milton was sufficiently known to all the learned in Europe through his works in Latin and English, as Edward Phillips, in his *Theatrum Poetarum*, observed, but also that his principles had begun to sway public opinion at home, that his revolutionary program had begun to turn the people of England away from Cavalier-Church orthodoxy toward Nonconformist concepts of toleration and a limited magisterial power. If Milton actually exerted such influence, he definitely threatened the Clarendon Code and emerged, even while he yet lived, as a source of strength to those Nonconformist and other groups which coalesced during the Popish Plot to form the Whig party.

see Masson, *op. cit.*, VI, 790 ff. For additional information concerning this story, see J. Milton French, "That Late Villain Milton," *PMLA*, LV (1940), 102–15, and Maurice Kelley, "Addendum: The Later Career of Daniel Skinner," *ibid.*, 116–18.

Chapter Three

THE ATTEMPTED WHIG REVOLUTION

THE WHIG PARTY made its first thrust for power as an organized political body under the leadership of the Earl of Shaftesbury during the national hysteria which followed the Popish Plot. A coalition of country interests and Nonconformist ideals, it drove the old Cavalier-Church group, now known as the Tory party, to the brink of disaster through a brilliantly led campaign to seize control of the government. Taking advantage of a widespread fear of Rome, which Titus Oates brought to a frenzied pitch by his alleged discovery of a Popish Plot to kill Charles II, Whigs struck at Tory power through three Bills of Exclusion, all of them designed to assert the supremacy of Parliament by preventing the succession of James, the Catholic Duke of York. The first Bill of Exclusion passed the Commons in the Parliament of 1679. The second Bill of Exclusion passed the Commons in the next Parliament and was taken to the House of Lords by William Lord Russell, where it was rejected by a vote of sixty-three to thirty. The third Bill of Exclusion, after some debate in the Commons, was read on March 28, 1681, at the colorful Parliament at Oxford; but on that very day Charles II asserted royal authority by dissolving Parliament and in so doing defeated Whig efforts to exclude York from the throne. Disorganized and fearful, Whigs fled Oxford to await royal revenge, which followed close on their heels. On July 2 Shaftesbury was sent to the Tower on the charge of high treason, only to emerge, after escaping capital punishment, a broken leader of a much-weakened Whig party; and in 1683 Lord Russell and Algernon Sidney, implicated in a supposed Rye House conspiracy to kill the King and seize power, were convicted of high treason and sent to the block. Through astute maneuvering, Charles II not only thwarted Whig attempts to gain control of the government but also so consolidated Tory strength that he was able to invoke some of the old oppressive acts of the Clarendon Code; and when he died in 1685, after ruling four years without Parliament, he passed the Crown to his Catholic brother James without opposition. The main tangible evidence of the attempted Whig Revolution during these years was a press made free through the lapse of the Licensing Act in 1679, a breach in Tory solidarity which James II and his "loyal" Parliament closed in 1685 by renewing the Act.

Milton served the Whig party well in its attempt to break Tory strength and seize control of the government. Tories, it is true, cheerfully employed him when his positions, as they sometimes did, argued their cause; but his main contribution to the political life of his country at this time flowed through Whig pamphleteers and high-ranking members of the Whig party. *Areopagitica*, for example, appeared in two separate adaptations to argue for a free press and against a renewal of the Licensing Act. *Pro Populo Anglicano Defensio* inspired Thomas Hunt and Samuel Johnson, two popular Whig pamphleteers, to write tracts which turned opinion against Tory principles and practice and inclined many people to favor the Bills of Exclusion. Moreover, Lord Russell and Algernon Sidney, both Whig leaders of high standing, lost their lives for holding and acting upon principles which derived either directly or indirectly from Milton. Milton's principles, indeed, proved so effective and useful that Tories attempted to counter their influence by spreading disquieting stories about Milton himself, the most fascinating of which was that he had been a Jesuit in disguise and had died in the Roman communion. By the time Charles II laid down the scepter Tories recognized, if their opponents did not, that Milton had become an oracle of the Whig party.

I

Milton contributed to the first phases of the attempted Whig revolution through Charles Blount's *A Just Vindication of Learning* in 1679 and William Denton's *An Apology for the Liberty of the Press* in 1681, two unlike but unmistakable adaptations of *Areopagitica*. The reason for the appearance of these adaptations early in the Whig thrust for power may be quickly told. In May of 1679 a Whig Parliament deliberately allowed the old Press Act of 1662 to lapse, with the result that the judiciary, primarily through Chief Justice Scroggs, attempted to enforce the Tory policy of the imprimatur by court decisions, many of which aroused public disfavor. Stringent decisions against printers and printing, coupled with other questionable actions, engendered so much opposition against him that he was summarily impeached, during which proceedings arose a great pamphlet war in which Chief Justice Scroggs defended the right of the courts to regulate printing despite the expiration of the Licensing Act, while Whigs, naturally enough, maintained the desirability of a free press. From the lapse of the Act to the dissolution of Parliament in 1681 a lively battle over freedom of thought and expression resounded through England.

Battle was joined when Benjamin Harris printed in 1679 *An Appeal From the Country To the City*,[1] a pamphlet in which Charles Blount, its author, painted in terrifying colors the fate of London should Papists gain control of the city. For printing such a tract, Harris was brought to trial before Chief Justice Scroggs, who stated the position of the courts succinctly. He claimed that the judiciary had met at the King's command and had unanimously declared "That all Persons, that do Write, or Print, or Sell any Pamphlet, that is either Scandalous to Public, or Private Persons; such Books may be seized, and the Person punished by Law." He declared furthermore that according to this agreement among judges all books scandalous to the government could be seized and all persons "Exposing" them punished. Reporters of news could be similarly indicted and punished, if what they wrote was in error, even though their accounts were neither "Scandalous, Seditious, nor Reflective upon the Government, or the State."[2] Moreover, in a speech before the King's Bench, the Chief Justice amplified these positions by explaining the duties of his own court as they bore upon the clash between printers and the judiciary. He declared that the proper business of his court was "to take care to prevent and punish the mischiefs of the Press," that such had to be done for the safety and peace of the nation. For, he continued, if men could with safety write and print what they pleased, the country would be overrun with the lies and libels of the Papists, the factious, and mercenaries alike, much to the discomfort of the government.[3] With these positions Roger L'Estrange fully agreed, though he perhaps privately deplored that the judiciary had attempted to take over his former office of Surveyor of the Imprimery, which he had found

[1] *An Appeal From the Country To the City, For the Preservation of His Majesties Person, Liberty, Property, and the Protestant Religion* (London, 1679).

[2] *A Short, But Just Account of the Tryal of Benjamin Harris, Upon an Information Brought against him For Printing and Vending a late Seditious Book* (London, 1679), p. 6.

[3] *The Lord Chief Justice Scroggs his Speech in the Kings-Bench the First Day of This Present Michaelmas Term 1679* (London, 1679), p. 7.

personally lucrative. But whatever his private thoughts he publicly defended the design of the courts to suppress what they considered subversive, particularly since, as he claimed, unlicensed printing could lead, as it had during the Puritan Rebellion, to the collapse of established religion and of constituted authority and government.[4]

Such an attempt by the judiciary and by Tory pamphleteers to muzzle the press called out strong replies from Whig forces in England. Pamphlets and broadsides, many of them scurrilous and abusive, attacked Chief Justice Scroggs for the stand he had taken, as well as Roger L'Estrange for his personal interest in the lapse of the Press Act. One broadside depicted the Chief Justice as a wild bull, bellowing over his impeachment and lamenting that he had ever been required to act as a judge in such troublesome and seditious times. "A Plague of my Starrs," he was represented as saying, "that ever I shu'd be Born in a Time of Printing! by *Wakemans* Soul, I hope *he's* Frying in Hell, that first invented that Heretical Art." Opposition continued to plague him in spite of his belief that he had "sent all those mangy Booksellers, Printers, &c. to the Devil by whole Sale" and had "set up an *Inquisition* against Printing."[5]

But L'Estrange fared even worse, standing, as he did, in the minds of Whigs as a symbol of tyrannical power. They twitted him in that he was now out of a job, in that he had lost his lucrative position as Surveyor of the Imprimery with the lapse of the Licensing Act. "He is still big with the *Press*," one rollicking attack ran; "He is sore grieved at the *Press*, 'tis the *Press* had made the people mad, because he cannot hang his Padlock on it again, that he might stifle all Pamphlets against the Papists, and put the *Guinies* and *Crowns* in his Pocket; oh! those were the Golden days he would fain see again, but in the mean time this *Licenser* is turning *Physician*, and he will forsooth either quickly cure or kill the people."[6] But not all attacks ran in such a humorous vein; some seriously questioned whether he was qualified to act as a licenser or competent enough to discuss the issues under debate. "'Tis the Opinion of more Doctors then one, that he had better have let it all alone," it was observed. "He has only exas-

[4] *A Seasonable Memorial in Some Historical Notes upon the Liberties of the Presse and Pulpit* (2d ed.; London, 1680), *passim.*

[5] *The Bellowings of a Wild-Bull* [London, 1680], p. 3.

[6] *The Observator Observ'd: or, Protestant Observations upon Anti-Protestant Pamphlets* (Friday, May 6, 1681), No. 1, sig. A1r.

perated, exagitated and boutfeud, by accusing almost a third part of the Protestants of the Kingdom of Plots and Contrivances, vilifying and discountenancing the Kings Evidence and distracting the minds of People in general; and still the Burthen of his Song is, oh the *Exorbitont Liberty of the Press;* as if he only wrote for his Licensers Place, and the sweets of Domineering at *Stationers-Hall.*"[7] Such was the tenor of opposition to Roger L'Estrange between 1679 and 1681. Whigs not only resented the judgments of Chief Justice Scroggs but also violently opposed the office of licenser and its former incumbent and hence raised their voices in protest in a general offensive against any renewal of the old Press Act. That the Act was not renewed for six years testifies to the success of Whig efforts.

Now, Charles Blount contributed to this Whig offensive in *A Just Vindication of Learning* shortly before the Press Act expired. Addressing the Whig Parliament, which had assembled on March 6, 1679, he called attention to the late Act which was "*so near Expiring*" and asked that body to consider his arguments against its renewal. Most of his contentions came from *Areopagitica,* which Milton had also addressed to Parliament; indeed, Blount followed the main lines of Milton's oration, cutting here, adding there, sometimes paraphrasing and sometimes transcribing verbatim. A few parallels will reveal the manner and extent of his adaptation.

Blount began his address to Parliament by establishing the importance of books to the nation. He informed the representatives of the people of England that books recorded history, excited men to imitate past glories, and contained the forms of divine worship. Books thus being so useful to human society, Blount agreed with Milton, that "You had almost as good kill a Man, as a good Book; for he that kills a Man, kills but a Reasonable Creature, Gods Image: Whereas he that destroys a good Book, kills Reason it self, which is as it were the very Eye of God."[8] This paraphrase of Milton's famous passage received proper credit in Blount's text; but through the course of his argument Blount followed the scheme and phraseology of *Areopagitica* as though both were his own. The first step of his argument, for example, in which he contended that in ancient Greek and Roman days the imprimatur was unknown and that the Council of Trent and the

[7] J. P., *Mr. L'Estrange Refuted with his own Arguments* (London, 1681), p. 35.
[8] *A Just Vindication of Learning: Or, An Humble Address to the High Court of Parliament In Behalf of the Liberty of the Press* (London, 1679), p. 3.

Spanish Inquisition "produced these two Monsters, an *Index Expurgatorius*, and a *Licenser*," came from Milton's opening section, though Blount greatly reduced it.[9] This argument, it might be observed, would still be effective in view of the national anger for, and fear of, popery, which Titus Oates and his companions in perjury had stirred up in England—a point Blount would not be likely to forget.

To his credit, however, he touched lightly on this association of licensing and the Catholic Church to emphasize and follow more closely Milton's rational arguments. In his second division, he contended, as Milton had before him, that a Licensing Act was "the greatest Affront and Discouragement that can be offer'd to Learning and Learned men," that an imprimatur could offer nothing but displeasure and indignity to a free and knowing spirit.

A Just Vindication	Areopagitica
What advantage is it to be a Man, over it is to be a Boy at School, if we have only 'scap'd the Ferula, to come under the Fescu of an *Imprimatur*? When a man Writes to the World, he summons up all his Reason and Deliberation to assist him; he Searches, Meditates, is industrious in Consulting and Conferring with his Judicious Friends; after all which, he takes himself to be inform'd in what he Writes, as well as any that writ before; if in this the most consummate act of his fidelity and ripeness, no years, no industry, no former proof of his Abilities, can bring him to the state of Maturity, as not to be still distrusted, unless he carry all his considerate diligence, all his midnight watchings and expence of *Palladian* Oyl, to the hasty view of an *Unleasured Licenser*, perhaps much his Younger, perhaps much his Inferior in Judgment, perhaps one who never	What advantage is it to be a man over it is to be a boy at school, if we have only scapt the ferular, to come under the fescu of an *Imprimatur*? . . . When a man writes to the world, he summons up all his reason and deliberation to assist him; he searches, meditats, is industrious, and likely consults and conferrs with his judicious friends; after all which done he takes himself to be inform'd in what he writes, as well as any that writ before him; if in this the most consummat act of his fidelity and ripenesse, no years, no industry, no former proof of his abilities can bring him to that state of maturity, as not to be still mistrusted and suspected, unlesse he carry all his considerat diligence, all his midnight watchings, and expence of *Palladian* oyl, to the hasty view of an unleasur'd licencer, perhaps much his younger, perhaps far his inferiour in judgement, perhaps one who never

[9] *Ibid.*, pp. 4–5. Compare with *Areopagitica* in the Columbia edition of *The Works of John Milton*, IV, 299–306.

knew the Labour of Book-writing, or perhaps one altogether ignorant of that Art or Science whereof the Author Treats. (p. 6.)	knew the labour of book-writing, and if he be not repulst, or slighted, must appear in Print like a punie with his guardian. . . . (*Works*, IV, 324–25).

Such a comparison illustrates Blount's method and manner; and as he developed his plea that Parliament allow the Press Act to lapse, he saw that he could do no better than this, that he would do best to follow the movement of Milton's thought, as well as his turn of phrase. Hence he declared that a Licensing Act prejudiced a book, that it undervalued and vilified the whole nation, that it reflected upon the clergy and upon the Church, and that it vitiated any objections that Englishmen might raise against either Mecca or Rome. A few more random comparisons will demonstrate beyond doubt that in arguing in this way Blount had his eyes squarely focused on *Areopagitica* and that he presented to the Whig Parliament of 1679 only a condensed form of what Milton had already said.

A JUST VINDICATION	AREOPAGITICA
I know nothing of the *Licenser*, but that I have his own hand for his arrogance; who shall warrent me his Judgment? (p. 7.)	I know nothing of the licencer, but that I have his own hand here for his arrogance; who shall warrant me his judgement? (IV, 326.)
Truth and Understanding are not such Wares as to be Monopolized and Traded in Tickets, Statutes and Standards. (p. 9.)	Truth and understanding are not such wares as to be monopoliz'd and traded in by tickets and statutes, and standards. (IV, 327.)
It reflects upon our Church and Clergy, of whose labours we should hope better . . . as that the Whiff of every new Pamphlet should stagger them out of their Catechism and Christian walking. (p. 10.)	And in conclusion it reflects to the disrepute of our Ministers also, of whose labours we should hope better . . . as that the whiffe of every new pamphlet should stagger them out of thir catechism, and Christian walking. (IV, 329.)
Let her and Falsehood grapple; who ever knew Truth put to the worst in a free and open Encounter? (p. 14.)	Let her and Falshood grapple; who ever knew Truth put to the wors, in a free and open encounter. (IV, 347.)

Toward the conclusion of his address to Parliament, Blount turned to Jeremy Taylor's *Liberty of Prophesying* for further evidence to buttress his plea; but his main arguments, as the foregoing comparisons show, followed the structure and wording of *Areopagitica*. He omitted many of the great passages in the original, to be sure, as well as the Puritan dream of reformation in England; no visions of an awakening nation mewing her mighty strength and trembling to catch the accents of Truth inspired Blount's address. But the rational arguments for a free press remain, often unspoiled by so much as the change of a word. Whoever listened to *A Just Vindication of Learning* simply heard Milton's oration arranged to fit the needs of a later day.

William Denton, a physician and a violent anti-Catholic pamphleteer, added his voice to Blount's in the general Whig offensive against a renewal of the Licensing Act. Though not officially identified with the Whig party, he nevertheless expressed Whig views, both during the attempted revolution and after the Revolutionary Settlement, when he became an exponent of the Williamite cause. His contribution to Shaftesbury's thrust for power resides chiefly in an unwieldy and rambling work entitled *Jus Cæsaris Et Ecclesiæ vere Dictæ*, in which he made a "Summe of Mr. *J. M.* His Treatise" of civil power, referred to *The Tenure of Kings and Magistrates*, and adapted *Areopagitica* under the title *An Apology for the Liberty of the Press*.[10] This adaptation has little to recommend it; but it is another clear instance of how Milton's rhetoric, as Royalists in the Restoration feared, made inroads on the minds of men and inspired them to march to the measure of his thought.

William Denton made no attempt, like his predecessor Charles Blount, to follow the structure and main arguments of *Areopagitica*. As an anti-Catholic pamphleteer, he seemed most impressed by Milton's historical account of the growth and development of the imprimatur under the approval of the Church of Rome. At any rate, he spent a good deal of time in his *Apology* pointing out how licensing had arisen under the popes and flourished in the Church, for which information he went to the first part of Milton's essay. Though he garbled his source, unwisely attempting, as his whole adaptation re-

[10] London, 1681; pp. 1–3, 67. The *Apology* is attached at the end, with separate pagination.

veals, either to conceal his theft or to improve upon his original, it is evident that he had *Areopagitica* directly before him:

An Apology

In the primitive Church *Heretical Books* were examined and declared to be such by the *Councils*, but not prohibited by them, nor by the *Pope*, but by the *Prince*. . . . This was the manner of the *Church*, until the year 800. since which Times the *Popes* of *Rome* have by Usurpation declared divers Writers to be *Hereticks* and *heretical*, that will not subscribe to the Canons of that *Conventicle of Trent.*

But all this while the *Press* was not guarded, nor *Transcribing* forbidden, but left free: Books only, and those but few censured and prohibited until after the year 1200. and then also but sparingly, until about the time of *Wickliff Husse*, and *Jerome* of *Praghe*, which was about 1371. in the days of *Edw.* 3d. *Rich.* 2d. and *Pope Martin* 5th. who by his *Bull excommunicated* all Sects of *Hereticks* in their esteem, especially *Wicklefists* and *Hussites*, and had recourse also unto a stricter *Guardianship* of the *Press* . . . (p. 2.)

Areopagitica

And that the primitive Councels and Bishops were wont only to declare what Books were not commendable, passing no furder, but leaving it to each ones conscience to read or to lay by, till after the yeare 800. is observ'd already by *Padre Paolo* the great unmasker of the *Trentine* Councel. After which time the Popes of *Rome* engrossing what they pleas'd of Politicall rule into their owne hands, extended their dominion over mens eyes, as they had before over their judgements, burning and prohibiting to be read, what they fansied not; yet sparing in their censures, and the Books not many which they so dealt with: till *Martin* the 5. by his Bull not only prohibited, but was the first that excommunicated the reading of hereticall Books; for about that time *Wicklef* and *Husse* growing terrible, were they who first drove the Papall Court to a stricter policy of prohibiting. (IV, 302–3.)

Such an account, appearing at a time when many still shuddered at the thought of the Popish Plot, would prejudice the people of England against any Press Act, as William Denton well knew; and for this reason he made much of Milton's historical survey of how the office of Licenser came into being. But he by no means confined his *Apology* to a paraphrase of the first part of *Areopagitica*. Like Charles Blount, he was moved by Milton's rational arguments and attempted to make them his own; unlike Blount, however, he changed Milton's phrases until they only faintly echoed their original eloquence. A few typical instances of Denton's rewording, compared with pertinent excerpts from the original essay, will illustrate the nature of his whole adaptation:

AN APOLOGY

God himself never created men, nor never gave talents of Reason or Judgment, subject and captivate unto the Reason and Judgment of others, but hath endued and trusted every man with his own proper talent of Reason to make his own choice, according to which only he shall be judged at the Judgment of the great Day. . . . What wisdom can there be to choose or refuse? or what praise or dispraise, reward or punishment, can equally be distributed by doing, or not doing good or evil, without full knowledge of good and evil, and that left to our own free choice? (p. 4.)

AREOPAGITICA

[W]hen God gave him reason, he gave him freedom to choose, for reason is but choosing; he had bin else a meer artificial *Adam*, such an *Adam* as he is in the motions. We our selves esteem not of that obedience, or love, or gift, which is of force: God therefore left him free. . . . It was from out the rinde of one apple tasted, that the knowledge of good and evill as two twins cleaving together leapt forth into the World. And perhaps this is that doom which *Adam* fell into of knowing good and evill, that is to say of knowing good by evill. As therefore the state of man now is; what wisdome can there be to choose, what continence to forbeare without the knowledge of evill? (IV, 319, 310–11.)

This device was first set on foot by *Antichristian mystery*, and design to smother *Light* and *Truth*, that the Contrivers might the more cleverly set up the Kingdom of Antichrist, in *Cimerian darkness of ignorance*, and if it were possible to hinder all reformations of their Lives and Doctrines, and to insinuate and establish Falshood. *Turkish policy!* To uphold their *Alcoran*, they prohibit Learning and Printing . . . Who ever knew her put to the worse? Let *Truth* and *Error* enter like fair Combatants and

[Licensing] hinders and retards the importation of our richest Marchandize, Truth: nay it was first establisht and put in practice by Antichristion malice and mystery on set purpose to extinguish, if it were possible, the light of Reformation, and to settle falshood; little differing from that policie wherewith the Turk upholds his *Alcoran*, by the prohibition of Printing. . . . And though all the windes of doctrin were let loose to play upon the earth, so Truth be in the field, we do injuriously by licenc-

Wrestlers into the Lists; confuting by dint of Reason is the only *Cornish Hug* that can lay flat. (p. 6.)

ing and prohibiting to misdoubt her strength. Let her and Falshood grapple; who ever knew Truth put to the wors, in a free and open encounter. (IV, 337, 347.)

Denton thus turned Milton's ringing defense of a free press into a poor thing indeed. But the arguments in his *Apology*, however mangled in phrase, retain some of their original strength and truss up an essay which, had it not found its source in *Areopagitica*, would have fallen completely apart, like some of Denton's other effusions. Whatever effectiveness *An Apology for the Liberty of the Press* had in the conflict over the Licensing Act derived directly from Milton.

The extent to which Charles Blount and William Denton turned public opinion against the renewal of the Press Act and hence the measure of Milton's contribution to this phase of the attempted Whig revolution will perhaps never be known. As a vigorous Whig pamphleteer, Blount no doubt convinced some that the press should remain free. At any rate, his adaptation of Milton aroused enough interest to merit comment in *Heraclitus Ridens*, a Tory paper devoted to discussions of events of the times. This comment appeared in a dialogue between Earnest and Jest, two symbolical characters who regularly appraised, somewhat wittily, party activities. To Jest's observation that it was high time Whigs wearied of their rebellious disciplines, Earnest replied that their tactics of keeping the nation in ferment to achieve their ends disclosed that they had. "For instance, there was the *Liberty of the Press*, how earnestly was it contended for, the denial of it said to be Relique of Popery, old *Milton*'s Arguments and Word were drest up into an Address to the Parliament for it."[11] Yet when they achieved it, Earnest continued, when they plied the world with papers and pamphlets, they soon found their own artillery turned against them and so wearied of the sport that they were the ones now most likely to complain of the licentiousness of the press. Unfortunately, Earnest failed to report whether Blount's adaptation, to which he here referred, had any specific effect on the representatives of England; but he recognized it as an instrument of Whig policy and implied that it had helped secure a free press. Such a singling out of *A Just Vindication of Learning* for discussion in the

[11] *Heraclitus Ridens* (Tuesday, August 8, 1682), No. 80.

Tory press is in itself an indication that it had made its mark in party contentions.

Whether William Denton's *Apology* exerted any influence, however, is less certain. His writings stirred enough interest to gain for him three definite, though unknown, adversaries;[12] and he appeared in an anti-Catholic tract addressed to the Earl of Shaftesbury.[13] His adaptation of Milton thus probably came to the attention of many, though apparently no one viewed it seriously enough to comment upon it. But if the effect of Denton, in the general Whig offensive to keep the Press Act from being renewed, must remain unknown, it is clear that he himself believed that Milton had spoken with such eloquence and force to the issues of a free press that he wanted him to speak again at this new period of crisis, hoping that his arguments would sway the people of England. *Areopagitica* at the very least converted two men, and their adaptations of it perhaps convinced others of the iniquity of licensing acts and of the desirability of freedom of thought and expression.

II

Milton contributed more tangibly to the attempted Whig revolution in the debates over the succession of James, Duke of York. These debates presented nothing fundamentally new; they indeed carried on the conflict which had crystallized in the Puritan Rebellion and had continued in the early years of the Restoration. But Whig attempts to exclude York from his hereditary throne because he openly professed the Catholic religion forced both Tories and Whigs to amplify and refine the old arguments on liberty of conscience and the power of kings to fit the new situation. Tories, in support of a possible Catholic successor, took the old doctrine of absolutism to new metaphysical heights; Whigs, fearful of Rome, developed in great detail the theory of compact. Since Milton figured prominently in these debates and gained alien companions as the conflict continued, any appraisal of his influence at this time necessitates an examination of the old arguments in view of their new refinements and amplifications.

12 *Jus Cæsaris Et Ecclesiæ vere Dictæ,* sig. a2. Denton referred to these enemies as R. P., I. S., and P. W.

13 *A True and Perfect Narrative of the Inhumane Practices (occasioned by the Damnable Positions) of Jesuites and Papists, Toward Protestants at Home and Abroad* (London, 1680), p. 7.

The debate between Tories and Whigs over the succession of York rose from the Popish Plot to a peak of fury at the executions of Lord Russell and Algernon Sidney, only to subside after Charles II had secured the throne for James in the face of the attempted revolution. In this clash many issues received detailed attention; but the "Subject of common *Discourse*"—indeed, the most fundamental question in the Whig-Tory struggle for power—was "*Whether Kings have their Power* immediately *from God, or whether it be conferred upon them by the People.*"[14] Tories argued almost to the man "*That God is the immediate Author of Soveraignty in the King, and that he is no Creature of the Peoples Making*";[15] that "The King hath His Title to the Crown, and to His Kingly Office and Power, not by way of Trust from the People, but by inherent Birthright, immediately from God, Nature, and the Law."[16] In support of such propositions, Tories arrayed a battery of arguments. John Nalson, for example, in *The Common Interest of King and People*, claimed that papal supremacy and Presbyterian popular supremacy could in no wise allow of prerogative, property, and liberty; that only through English monarchy, which was hereditary, absolute, and independent, could such be secured.[17] But Sir Robert Filmer's *Patriarcha*, written earlier but not published until 1680, best argued the Tory cause. Filmer contended that the first kings were fathers of families, and that as such they possessed absolute power and their heirs the right of succession. Regal government, therefore, with its absolute powers and its rights of primogeniture, sprang not from any artificial agreement but from the very bowels of nature herself, as shown in the most ancient and natural of organizations, the family. Now, Filmer continued, since regal and paternal power are one and the same and both natural, it logically followed that "*It is unnatural for the People to Govern, or Chose Governours.*"[18] This position established, Filmer next moved to his most telling argument, that "*Positive Laws do not infringe the Natural and*

[14] Paul Lathom, *The Power of Kings from God. A Sermon Preached in the Cathedral Church of Sarum, The XXIX. Day of June, 1683* (London, 1683), p. 25.

[15] *A Letter to a Friend. Shewing from Scripture, Fathers, and Reason, How False That State-Maxim is, Royal Authority is Originally and Radically in the People* (London, 1679), p. 9.

[16] W. P., *The Divine Right of Kings Asserted in General: Ours in Particular; both by the Laws of God, and this Land* [London, 1679], p. 2.

[17] *The Common Interest of King and People: Shewing the Original, Antiquity and Excellency of Monarchy* (London, 1678). Nalson devoted chapters viii, ix, and x to an attack upon Presbyterianism, which he considered particularly dangerous to monarchy.

[18] *Patriarcha: Or the Natural Power of Kings* (London, 1680), the title and substance of chapter ii.

Fatherly Power of Kings,"[19] for proof of which he turned to the Old Testament story of Samuel, Christ's injunction to give Caesar his due, Bracton's famous pronouncements in *De Legibus*, and James I himself, to name but a few of his impressive list of authorities. He fully agreed with Ulpian, the great Roman jurist, who had declared that "*Princeps, Legibus solutus est.* The Prince is not bound by the Laws."

To such arguments for absolute regal supremacy and for the natural right of York to inherit the kingdom, the Anglican clergy added a chant of divine right, particularly in their thirtieth of January memorial sermons, which became at this time, and continued to be through the rest of the seventeenth century, mere instruments of Tory propaganda.[20] Edward Pelling, for example, in an anniversary sermon entitled *David and the Amalekite Upon the Death of Saul*, defended the absolute power of kings by elaborately defining the meaning of a then much-abused term, the "Lord's Anointed." A king may be said to possess this title in a twofold respect, Pelling began; "In respect of that *outward*, *Ceremonial* Unction" the king may be called the anointed of the Lord because he is a sacred person, separated from the people by ceremonial rites and forms. This distinction was clear and hence needed little further development. The inward unction, however, which flowed from God and hence allowed the king to partake of divinity, was more mystical and thus required a fuller account. "In respect of that *inward* and *essential* Unction," Pelling explained, "which he receives at the very first *minute* of his Kingship, and by which he is Sanctified and set *apart* and *above* all others in that very Article of time, and which from that day forward is *inseparable* from his Person," the sovereign, because of the "Supreme *Power*" given him, the "Sacred *Authority*" vested in him, the "inviolable *Majesty*" inseparable from him, and the "Divine *Image* and *Impress*" whereby "he bears a *different* and *singular* character, and becomes *Hallowed*," all of which he owes "neither to *Priest* nor *People*, but to *God* alone"—because, Pelling concluded, "this *Power*, *Authority*, *Majesty*, *Image*, and *Character* is given him by the *Lord* only, therefore he is called, *The Lord's Anointed*, that is, a Person made so *Sacred* by God by the Communication of his *own* Authority, that now he cannot be treated

19 *Ibid.*, the title and substance of chapter iii.

20 See Helen W. Randall, "The Rise and Fall of a Martyrology: Sermons on Charles I," *The Huntington Library Quarterly*, X (1947), 135–67.

with rudeness or violence, without Dishonouring God's own Majesty and striking at the Face of God *himself*."[21]

Few dared speculate further than this on the absolute power of kings by divine right; but such sentiments expressed in a very real sense Tory feeling in the debates over the succession. So great was party fear over Whig attempts to assert the authority of Parliament and exclude York from the throne that Tories not only invoked the old arguments drawn from the laws of nature and God but also embroidered them in ways that would have surprised even the most ardent Royalist of an earlier day. Claims of absolute power for the throne could not be pushed any further without appearing ridiculous, if indeed they had not already become so.

Even as Tories at this time took the theory of absolute power to its logical extreme, so they developed the doctrine of passive obedience to make it become the singular article of Anglican faith. This doctrine, of course, had long been an adjunct to the Anglican service as expressed in homilies on obedience and against disobedience to kings; but during the debates over the succession it became less a moral injunction and more a Tory weapon to convince people that under no circumstances whatever could rebellion against authority be condoned. Some years before the controversy reached an acrimonious height, George Hickes, an inveterate Tory Churchman, declared "that a King ought not to lose his Crown, for not being a Christian, or for renouncing the Christian *Religion* as *Julian* did." Since to Hickes this was clear, it was equally evident "that neither the Duke nor any other *Prince* ought to be debarred from the Crown, which is the greatest and most sacred of Temporal Rights." As Hickes developed his argument for the succession of York, he invoked the doctrine of passive obedience and claimed it to be the unique possession of the Anglican Church—a doctrine, he explained, founded on the example of the primitive Christians, whose only weapons even against pagan kings had been "*Tears, Arguments* and *Prayers*." How different, in view of this, were the "Church of *Rome*" and "the Kirk of *Scotland*; both of which" had "actually *Excommunicated* and *Deposed Lawful* and *Rightful Princes*, under the Notion of being *Hereticks*, and *Enemies* to Christs Kingdom; forgetting both alike the *Precepts* and *Examples* of our *Saviour* and his *Apostles*, on which the Church of *England* hath

[21] *David and the Amalekite Upon the Death of Saul. A Sermon Preached on Jan. 30, 1682* (London, 1683), p. 7.

grounded the contrary Doctrine, as well as on right reason."[22] But Hickes not only claimed for the Church of England a unique policy toward kings; he realized that the doctrine of passive obedience could be used as a weapon to fight against both Geneva and Rome, and hence against Whigs, and that it could be as effective as the theory of divine right, to which it was inextricably bound. Sovereign princes, as God's ministers, he maintained, held the supreme power of the sword; hence it followed that "the first Table of every government, and by the Gospel, which confirms them, that *passive obedience*, or *non-resistance* becomes the double duty of Christian subjects, who cannot take up the Sword against their Sovereign without resisting God, whose Minister he is, and making themselves justly liable to the stroak of that Sword, which God hath put in his hand."[23] This doctrine, which became during the debates over the succession one of the most powerful weapons in the Tory arsenal, placed Whigs on the defensive in that their attempts to block James from the throne could be termed resistance against God himself.

Whigs continued to press for the exclusion of James, however, and in consequence Tories, as a later commentator observed, "by a well design'd Zeal were carried on to enlarge the Notion of *Non-Resistance* beyond the limits their cooler Reasonings would allow."[24] Francis Turner, for example, an ardent Tory consecrated Bishop of Ely in 1684, struck directly against Whig maneuverings to pass Bills of Exclusion by presenting, in *A Sermon Preached before the King*, a hypothetical case of a tyrant, asking whether, under such circumstances, good Christians should continue to practice the doctrine of passive obedience. Suppose a tyrant sat on the throne, he declared to his audience; would it be lawful then to depose him? "Is the greatest Misgovernment a sufficient pretence for any *Pope* or *Consistory* upon Earth to Depose a Soveraign Prince? To Legitimate Treason, Rebellion, the Parricide of a King by his Subjects?" Before Turner answered these questions so pertinent to political disputes of the day, he laid open to his congregation a test case,—"as hard a case as ever was, or perhaps as can be supposed, that is, the Case of *Julian the Apostate* Emperor." Turner then told at some length the story of the

[22] *The Judgment of an Anonymous Writer* (2d ed.; London, 1684), pp. 2–3.

[23] *A Discourse of the Soveraign Power, in a Sermon Preached at St. Mary Le Bow, Nov. 28. 1682* (London, 1682), pp. 26–27.

[24] *The True Notion of Passive-Obedience Stated* (London, 1690), p. 1.

primitive Christians under this apostate prince: how Julian had renounced his baptism and had turned a very plague to the Church, how he had even tempted his Christian subjects to apostasy, how for these actions he had been accused of committing an unpardonable sin against the Holy Ghost, for which he had been excommunicated "even to *Anathema Marantha*, that is, *till the Lord come to Judgment*." "Now in this case," Turner then asked, "was it lawful for Christians to cast off Him that had so openly and maliciously cast off his Christianity?" The answer was a ringing "No!" The judgment of the whole Church spoke to the contrary. Its members, in fact, "thought themselves oblig'd, by S. *Pauls* Apostolical Canon, *to make Supplications and Prayers* even for Him, that whatsoever he was, and howsoever he behav'd himself toward them, *they might still lead a quiet and peaceable life in all godliness and honesty*." And, Turner continued, "they had the Grace they pray'd for, they did live peaceably under him, they never took upon them to *Unking* him, they drew out no Forces against him, but only their *thundring Legion* of Prayers and Tears." This was the practice of the Church, he concluded, and it conformed "to the Doctrine of all her Ancient Fathers, none excepted."[25]

Such a tale, of course, could signify only one thing to the royal congregation before whom Turner preached. All present at that time would perforce interpret it to mean that every Englishman, as shown by the example of the primitive Christians, should obey the powers that reigned, that every Christian, by the same token, should accept the succession of York, despite his espousal of Rome and the risk that he might be a tyrant. The story of Julian the Apostate, indeed, served Tories well; and they pressed from it every ounce of meaning to make it speak in opposition to the Bills of Exclusion and in behalf of the Stuart succession.

But Whigs challenged these doctrines which Tories had pressed to such unwarranted extremes both by analyzing their pertinence to debates over the succession and by offering in their stead theories which to them seemed more rational. "Monarchy is far from being *de Jure Divino*, or by the Law of Nature," Whigs generally cried, "but ariseth by consent."[26] And on this assumption they at once an-

[25] *A Sermon Preached before the King on the 30/1 of January 1680/1. Being the Fast for the Martyrdom of King Charles I. of Blessed Memory* (London, 1681), pp. 22–24.

[26] W. G., *The Case of Succession to the Crown of England Stated, In a Letter to a Member of the Honorable House of Commons* ([London], 1679), p. 8.

swered Tory polemics and reared their own arguments. Many Whig voices sounded in concert in support of this proposition and of the kind of government it premised, but none spoke with more vigor or with greater effectiveness than Thomas Hunt, a lawyer turned pamphleteer, and Samuel Johnson, the politically active chaplain of Lord Russell.

Thomas Hunt voiced Whig theory best in his famous *Postscript*, a collection of several pamphlets, some of which had been written as early as 1679. Addressing himself to the specific problem of the succession, he attacked as a matter of course Tory doctrines of divine right and passive obedience as they had been maintained by Sir Robert Filmer and the Anglican clergy. He found no support anywhere, either in nature or in Scripture, that "Monarchy is *jure divino*, unalterable in its descent by any Law of man, for that it is subject to none";[27] such a doctrine indeed he believed derived from "*crude speculations*." Nor could Hunt agree with the Anglican interpretation of the primitive Christians under Julian the Apostate. After all, the Church did curse and anathematize that renegade emperor, actions which to Hunt could hardly mean passive obedience.[28] Through the whole of the *Postscript*, Hunt attacked doctrines central to the Tory position; and side by side with this attack stood arguments for Whig policy to exclude James from the throne.

Hunt prefaced these arguments by defining in Whig terms the nature of government. "Nothing is so intirely, perfectly, and abstractly Civil, as Government," he began, "the perfect Creature of men in society, made by pact and consent, and not otherwise, most certainly not otherwise: and therefore most certainly ordainable by the whole Community, for the safety and preservation of the whole, to which it is in the reason and nature of it intirely design'd."[29] Hunt thus conceived of government as an organization created by man, by his own consent and for his own good; and from this conception it followed that "universal consent," not the king, made the laws by which this organization was governed. This concept of government allowed Hunt to argue specifically for the exclusion of James. If popery, he said, "which is the greatest mischief that ever threatned this Kingdom," can be "kept out by a Law," then England

[27] *Mr. Hunt's Postscript For Rectifying some Mistakes in some of the Inferiour Clergy, Mischievous to our Government and Religion* (London, 1682), pp. 33 ff.

[28] *Ibid.*, p. 152.

[29] *Ibid.*, sigs. c3v–c4.

"ought to have such a Law; and nothing can hinder such a Law to be past for that purpose, but want of an universal desire to have it."[30] Hunt went so far as to suggest that James should agree to an exclusion for the peace of the nation; such at least would allow him to live long and to see good days, which was not his fate once the Duke put on the crown. But his most telling argument was that laws sprang from the consent of the people, that therefore if enough Englishmen wanted to keep James from the throne they had only to agree through law to do so. That a king, as Tories argued, could by divine right overrule the will of the people by making and executing laws detrimental to their good, and that subjects, in accordance with passive obedience, had no right to resist regal encroachments upon their civil and religious liberties appeared to Hunt as positions both absurd and abhorrent. Most Whigs agreed with him that such doctrines flew in the face of reason and grievously affronted the dignity of man.

However cogently Hunt argued the Whig cause in his *Postscript*, Samuel Johnson apparently spoke with even greater effectiveness in his *Julian the Apostate*, a direct answer to the Anglican doctrine of passive obedience as expressed by George Hickes. In this volume Johnson attacked specifically and in detail the popular story told about Julian, and through his logic, as well as his historical interpretations, turned many away from that singular article of Anglican faith by which the clergy had supported the succession of James. Johnson began his attack by sketching a short account of Julian's life in which he declared that the Anglican interpretation of the primitive Christians under that apostate prince not only was historically inaccurate but also had been irresponsibly applied to the present. Rather than submitting to Julian and sending up only a thundering legion of prayers and tears, he observed, the primitive Christians had actually called him names, had derided the shape of his body, and had prayed not for but against him. Moreover, he continued, when the news came of Julian's death, Christians fell to dancing and rejoicing; and rumor reported that he had met death not by enemy action but by his own troops.[31] Johnson had found, then, that historical facts would not support the Anglican story. Furthermore, reflection upon the actual behavior of the primitive Christians convinced him that Tories

[30] *Mr. Hunt's Postscript*, p. 30.

[31] *Julian the Apostate: Being A Short Account of His Life; The Sense of the Primitive Christians about his Succession; And their Behaviour towards Him* (London, 1682), pp. 1–64.

had misinterpreted the story of Julian and that, rightly understood, it argued not for the succession of James but for his exclusion. He recalled that Christians had not been moved by Julian's injunction that they submit to his will, even when Julian had invoked the doctrine of divine right and had turned for support to the laws of nature and of God. Julian indeed might as well have fallen among barbarians, so ill was his treatment at Christian hands. And Christians had a right to treat Julian thus, he explained, for by this time Christianity had been established by law. Johnson admitted, to be sure, that with the primitive Christians before Constantine's time matters were different: they suffered under a tyrannical yoke because Christianity had not yet been established and hence could not legally resist authority which threatened their faith. But when Julian came to the throne, he found Christians in full and quiet possession of their religion, which they had enjoyed without interruption for almost fifty years; hence "to have this Treasure wrested out of their hands, by one that had been bred up in the Bosom of the Church, who profess'd himself a Christian, and never pull'd off his Masque, till it was too late for them to help themselves; this was enough to raise, not only all their Zeal, but all their indignation too."[32]

Christians under Julian, then, rightly resisted encroachments on their religion because the laws of the Empire stood on their side, whereas before Constantine recognized Christianity the laws of the land had militated against them and hence they had no right to resist. Now this distinction, as Johnson further explained, not only invalidated the Anglican story of the primitive Christians under Julian but also made it inapplicable, at least as Tories had used it, to the debates over the succession of James. After all, Englishmen under Charles II also enjoyed their religion by established laws of the land; hence they could lawfully resist the threat of a popish successor. In view of this, Johnson wondered "at those Men, who trouble the Nation at this time of the day, with the unseasonable prescriptions of Prayers and Tears, and the Passive Obedience of the *Thebæan* Legion, and such-like last Remedies," which were proper "only at such a Time" when the laws of the country militated against their religion.[33]

Such answers to Tory contentions, coupled with arguments for the supremacy of law as enacted in Parliament, soon split England

[32] *Ibid.*, pp. 68–69. [33] *Ibid.*, pp. 73–74.

into two broad, hostile camps. Those who defended hereditary succession of the Crown by the doctrines of divine right and passive obedience passed simply as monarchists; those who openly or tacitly supported the Bills of Exclusion by invoking the theory of compact and by claiming the right to resist regal encroachments on religion established by law passed simply as antimonarchists. Such a cleavage, so broad and inexact, scorned fine distinctions and created several strange, but nevertheless logical, party alignments, a situation which Tories quickly exploited for the purpose of discrediting Whig theory and policy. Presbyterians, for example, though usually ardent supporters of kings, historically opposed monarchy by divine right and hence their exponents, like Knox and Buchanan, fell into the Whig fold. Moreover, Jesuit political writers, like Suarez and Bellarmine, also opposed divine right, though for quite different reasons, and hence they too fell into the Whig fold. Furthermore, both Presbyterians and Jesuits defended the right of a people to rise up against a tyrannous king. Such similarities allowed Tories to associate Geneva and Rome and to make it appear that Whigs, with their Presbyterian inheritance, advocated Papist principles of government. Henry Maurice, for example, in a typical Anglican sermon commemorating the execution of Charles I, stated that the Faction and Rome "both Agree in the Fundamentals of *Rebellion*, and the Lawfulness and Merit of *Resisting the Higher Powers*"; and he went ahead to trace England's troubles to the arguments the Faction borrowed "from their *Catholick Authors*," claiming that "the Sermons and Speeches of the *Party*, had deriv'd all the Art and Colour of Their *Treason*."[34] Edward Pelling, in a similar sermon, made the same identification and also traced the principles of the Whigs, as well as those of their forebears in the Puritan Rebellion, to "the *Proper Creed* of the *Jesuites*."[35]

By the time of the Rye House conspiracy the identification of Geneva with Rome, long a loose association in the Anglican mind, had become a fixed pattern of thought as well as a weapon of political propaganda. Thus Nathaniel Bisbie, in a sermon on Guy Fawkes Day, told his congregation that "verily *Bellarmin*, *Sanctarel*, *Mariana*,

[34] *A Sermon Preached before the King at White-Hall, On January the 30, 1681* (London, 1682), p. 32.

[35] *A Sermon Preached On the Anniversary of That Most Execrable Murder of K. Charles The First Royal Martyr* (London, 1682), pp. 13–14.

are not more fulsome in their Tenents, nor more antiregal, antimonarchical in their Positions, than *Knox, Buchanan* and *Cartwright* of old; or than their offspring of late have been, still are, and are ever likely to be."[36] Moreover, Edward Pelling, in a subsequent sermon of thanks for the deliverance of England from the Rye House conspirators, declared that "*Azorius* the Jesuite, endeavouring to prove the *Lawfulness* of *Deposing Kings*, urgeth several Presidents for it, and among other Examples which he mentioneth, he saith, That it was a *common Practice in Scotland*."[37] And finally William Bolton, in another thanksgiving sermon, made it clear why "good Christians" could not be blamed for naming the Jesuits and the Presbyterians together, "seeing that both of them were setled in the World in the same unhappy year. *viz* 1541. The one by *Ignatius Loyola* at *Rome*; The other by Mr. *Calvin* at *Geneva*: and all their practice ever since hath been, like *Simeon* and *Levi*, sworn Brethren in Iniquity, to plot and conspire the death and ruine of Princes."[38] If good Christians could not be blamed for mentioning Geneva and Rome in the same breath, good Tories could hardly be expected to do less; indeed, from the Popish Plot to the succession of James, Tories saw Presbyterians and Papists alike as mortal enemies of the Anglican Church and of the government of Charles II.[39]

This identification in crime was not simply a Tory device for discrediting the Whig party. In actual fact, the Whig theory of natural rights, of an original compact, and of the humanistic and utilitarian basis of the State differed little from Jesuit doctrines.[40] But Tories no doubt shrewdly calculated the effect their identification would have on an England which still held green the memory of Guy Fawkes, shuddered at the Irish Massacre, and accepted, in some quarters at least, the legendary Catholic origin of the great fire of London. That Tories repeated the identification so often and in such detail indicates that the device of association successfully turned many people away from the Whig fold.

Debates over the succession of James and the Bills of Exclusion

[36] *The Modern Pharisees: Or A Sermon On the xxiij. of S. Matt. v. 15* (London, 1683), p. 22.

[37] *A Sermon Preached upon September the 9th, 1683* (London, 1683), p. 15.

[38] *Core Redivivus, In a Sermon Preached At Christ-Church Tabernacle in London, upon Sunday, September 9. 1683* (London, 1684), p. 15.

[39] See particularly *The Royal Guard: Or The King and Kingdoms Sure Defensative* (London, 1684).

[40] See J. Neville Figgis, "On Some Political Theories of the Early Jesuits," *Transactions of the Royal Historical Society*, New Series, XI (1897), 94.

during the attempted Whig revolution thus forced both parties to elaborate their doctrines for the purpose of defense and attack—a process which not only revealed historical alignments in the realm of theory but also drove Tories, in their desperate efforts to block rising Whig power, to extreme positions of absolute regal authority by divine right and of absolute passive obedience in subjects. Tories believed, and apparently convinced a good part of the nation, that such positions would serve the best interests of England, would secure the hereditary succession of the crown and hence would assure stability in Church and State. Since Charles II appeared friendly to their religion and cause, Tories failed at this time to realize that the real threat to the established Church and State lay not in Whig or Jesuit theories but in their own doctrines pressed into action by a popish successor. The time had not yet arrived to disclose the validity of Whig contentions.

III

Whigs employed Milton extensively in their arguments with Tories over the succession of James and the Bills of Exclusion. Sir James Tyrell, a historian of Whig political theory, answered Sir Robert Filmer's *Patriarcha* with a volume entitled *Patriarcha Non Monarcha*, in which appear many arguments reminiscent of Milton's revolutionary program for man and society. The gist of his book, in a sense, is a plea for a limited, constitutional monarchy, with king and subjects alike governed by law. Furthermore, he showed an acquaintance with Milton's arguments against Salmasius[41] and spoke of Filmer's *Observations* upon Hobbes, Milton, and Grotius, which had appeared first in 1652.[42] These observations on Milton, which Tories recalled to the nation's memory by reissuing Filmer's *The Free-holders Grand Inquest* and *The Power of Kings*,[43] could have spurred Tyrell to answer *Patriarcha* with principles of government gleaned from *Pro Populo Anglicano Defensio*. But it would be an error to claim for Tyrell more than a general affiliation with Milton, more

[41] *Patriarcha Non Monarcha. The Patriarch Unmonarch'd: Being Observations on A Late Treatise and Divers Other Miscellanies, Published under the Name of Sir Robert Filmer Baronet* (London, 1681), sig. [A3].

[42] *Ibid.*, pp. 96–97.

[43] These new issues appeared in 1679 and 1680, respectively; the title page of the first and the Preface of the second mentioned *Observations Concerning the Originall of Government.* For another mention of Milton at this time, see George W. Whiting, "A Whig Reference to 'Paradise Lost,' 1682," *The Times* [London] *Literary Supplement* (June 7, 1934), p. 408.

than intellectual friendship and likeness of mind; and it appears that whatever he absorbed from Milton's works had little effect in the attempted Whig revolution. The same cannot be said, however, of Thomas Hunt and Samuel Johnson, those two seasoned veterans of the Whig-Tory struggle for the possession of men's minds. Their most effective books, *Mr. Hunt's Postscript* and *Julian the Apostate*, derived significantly from Milton's *Pro Populo Anglicano Defensio*; and, as later analysis will show, arguments from this tract flowing through these men moved many to favor the Whig cause.

Tories recognized that both Hunt and Johnson had made use of Milton's tract and took immediate steps to inform the nation of the extent of their debt. Roger L'Estrange, still free to carry on a private campaign through his paper, *The Observator*, disclosed this debt first on August 16, 1682, in a dialogue between Tory and Whig, two politically initiated characters who habitually addressed themselves to topics of national importance. On this particular day, they discussed the privileges of Parliament, a subject of sufficient breadth to allow comment on party principles and practice, both in their own day and during the Puritan Rebellion. Tory opined that the Parliament of '41 had "Acted by the Principles of *Knox*, *Buchanan*, *Junius Brutus*, *Doleman*," as evidenced by popular discourses in its defense by "*Rutherford*, *Pryn*, *Milton*, *Bridges*, *Goodwyn*," to which Whig replied that his party now acted in accordance with "The very Same *Authorities*, and *Maxims*." "Nay," Whig continued, for the "better Conduct" of his party's affairs the "most *Dangerous* of those *Authors*" had been now "turn'd into *English*; As *Doleman*, *Milton*, against *Salmasius*, *&c*," and where the party had "them not in *Gross*," it had "the Venome of them yet by *Transfusion:* Only *Disguis'd*, and Slyly Convey'd" into "*HUNTS*, and *JULIANS*, the *Oracles* of the Age," if their own words might be taken, "for the *True-Protestant Doctrine* of *Loyalty*, and *Obedience*."[44] Apparently, such tactics helped the Whig cause. At any rate, L'Estrange returned to the matter several months later, devoting a complete issue of *The Observator* to Thomas Hunt and his political activities, which to the former Surveyor of the Imprimery reeked with dishonesty and revealed true Whiggish character. "If he had put only *THOMAS* to his Books," L'Estrange

[44] *The Observator* (Wednesday, August 16, 1682), No. 190. See also Anthony Wood, *Athenæ Oxonienses*, ed. Philip Bliss (London, 1820), IV, 82–84, for an account of these and other accusations.

observed, "and left the Reader to Supply his *Surname*, it should have been either *Parsons, White*, or *Milton*; for *there is* NOT ONE MASTERLY STROKE *in his whole* PREFACE, & POSTSCRIPT, which he has not taken out of DOLEMANS (in truth *Parsons*) *Conference about the next Succession to the Crown of* England; WHITES *Grounds of Obedience and Government*; Or MILTONS APOLOGY *pro Populo Anglicano.*" L'Estrange then disclosed that Hunt's use of "*White*, and *Milton*" had been detected at large in *A Vindication of the Primitive Christians*, a reply not only to *Mr. Hunt's Postscript* but also to Johnson's *Julian the Apostate*. Behold, then, L'Estrange indignantly exclaimed, "Behold your DOGMATIZING POLITICASTER; an *Empty, Talking Plagiary.* Behold your ADVOCATE; that has only *Lickt up the Vomit* (as he says) of the EXECRABLE DEFENDER of your SOVEREIGNS *Murder.*"[45] Since *The Observator* achieved a comparatively wide circulation during the attempted Whig revolution, few interested in politics could have missed these dramatic disclosures of Whig practice.

L'Estrange, however, simply announced with a dramatic flourish that Hunt and Johnson had plagiarized *Pro Populo Anglicano Defensio*; it remained for Thomas Long, whose *A Vindication of the Primitive Christians* he had mentioned, to work out the details and to cite chapter and verse. As an ardent Churchman, Long approached his task with a holy zeal to expose how and from whom Whigs had derived principles so dangerous to the Tory policy of securing the succession of James. Speaking first in general terms, he recalled how writers during his own time, including Johnson and Hunt, had drawn their political principles from rebels of an earlier day. "Prynne, Burton, *and* Bastwick, *were the Great Grandsires of this monstrous Progenie*," he declared; "*The* Covenanters, Nye, Marshal, *and the* Smectymnuans, *were their genuine Off-spring. To these succeed (notwithstanding the peremptory Vote for Exclusion)* John Goodwin, Owen, Harrington, *and* Baxter; *all right Commonwealths-men; with* Milton, *and* May, *and many others, whose Writings have by men of like Principles been reviewed, reprinted, and recommended to the present Age.*"[46] But if Long saw the political ills of his day stemming from a great progeny of rebels, he singled out Milton from

[45] *The Observator* (Monday, January 22, 1682), No. 276. See also *The Loyal Protestant* (September 14, 1682), No. 207, for a notice of the answer to Johnson's *Julian the Apostate*.

[46] *A Vindication of the Primitive Christians, in point of Obedience to their Prince, against the Calumnies of a Book intituled the Life of Julian* (London, 1683), sig. Bv.

among them as one of the most villainous and influential. He declared that Milton was the "great Exemplar and Tutor" of radical writers, the regicide "whose very *Sores* and *Impostumes* these Authors suck, and spit them out to poyson the People";[47] he designated *Julian the Apostate* a "*Notorious Plagiary*," Johnson having taken "his *whole design* (as Mr. *Hunt* had done before him) from an *Argument* of that *profligate Villain, John Milton*"; and he stated unequivocally that both Johnson and Hunt had drawn "their whole *Scheme* from *John Milton's Defence* of that most execrable Murther committed on the *Royal Martyr*."[48] Such grave accusations, if they were to remain politically significant, asked for supporting details; hence Long joyfully supplied specific citations in a lengthy comparison which he believed would make good his claims.

Even a glance at Milton's *Pro Populo Anglicano Defensio, Mr. Hunt's Postscript*, and *Julian the Apostate* reveals similarities in spirit and content. All three exhibited a profound hatred and distrust of Rome; all three argued cogently against the theory of divine right and the doctrine of passive obedience; all three denied hereditary succession to the throne and stressed the superiority of law over kings. Long failed to mention all these similarities, but he no doubt had them in mind when he said that Johnson and Hunt had taken their whole scheme from Milton's defense of the Commonwealth. Specifically, Long recalled that Milton had said that "si rex Parlamentum prius dimiserit, quàm ea omnia transigantur quorum causa concilium indictum erat, perjurii reus erit"—"If the king shall dissolve Parliament before it have disposed of all those things wherefore the council was summoned, he is guilty of perjury."[49] Now, declared Long, "Mr. *Hunt* resembles him in this, as well as if there had been a *transmigration of Souls*"; and to substantiate his assertion he referred to the Preface of Hunt's *Postscript*.[50] Hunt, to be sure, had revealed in his Preface a definite irritation for Charles II for his having repeatedly dissolved Parliament when the Bills of Exclusion were under discussion; and he openly opposed those men whose design it was to "make Voices for the discontinuance of Parliaments, and for a Popish Succession."[51] These dissolutions of Parliament at the will of the

[47] *Ibid.*, p. 191. [48] *Ibid.*, pp. 291, 293.

[49] *The Works of John Milton*, VII, 438–39. The quotation here cited Milton himself took from an ancient manuscript, "The Manner of Parliament."

[50] *A Vindication of the Primitive Christians*, p. 184.

[51] *Mr. Hunt's Postscript*, sigs. b6r–v.

King but against the will of the people spelled to Hunt a kind of treason, a kind of perjury itself, in that such actions belied the real duty of princes. "The Affections of a Prince to his People," Hunt explained, "supersede his Affection towards any private Relation: So strong is the Tye of Duty upon him, from his Office, to prevent publick Calamities, as no respect whatsoever, no not of the *Right Line*, can discharge; nor will he himself ever think, if duly addressed, that it can."[52] Thus Hunt clearly intimated that it was the duty of Charles II to keep Parliament in session until the Bills of Exclusion had received proper attention, a position which reminded Long that Milton had said much the same thing. But perhaps little importance should be attached to this recollection of Long's, other than to note that both Milton and Hunt believed that Parliament should sit until all grievances of the people had been duly redressed. Such an affinity in spirit may indicate a transmigration of souls but hardly a tangible debt.

Long made a more convincing case, however, in his contention that Johnson drew directly from Milton for the proposition that the law was superior to the will of the king. It will be recalled that Milton had, in *Pro Populo Anglicano Defensio*, attacked Salmasius' argument that the will of the king was supreme, that the king was not subject to law and hence could not commit crimes, since he ruled by divine right. Indeed, through the whole of chapter viii Milton undermined what Salmasius had said by referring to English chronicles and to authorities on law. He pointed out, furthermore, that it was the duty of kings not to make laws but to enforce the laws that the people had made, and he therefore accounted a king who acted in opposition to law a lawbreaker himself. In support of this general position, Milton brought forward the authority of the ancient and famous lawyer, Bracton, whose observations on the relation of kings and the law helped him dispose of Salmasius. He referred specifically to Book I, chapter viii, of Bracton's *De Legibus*, from which he excerpted a brief passage: *Non est rex, ubi dominatur voluntas, et non lex*; or,

> There is no king in the case
> Where will rules and law takes not place.[53]

[52] *Mr. Hunt's Postscript*, sig. b7v.

[53] *The Works of John Milton*, VII, 442–43. For the full text of Bracton, see *Henrici de Bracton de Legibus & consuetudinibus Angliæ* (Londini, 1596), the edition which Milton could have used.

Upon the heels of this reference, in support of the same proposition, Milton submitted two more quotations from Bracton, both from Book III, chapter ix:

Et. l.3.c.9 *rex est dum benè regit; tyrannus, dum populum sibi creditum violentâ opprimit dominatione.* Et ibidem, *exercere debet rex potestatem juris, ut vicarius et minister Dei: potestas autem injuriæ diaboli est, non Dei: cum declinat ad injuriam rex, diaboli minister est,*

or,

And in his third book, Chapter ix. "A King is a king so long as he rules well; he becomes a tyrant when he crushes with despotic violence the people that are trusted to his charge." And in the same chapter, "The king ought to use the power of law and right as God's servant and vicegerent; the power to do wrong is the Devil's, and not God's; when the king turns aside to do wrong, he is the servant of the Devil." [54]

This argument of Milton's for the supremacy of the law over the will of the king, together with his appropriate quotations from Bracton, apparently made a deep impression upon Thomas Long when he read the *Pro Populo Anglicano Defensio.* For when he came across the same argument in *Julian the Apostate*, supported by the same quotations in the same order, he recalled that he had seen he whole sequence before in Milton's *Defensio*, page 81, Johnson differing from Milton only in that he had become more expansive, "as if these Arguments which that *Mercenarie man* made use of to justifie the death of *Charles* the first, were not enough."[55] Long's recollection was wholly accurate. Johnson answered Tory contentions with arguments taken from the vast storehouse of Milton's attack upon Salmasius—particularly the Tory concept of royal prerogative as George Hickes had advanced it, which Johnson described as a "bottomless Pit of Arbitrary Power and Self-Will." To demonstrate that "There is no Authority upon Earth above the Law, much less against it," Johnson directed the attention of George Hickes to Bracton, citing first from Book I, chapter viii, of *De Legibus*, then from Book II, chapter xxii; Book I, chapter ii; and Book II, chapter xxiv, only to return again, in more detail, to Book I, chapter viii, which he immediately followed by quotations from Book III, chapter ix. In this last sequence Johnson

[54] *The Works of John Milton,* VII, 442–43.

[55] *A Vindication of the Primitive Christians,* p. 181. See p. 81 of the 1651 edition.

followed exactly the order of Milton's quotations from Bracton, simply enlarging them, as Thomas Long observed, to make his case stronger:

Ipse autem Rex non debet esse sub homine, sed sub Deo, & sub Lege, quia Lex facit Regem. Attribuat ergo Rex legi quod Lex attribuit ei, videlicet dominationem & potestatem. Non est enim Rex ubi dominatur voluntas & non Lex. Et quod sub Lege esse debeat, cum sit Dei Vicarius, evidenter apparet ad exemplum Iesu Christi, cujus vices gerit in terrâ, &c. qui noluit uti viribus sed ratione & judicio. [marginal note: Lib. I. cap. 8.]

Potestas sua juris est, non injuria. Exercere igitur debet Rex potestatem juris, sicut Dei Vicarius & Minister in terrâ, quia illa potestas solius Dei est, potestas autem injuriæ Diaboli & non Dei, & cujus horum opera fecerit Rex, ejus Minister erit, cujus opera fecerit. Igitur dum facit justitiam Vicarius est Regis æterni, Minister autem Diaboli, dum declinet ad injuriam. [marginal note: Lib. 3. cap. 9.][56]

That both Milton and Johnson should make use of *De Legibus* to bolster their arguments should cause no surprise, for Bracton was, as Milton declared, an ancient and famous lawyer, whose pronouncements on English law commanded respect in the seventeenth century. Moreover, political contestants on both sides referred often to the much-mooted Book I, chapter viii, in support of their particular causes, as witness John Bradshawe at the trial of Charles I and Sir Robert Filmer in defense of absolute regal authority. Furthermore, Samuel Johnson, on the advice of his patron, Lord Russell, had made a study of Bracton in order to become familiar with the constitution of England and hence would be likely to cite him whenever occasion demanded.[57] But it is singular that Johnson should quote the same passages Milton originally employed, in the same order in support of the same propositions. Unless both drew from a common expositor, it seems evident that Johnson found his cue to employ Bracton in this way in the *Pro Populo Anglicano Defensio*, and that he then enlarged Milton's quotations in order to give his positions greater authority.

Long presented his strongest case, however, when he observed that Johnson, and to a lesser extent Hunt, followed the letter and spirit of Milton's interpretation of the behavior of the primitive

[56] *Julian the Apostate*, pp. 83–84.

[57] *The Works of the Late Reverend Mr. Samuel Johnson, Sometime Chaplain to the Right Honourable William Lord Russel* (2d ed.; 1713), p. iii.

Christians under the emperors Constantius and Julian. In *Pro Populo Anglicano Defensio*, Milton had spent a good deal of time refuting the contentions of Salmasius that the primitive Christians had never taken up arms against royal authority and that for this reason they should be considered as models of Christian behavior. Milton replied with a flat denial of such a reading of early church history. Pointing to references from the church fathers and from early historians, Milton demonstrated that the primitive Christians for the most part could not rebel, that whenever they could they did, and that their behavior in any event could hardly be taken as a model for Christians to follow. The first proposition Milton dismissed rather briefly: Christians in primitive times lived on a low social scale and simply lacked strength to resist powerful kings. The second and third propositions, however, he developed in a good deal of detail. He disclosed that the inhabitants of Constantinople, for example, had resisted their Arian emperor, Constantius, by actual force of arms. Even when Constantius sent Hermogenes "with troops to depose Paul the orthodox bishop," Milton wrote, "they charged him [Hermogenes] and repulsed him, fired the house whither he had betaken himself, mangled and half-burned him, and at last killed him outright." Furthermore, Milton continued, "When Julian was not yet apostate, but virtuous and valiant, certain persons saluted him as Emperor, against the will of Constantius their actual emperor. How now? Are they not amongst the number of those primitive Christians whom you place as a pattern for us?" To these instances Milton added further historical evidence to refute the claim Salmasius had made. "When Constantius, by letter openly read to the people, sharply forbade this action of theirs, they all cried out that they had but done what their Provincial and the army and the authority of the commonwealth had decided. The same persons declared war against Constantius, and, as much as in them lay, deprived him of his empire and his life."[58] Milton thus made it abundantly clear from historical authority that the rebellious behavior of the primitive Christians, rather than supporting the doctrine of passive obedience, eloquently argued against it; early Christians had indeed not only rebelled against their kings but had done so under the sanction of law.

[58] *The Works of John Milton*, VII, 253–55. Milton's interpretation of the behavior of the primitive Christians, and hence that of the Whigs, was essentially accurate. See B. J. Kidd, *A History of the Church to A.D. 461* (Oxford, 1922), II, chaps. v, vi, and vii.

Now Thomas Hunt in his *Postscript*, in answer to a "worthy Gentleman" who had argued as Salmasius had done, presented the same example of rebellion among primitive Christians that Milton had employed against his opponent. Hunt observed that his adversary had supported the succession of James, that he had argued against the Bill of Exclusion by stating "That the Orthodox did not Depose the *Arrian* Emperours," an observation which was to be interpreted that Christians in England should not tamper with hereditary rights to the throne. Hunt, like Milton, made use of events during the reign of Constantius to show that his opponent's contention actually argued against him, referring specifically to happenings as recorded by Socrates, the ecclesiastical historian, who had written that "when the Souldiers of *Constantius* the *Arrian* Emperour were by his command sent to enforce them to be come *Arrians*, they took Arms in defence of their profession of Religion."[59] This reading of the behavior of the primitive Christians under Emperor Constantius compelled Long to observe, despite the reference to Socrates, that Hunt had "taken honest *John Milton* into his Consult; who says, *Chap.* 44 [*i.e.*, p. 44] of the *Primitive Christians* (Idem bellum *Constantio* indixerunt, & quantum in se erat, Imperia & vita spoliarunt) *That they waged War with* Constantius, *and as much as in them lay, spoiled him of his Life and Empire.*" Nor was Long content to let his observation rest with this exposé; he stated further that Milton's reading of history, "how *notoriously false* soever, Mr. *Hunt* is ready to assert the truth of it, and makes an offer of as *good Authoritie* for it, as even *Milton* did for the *Kings Condemnation.*"[60] Whether Hunt took Milton or Socrates into his consult can perhaps never be known, for both told similar stories about Constantius and the primitive Christians. Milton related his concisely and for a definite political purpose; Socrates, as a historian, spoke at greater length and without noticeable bias.[61] It is therefore not improbable, as Long suggested, that Hunt found his inspiration in Milton's *Pro Populo Anglicano Defensio* and then weighted his argument with the authority of an ecclesiastical historian.

If some misgivings cluster about Long's assertions that Hunt

[59] *Mr. Hunt's Postscript*, pp. 152–53.

[60] *A Vindication of the Primitive Christians*, p. 245.

[61] See *Patrologia Graeca*, ed. J. P. Migne (1864), Vol. LXVII, which contains the works of both Socrates and Sozomen. Hunt's reference may be found in Socrates' *Historia Ecclesiastica*, Book II, chapter xxxviii.

drew from Milton for his story of Constantius, no doubt should arise over his contention that Johnson found his interpretation of the behavior of the primitive Christians under Julian in the *Defensio*. Indeed, Johnson simply developed in great detail and in the same order the tale of Julian as Milton had told it, as a comparison of their versions will immediately make clear. Milton had continued his refutation of Salmasius, after his discussion of Constantius, by examining how Christians behaved under Julian, the apostate prince, particularly how Antiochians acted toward him, that group among early Christians usually considered the most devout. "Quid Antiocheni, homines apprimè Christiani?" began Milton; then he continued:

After Julian apostatized, I suppose they prayed for him, when they used to brave him to his face, and defame and revile, and scoff at his long beard and bid him make ropes of it! Think you they used to pray for the health and long life of one upon the news of whose death they offered thanksgivings, made feasts, and gave public demonstrations of joy? Nay, is it not reported that he was killed by a Christian soldier in his own army? Sozomen, a writer of ecclesiastical history, does not deny it, but commends him that did it, if the fact were so: "For it is no wonder," says he, "that some one of his own soldiers might think within himself that not only the Greeks but all mankind hitherto had been wont to praise tyrant-killers, who go unhesitating to death to procure the liberty of all: so that that soldier ought not rashly to be condemned who in the cause of God and of religion was so zealous and valiant." These are the words of Sozomen, a contemporary author, and a good and religious man; by which we may easily apprehend what the general opinion of good men in those days was upon this point.[62]

Such an interpretation of how the most devout of early Christians acted toward Julian would belie, as prior analysis has shown, the unique Anglican doctrine of passive obedience and the main Tory claim that Englishmen, whatever the circumstances, should never rebel against a prince on the throne. In view of this, it could be expected that Samuel Johnson, in his quarrel with George Hickes over passive obedience and the succession of James, should pick up the story of the primitive Christians as Milton had told it, embroider it, and strengthen it with the same historical authority; and that Long, with his knowledge of the *Defensio*, should recognize and point out that Johnson had simply embellished what Milton had said. Thus when Johnson,

[62] *The Works of John Milton*, VII, 254–55.

in *Julian the Apostate*, began to scoff at Anglican claims that the primitive Christians should be considered as models of behavior toward princes, and when he quoted a passage from Sozomen to prepare Englishmen (according to Long) for rebellion during the attempted Whig revolution, it came to Long's "remembrance that *Milton* (*Cromwel's* Secretarie) in his *Defence of the People of* England for murthering King *Charles* the First of blessed memorie, made use of the same quotation, *totidem verbis*, p. 44. From him also he took the Theme on which he declaims in so many Chapters. For thus *Milton:* Quid Antiocheni homines apprime Christiani?"[63] At this point, Long translated Milton's interpretation of how the Antiochians had treated Julian the Apostate; then, referring to the actions and thoughts of the primitive Christians as described by Milton, Long declared that these were the "*Pillars*" upon which Johnson, that "*English Solomon*," had raised himself to that "*Temple of Honour*; which yet may prove but as so many *Pillars of Smoak* to the eyes of all that shall inspect them." As a parting injunction, not lacking in irony, Long asked that his readers inspect with him these insubstantial pillars, to observe with him "what worthie *Lectures*" Johnson had developed from "these *Texts* of *Milton*" in chapters iii through ix of his *Julian the Apostate*.[64]

Long's analysis of these chapters in *Julian the Apostate* revealed, indeed, that Johnson simply followed step by step the order by which Milton had developed his story about the conduct of Christians toward princes in primitive times. Chapter iii, for example, entitled "Their Behaviour towards him in Words," told how the Antiochians, in their descriptions of Julian, "derided the shape of his Body, his Gate, his Goat's Beard, every thing that belonged to him," how they said "that his Beard was fit to make ropes of."[65] Such colorful passages, as well as others in chapter iii, merely expanded Milton's own observations on the most devout of the primitive Christians. Furthermore, chapter iv, "Their Actions"; chapter v, "Their Devotions"; and chapter vi, "Their Prayers and Tears," expanded in even greater detail the observation Milton had made concerning the prayers of the Antiochians, answering positively and with a wealth of examples the question Milton had asked, "Think you they used to pray for the

[63] *A Vindication of the Primitive Christians*, p. 180.
[64] *Ibid.*, pp. 180–81.
[65] *Julian the Apostate*, pp. 33–34.

health and long life of one upon the news of whose death they offered thankgivings, made feasts, and gave public demonstrations of joy?" These chapters made it clear that neither in their actions nor in their devotions did the primitive Christians show a respect for Julian commonly associated with the doctrine of passive obedience, that quite to the contrary they did all they could to resist him. Moreover, chapter vii, entitled "Julian's Death," picked up the latter part of Milton's query and gave a detailed account of the joy which possessed Christians when news came of the Apostate's demise:

> And thus the News, as fast as it arrived, was every-where entertained with all the demonstrations of joy and gladness. His old Friends, the *Antiochians*, as soon as they heard of his Death, kept Feasts, and publick joyful Meetings; and they not only had Dances in their Churches and Chappels of the Martyrs, but likewise in their Theatre they proclaimed the Victory of the Cross. . . .[66]

Finally, the conclusion of chapter vii stated positively Milton's query, Was not Julian, according to report, "killed by a Christian soldier in his own Army?" and presented the passage from Sozomen which Milton also had used as an appropriate commentary upon the person who had caused Julian's death:

> Some say he was killed by a *Persian*; but the more general and prevailing Report is, That he was kill'd by one of his own Souldiers.[67]
>
> And *Libanius* writing after this fashion, insinuates, that he who kill'd *Julian* was a Christian; which it may be (says the Historian) was true. This [is] a strange Concession, but you will more wonder that he should justify such a Traiterous Assassination, and yet he does in the following words. "For it is not improbable, that some one of the Souldiers might take into consideration, how the Heathens, and all Men to this day, do still praise those who long since have killed Tyrants, as Men that were willing to die for the Common Liberty, and defended in that manner their Country-men, Kinsmen, and Friends. And you can hardly blame him, who shews himself so couragious for God, and for that Religion which he approves."[68]

Chapter vii brought Johnson's specific "Lectures" on the texts of Milton to a close, though chapter ix, entitled "Reflections on the Behaviour of these Christians," followed the order of Milton's cita-

[66] *Ibid.*, p. 58.
[67] *Ibid.*, p. 59.
[68] *Ibid.*, pp. 60–61. See also *Patrologia Graeca*, in the *Historia Ecclesiastica* of Sozomen, Book VI, chapter ii, where Sozomen tells the story about the death of Julian, as recorded by Libanius.

tions from Bracton's *De Legibus*, as has already been seen. Such similarities in the order and development of *Julian the Apostate* and of excerpts from pertinent parts of *Pro Populo Anglicano Defensio*, as well as many identities in purpose and tone, demonstrate without doubt the validity of Long's claim that the whole scheme for Johnson's book came directly from Milton. Every indication points to the conclusion that Johnson had Milton's *Defensio* before him when he sat down to write, that he ran his fingers through its pages and jotted down his general headings, which he then expanded and refined to meet the exigencies of the attempted Whig revolution.

During the Whig attempt to seize power, Tories thus announced in their press and demonstrated in a tract that Samuel Johnson and Thomas Hunt had silently stolen some of their most important positions from authors of an earlier time. Why they took such pains to point out the debt these men owed to *Pro Populo Anglicano Defensio*, as well as Whig silence concerning the source of their views, is of course evident. Accusations of plagiary, supported with citations of chapter and verse, would discredit Whig methods and cast doubts on party integrity. Furthermore, Milton still offended the nostrils of many because of his attack upon the person of Charles I, and hence it would be as politically unwise for Whigs to reveal where they found some of their best arguments as it would be profitable for Tories to do so. Such spirited exposés testify to the importance of Johnson and Hunt, and continued attacks on their principles to their political influence. Roger L'Estrange, for example, devoted several almost complete issues of *The Observator* to discussions arguing against *Mr. Hunt's Postscript* and *Julian the Apostate.*[69] Moreover, George Hickes, whose positions on passive obedience and regal authority, as already seen, inspired Johnson to write *Julian the Apostate*, replied to Johnson in *Jovian*, a book in which he reasserted his original doctrines;[70] and Edward Meredith, in *Some Remarques Upon a Late Popular Piece of Nonsence called Julian the Apostate*, questioned specifically Johnson's use of *De Legibus*, saying that Bracton's positions (and hence Johnson's) could not be allowed, since it was evident that laws made not the king, but the king the laws.[71] Others

[69] See particularly issues for June 19, 1682 (No. 157), January 18, 1682 (No. 274), January 20, 1682 (No. 275), January 22, 1682 (No. 276), and January 24, 1682 (No. 277).

[70] *Jovian: Or, An Answer to Julian the Apostate* (London, 1683).

[71] London, 1682; pp. 33–34.

turned to the attack in a more jocular vein. A "Tory Land" answer to *Julian the Apostate*, as reported in *The True Protestant Mercury*, cast aspersions on Johnson himself, declaring that his head was fit for nothing else than to be shot away when the party should want other bullets;[72] and John Dryden, in Part II of *Absalom and Achitophel*, sketched with a masterly hand the opinions and activities of Johnson as Ben Jochanan, making him and his cause appear both ridiculous and dangerous. But Dryden not only turned his talents on Johnson; in an acrimonious clash over the political implications of *The Duke of Guise* he ridiculed Hunt as the "*Jehu* of the Party."[73] Such specific attacks, coupled with many references, most of which displayed anger and fear, indicate that Johnson and Hunt seriously threatened Tory doctrines and hence the succession of James, and at the same time strengthened Whig theory and the policy of excluding York from the throne. That these two Whig controversialists should become known as "Postscript Hunt" and "Julian Johnson" is in itself a measure of the influence their books had in affairs of the day.

Johnson and Hunt spoke so significantly to the debate over the succession of York that Tories not only frankly admitted their influence but also officially recognized their threat to the Crown. Wa[lter] Williams, for example, in *An Answer to Sundry Matters Contain'd in Mr. Hunt's Postscript*, reported that on a trip through the country he had had occasion to talk with several late members of the Commons and that some of them, who before reading Hunt's book had held no particular feelings about the Bill of Exclusion, now, after reading it, viewed it with favor. Such an influence in places of such importance compelled Williams to add his "mite to the Mint," that is, to answer Hunt by maintaining that hereditary kingly government was the only government of divine institution in the world.[74] Samuel Johnson's threat to Tory doctrines is so well known that the full story of it need not be told here.[75] Suffice it to say that with the collapse of the attempted Whig revolution in 1683 the Privy Council questioned him about *Julian's Arts*, his unpublished answer to the *Jovian* of George Hickes; and that in November of the same year Chief Justice Jeffreys convicted him, on the evidence of *Julian the*

72 July 12 to July 15, 1682, No. 159.

73 *The Vindication: Or The Parallel of the French Holy-League* (London, 1683), p. 13.

74 London, 1682; pp. 5–11.

75 See *DNB* under "Samuel Johnson" for more details.

Apostate, of seditious libel and condemned his book to the hangman. Johnson was freed on bail, however, and continued his efforts with such vigor that, in the reign of James II, he was degraded from the priesthood and with the open approval of the King publicly whipped with three hundred seventeen stripes. Even after the Glorious Revolution ruffians broke into his house and threatened his life for books he had written. To these admissions of the importance of Johnson and Hunt may be added the judgment of the University of Oxford Convocation in its famous decree of July 21, 1683. Interested, as scholars should be, in cause and effect, the Convocation of the University searched into and laid open the "impious Doctrines" which, having been "studiously disseminated," had led to subversive activity during the attempted Whig revolution, particularly to the Rye House conspiracy, the purported plot to take the King's life. This search resulted in a list of twenty-seven subversive propositions, to which were subjoined the authors and books from which they were drawn—all of them, according to the Convocation, "fitted to deprave good manners; corrupt the minds of unwary men, stir up seditions and tumults, overthrow States and Kingdoms, and lead to Rebellion, murther of Princes, and Atheism it self."[76]

On this list Johnson and Hunt appeared several times, the proclamation blaming them both for helping disseminate the proposition that "Birthright and proximity of bloud give no title to rule or Government, and it is lawful to preclude the next heir from his Right of Succession to the Crown."[77] It further accused Johnson, together with Samuel Rutherford and John Brown, of having promoted the proposition that "The doctrine of the Gospel concerning patient suffering of injuries, is not inconsistent with violent resisting of the higher powers in case of persecution for religion"; and Johnson alone for claiming that "There lies no obligation upon Christians to passive obedience, when the Prince commands any thing against the laws of our country; and the primitive Christians chose rather to die then resist, because Christianity was not yet setled by the laws of the Empire."[78] Now Milton also appeared on this list as an author of other

[76] *The Judgment and Decree Of The University of Oxford Past in Their Convocation July 21, 1683, Against Certain Pernicious Books and Damnable Doctrines Destructive to the Sacred Persons of Princes, Their State and Government, and of All Humane Society* (Oxford, 1683), pp. 1–2, 7. This particular convocation included the vice-chancellor, doctors, proctors, and masters regent.

[77] *Ibid.*, Proposition 5, p. 3.

[78] *Ibid.*, Propositions 8 and 9, pp. 3–4.

subversive doctrines, as later discussion will show; for the present it need only be pointed out that the very positions the Convocation attributed to Johnson and Hunt as promoting the Whig effort to subvert Tory policy and seize control of the government derived in considerable measure from *Pro Populo Anglicano Defensio*. Milton's disciples thus received wide recognition and at the same time claimed official attention for advancing with their own power and skill principles they had absorbed from their master. To the extent their arguments turned public opinion against Tory doctrines and in favor of Whig propositions, so also did Milton's. More than Oxford University officially disclosed at this time, Milton contributed to the attempted Whig revolution.

IV

Milton's political principles flowing through his disciples or directly from his own revolutionary program for man and society not only influenced public opinion in general but also penetrated into the very highest of Whig councils. Lord Russell and Algernon Sidney, two powerful and influential Whigs, went to the block in 1683 for holding firm in their belief that they possessed the right to oppose regal power. Their trials, it is true, which followed their implication in the Rye House conspiracy, revealed that they had obscurely taken part in Whig discussions to resist the government of Charles II, and hence the Crown had an excuse to convict them of high treason and to ask for their heads. But the government prosecuted their cases with unusual vigor, not so much because either Lord Russell or Algernon Sidney had openly resisted regal authority, but because they had advocated principles unfriendly to the Crown and to the succession of James. Some of these principles came either directly from Milton, or from his disciples.

The task of revealing that Lord Russell drew from Milton the doctrines which sent him to his death on the very day of the Oxford decree presents genuine difficulties in that he left no body of political thought. On the day of his execution, however, he delivered to the sheriffs a paper containing, among other things, some indication of his political beliefs. The importance of this paper as a political document is attested by its reception in town and court. Within an hour after Lord Russell had walked to the scaffold, put his head on the block, and received the ax of the headsman for "Conspiring the Death of the King and the Subversion of the Government," this paper issued wet from the press to become the center of royal concern and public debate. According to Gilbert Burnet, its appearance "enflamed" the court.[79] The King and the Duke of York felt such concern that both Burnet and John Tillotson, who had been with Lord Russell during the last days of his life, were called in for questioning before the Cabinet Council. Tillotson had little to say, except that Lord Russell had shown him the paper before the execution and that proper remarks had been made. Gilbert Burnet was questioned in greater detail and was even accused of having written some of the sentiments, an accusation which, in his *History*, he vaguely denied, though he admitted that he had helped Lord Russell in matters of organization and form.[80] Both King Charles and the Duke of York, then, apparently believed that the paper spoke cogently to political issues of the day. Moreover, it aroused among pamphleteers violent emotions. It was soon taken up, its contents dissected, and its sentiments cursed or praised in accordance with Whig or Tory positions. The paper could hardly have aroused more interest if it had been a complete statement of Lord Russell's political doctrines.[81]

Unfortunately, the paper Lord Russell delivered to the sheriffs is not a complete statement. Quite to the contrary, it is somewhat cryptic, aside from the conventional statements of a man on the scaffold, and therefore needs to be read for full understanding in the light of Lord Russell's trial and of events immediately preceding his execution. He had been convicted chiefly on the Twenty-fifth Statute of Edward Third, which, as read by the Clerk of the Court, declared, in part, that to "COMPASS OR IMAGINE THE DEATH OF OUR LORD THE

[79] *Bishop Burnet's History of His Own Time* (London, 1724), I, 561.

[80] *Ibid.*, pp. 558–62. For further information on this matter, see *A Supplement to Burnet's History of My Own Time*, ed. H. C. Foxcroft (Oxford, 1902), p. 131. See also T. E. S. Clarke and H. C. Foxcroft, *A Life of Gilbert Burnet: Bishop of Salisbury* (Cambridge, 1907), p. 195. Here it is stated that, at the suggestion of Burnet, Lord Russell, in his paper delivered to the sheriffs, cleared the country leaders from the charge of suborning Titus Oates and deleted some lines "on the dangers of *slavery*." It thus appears that Burnet did more than help Lord Russell in matters of organization and form, as he claimed in his *History*. The suspicions of Charles II and the Duke of York were perhaps rightly justified.

[81] See, for example, *Animadversions upon a Paper, Entituled, The Speech of the Late Lord Russell, &c.* (London, 1683); *Animadversions on the Last Speech and Confession of the Late William Lord Russell* (London, 1683); *Some Succinct Remarks on the Speech of the Late Lord Russell* (London, 1683); *An Antidote Against Poison* (London, 1683); and *A Vindication of the Lord Russell's Speech and Paper, &c. from the Foul Imputations of Falshood* (London, 1683).

KING" was high treason.[82] Witnesses testified that Lord Russell, at the house of a Mr. Sheppard, had talked with other conspirators about plans for a rebellion and this talk in turn was connected with the Rye House conspiracy. "This," as Gilbert Burnet observed, "gave the greatest advantage to the duke and his party that was possible, for now they twisted the design of murdering the king with the other consultations that were among the lords, and made it all appear as one complicated thing, and so the matter went over England and over all Europe."[83] But as the trial proceeded, in spite of confused and uncertain testimony, it became evident that Lord Russell had no connection with the Rye House conspirators. The Lord Chief Justice himself, in his summary of the case, made this clear when he pointed out that testimony against the other Rye House conspirators had given "direct evidence of a Consult to kill the King," whereas that against Lord Russell had disclosed only "an act of contriving Rebellion and an Insurrection within the Kingdom," which he urged "as an evidence" and felt sure was "in it self an evidence to seize and destroy the King."[84] Lord Russell, then, was convicted not for taking a direct part in the Rye House Plot but for contriving rebellion and insurrection, for, in short, consulting with other members of the Whig party on the advisability of resisting the King in the struggle over the succession of York. On the right to resist kingly authority in this matter Lord Russell held strong convictions.

These convictions emerge from his conversations with Gilbert Burnet and John Tillotson during the week preceding his execution. Both these divines, bent on saving Lord Russell's life, visited the condemned man and attempted to persuade him that resistance to kings under any circumstance was unlawful. On one of these visits, Burnet found Lord Russell so moderate in his views that he thought Lord Russell had come to a "willingness" to be convinced of the "absolute illegality of resistance." Upon leaving Lord Russell, Burnet met Tillotson, in whom he confided this apparent willingness on Lord Russell's part, along with the request that Tillotson convey it to Lord Halifax, who in turn might relate it to the King in such a manner "as

82 *The Tryals of Thomas Walcot, William Hone, William Lord Russell, John Rous & William Blagg. For High-Treason, for Conspiring the Death of the King, and Raising a Rebellion in This Kingdom* (London, 1683), p. 50.

83 *A Supplement to Burnet's History of My Own Time*, p. 111.

84 *The Tryals of Thomas Walcot . . .*, p. 61.

to be the means of saving Lord Russell's life."[85] Lord Halifax did so, and reported to Tillotson that the King seemed more moved by this news than by anything he had heard before, whereupon Tillotson reported back to Lord Russell the King's feelings but found him not as convinced as Tillotson had supposed. Indeed, Lord Russell was far from convinced, in witness of which he showed Tillotson a passage from the paper he expected to deliver to the sheriffs on the day of his death:

> For my part, I cannot deny, but I have been of opinion, that a free nation like this might defend their religion and liberties, when invaded, and taken from them, though under pretence, and colour of law. But some eminent and worthy divines, who have had the charity to be often with me, and whom I value and esteem to a very great degree, have offered me weighty reasons to persuade me, that faith and patience are the proper ways for the preservation of religion; and the method of the Gospel is to suffer persecution, rather than to use resistance. But if I have sinned in this, I hope God will not lay it to my charge, since he knows it was only a sin of ignorance.[86]

This passage stirred Tillotson deeply and shattered his hopes, for its sentiments not only ran directly across the doctrine of passive obedience but also nullified the impression which had been conveyed to the King. Consequently, in order to clarify his part in the negotiations which had so signally failed, he composed a long letter stating the position of the Church on obedience to kings, which he dispatched to Lord Russell with the hope that its arguments might bring a last-minute change. In this letter Tillotson revealed his own views as well as those of the Church. First, he stated unequivocally "That the Christian Religion doth plainly forbid the Resistance of Authority." Second, he pointed to Lord Russell's claim that a difference existed between the case of the primitive Christians and present-day Englishmen, since Anglicanism was established by law, whereas primitive Christianity had not enjoyed legal status—a claim which he answered by saying that, though religion in England was established by law, yet the same law declared it "not Lawful under any pretence whatsoever to take up Arms." Third, he asserted that Lord Russell had expressed opinions contrary to the doctrines of all Protestant churches

[85] Lord John Russell, *The Life of William Lord Russell* (London, 1819), p. 212. See also Clarke and Foxcroft, *op. cit.*, pp. 194–96.

[86] Lord John Russell, *op. cit.*, p. 213.

and that, though "some particular Persons" had taught otherwise, they had been contradicted by the "generality of Protestants." In view of this, he begged Lord Russell to reconsider his stand and hoped by his letter to convince him that he had fallen into "a very Great and Dangerous Mistake, and being so convinced, that which before was a Sin of Ignorance" would "appear of much more heinous Nature" and "call for a very particular and deep Repentance."[87]

The letter expressing such sentiments came to Russell's hands the day before his execution; but, rather than changing his opinions, it apparently confirmed them. For, though at Burnet's request, as suggested by Tillotson, Lord Russell struck out the offending passage from his paper to the sheriffs, he remained unconvinced and unrepentant, declaring that his notions of law and of English government simply differed from those belonging to Burnet and Tillotson.[88] He went to the block firm in his original convictions.

The account of Lord Russell's trial and the record of his conversations with Burnet and Tillotson during the last days of his life both clarify and supplement the much-discussed paper delivered to the sheriffs. Lord Russell was quite right, as the trial disclosed and as the paper declared, in denying his complicity in any plot to kill the King, let alone the Rye House conspiracy, from which the Lord Chief Justice had virtually exonerated him. He made it clear that nothing had been sworn against him except some "consulting and discoursing," except "some Discourses about making some Stirs"; and this was not, he claimed, "levying War against the King, which is Treason by the Statute of *Edward* the Third."[89] He implied that the Court had considerably stretched this statute to cover his case, that he had been convicted not for any overt act but for holding illegal opinions in opposition to men powerful in both Church and State. He stressed, for instance, that he had lived and would die in the "Reformed Religion, a true and sincere Protestant, and in the Communion of the Church of *England*"; but he admitted that he "could never yet comply with, or rise up to the heights of some People," which was to say, in view of his conversations with Burnet and Tillotson, that he had held firm in his

[87] *A Letter Written to My Lord Russel in NewGate, the Twentieth of July, 1683* (London, 1683), p. 2.

[88] Lord John Russell, *op. cit.*, p. 215; and Clarke and Foxcroft, *op. cit.*, pp. 195–96.

[89] *The Last Speech & Behaviour of William Late Lord Russell, upon the Scaffold in Lincolns-Inne-Fields, A Little Before His Execution, on Saturday, July 21, 1683* (London, 1683). All references to this paper are from this edition.

convictions concerning resistance to kings in cases of religion and had rejected the doctrine of passive obedience. Moreover, he presented his plight as one growing out of his active role in the Whig party. He had been fearful of popery and had sided with Shaftesbury in the turmoils which had attended the Popish Plot. He had supported the Bills of Exclusion because he thought a popish successor would be a threat to the Anglican faith. "Earnestness in that matter," he declared, had "no small Influence" on his "present sufferings." Furthermore, from the time of the conflicts over the election of sheriffs, Lord Russell had feared "that the Heat in that Matter would produce something of this kind"; hence he was not now surprised to find the ax falling on him. A considerable part of the paper clearly implied that his opposition to the Crown could no longer be tolerated, that he had been tried and convicted for not complying with opinions of men high in Church and State, that he was important enough to be dangerous and hence his head had to roll, not for a direct attempt to waylay and kill Charles II, but for his possessing strong convictions and being willing to act upon them.

Lord Russell, then, was removed from the political scene because he had, prior to the Rye House Plot, acted upon his political principles and had clung, during the excitement the plot had engendered, to his conviction in the lawfulness of resisting kings in cases of religion; or, to phrase it another way, because he had not conformed to and could not, even in the face of powerful opposition, comply with the details of what Churchmen of the time believed was the singular article of the Anglican faith, the doctrine of passive obedience. From the evidence in John Tillotson's letter, it appears that he argued against this doctrine with a good deal of precision. It will be recalled that Tillotson stated in this letter that Lord Russell had drawn a distinction between the case of the primitive Christians and that of Christians under Charles II, whose similarities Anglican divines had so often presented in support of their doctrine. The distinction Lord Russell made, Tillotson explained, was that Christians under Charles II possessed their religion by law, whereas the primitive Christians had not. Such a distinction, of course, was highly significant because it meant that the example of the primitive Christians, upon which the defenders of the doctrine of passive obedience had built most of their case, could not be applied with any force or accuracy to the present. In short, it may be inferred from Tillotson's letter, as well as from the passage expunged from the paper Lord Russell was to deliver to the sheriffs, that Lord Russell attributed the obedience of primitive Christians before Constantine's time to the fact that the laws of the land stood against them, but stoutly maintained that when Christianity became established by law Christians could resist the encroachments of tyrannical kings. It followed from this that Christians under Charles II, far from being compelled to obey blindly their Prince, possessed the right to rise up in defense of their liberties whenever royal power invaded their religion, which had been and still was established by law. Lord Russell, then, held clearly defined beliefs on resistance to kings and on the doctrine of passive obedience, and knew how to defend them with precision and care. Moreover, they were exactly the same that Samuel Johnson expressed in *Julian the Apostate* and for which he was condemned in the Oxford decree. Since Samuel Johnson was Lord Russell's chaplain and since a close relation existed between them, it is impossible not to come to the conclusion that Lord Russell derived the position which sent him to his death from the author of *Julian.*

Contemporary witnesses confirm this conclusion. Tillotson spoke in his letter of particular persons who had "taught otherwise" than the Church; and Thomas Sprat, two years after the Rye House Plot, specifically mentioned that Lord Russell had been "seduced by the wicked Teachers of that most Unchristian Doctrine, which has been the cause of so many Rebellions, and was so conformable to his Presbyterian Education, That *it is lawful to Resist and Rise against Soveraign Princes for preserving Religion.*"[90] Neither Tillotson nor Sprat named the culprit; but Bartholomew Shower, a robust supporter of Court policy, intimated that he was none other than Samuel Johnson, who had made Lord Russell pursue his course to the very last, "because this might become any Heroick Christian drawn in Armour by the Pensil of the Author of *Julian:* and is not unlike to the practices of the ancient Christians, so shamefully disguised by the same Author."[91]

Roger L'Estrange developed this suggestion in some detail. In his *Considerations upon a Printed Sheet*, published under royal authority, he searched into the authorship of the paper Lord Russell de-

[90] *A True Account and Declaration of the Horrid Conspiracy Against the Late King, His Present Majesty, and the Government* (In the Savoy, 1685), p. 21.

[91] *An Antidote Against Poison*, p. 3.

livered to the sheriffs, claiming that, though Lord Russell should be held responsible for signing it, a behind-the-scenes genius had inspired its sentiments, that is, "Julian" himself, whose evil spirit, which made treason a virtue and repentance a sin, could be traced through its whole design. Now L'Estrange believed in the justness of Lord Russell's sentence; but he declared that Johnson, who had left Lord Russell in the anguish of his thought to answer for principles he had put in his mind, was *"Incomparably the Greater Criminal."* What could be more Luciferian, L'Estrange asked, "then to turn *Penitence* into a *Scandal;* And to *Preach* it for a Point of *Religious Honor,* in a *Christian,* not to *Discover* his *Complices* in a *Rebellion.* Surely the Author of this Paper was afraid of being Discovered himself; And therefore *Inculcates* the *Principle,* and *Recommends* it."[92] As L'Estrange developed his theme further, commenting on particular passages, he recalled how Lord Russell had been "somewhat *deeper Dyed* then *ordinary";* but he found this hardly surprising since he had all too frequently "most desperate *Seducers* at his *Elbow."* He even made Samuel Johnson responsible for Lord Russell's implication in the Rye House Plot, claiming that *Julian the Apostate* was "the very *Scheme* of this *Conspiracy,* and *Calculated* for the *Murder* of the *King,* and the *Dissolution* of the *State,"* and that "it was *the same Poysonous Position* that brought this *Unhappy Lord* to his *Ruine."*[93] L'Estrange next recalled how Tillotson had made friendly and pious visits to Lord Russell with the hope of dissuading him from his dangerous position, and how this godly man was troubled to find Lord Russell *"Possess'd* with the *Principle* of his Chaplains [*Julian the Apostate*] that *Resistance was Lawful in the Case of Religion, Liberties* and *Properties being Invaded."*[94] Then, with a final flourish, L'Estrange virtually exonerated Lord Russell and placed the blame for the tragedy on Samuel Johnson himself. The scandalous paper, he explained, had suggested that the unhappy execution had been a murder. Well, it was, but not in the sense the paper implied. It was in him "that *Poysoned this Unfortunate Gentleman* with that *Seditious Maxim* that brought him to the Block, and that afterwards Encouraged him to

[92] *Considerations upon a Printed Sheet Entituled the Speech of the Late Lord Russell to the Sheriffs: Together, with the Paper Delivered by Him to Them, at the Place of Execution, on July 21, 1683* (London, 1683), p. 37.

[93] *Ibid.*, p. 46.

[94] *Ibid.*, p. 47.

persist in't"; it was in him the "*Basest*, and the most *Treacherous* of *Murders*."[95]

L'Estrange thus openly accused Johnson of treacherously murdering Lord Russell by infecting his mind with seditious maxims. The one had laid down the rule, and the other had been the example; Johnson had directed the rebellion, and Lord Russell had carried it out. Though L'Estrange, in assuming that Lord Russell had actually taken part in the Rye House Plot, pushed his analysis beyond the realm of provable fact, no doubt should remain that the condemned man derived from his chaplain the principles which placed his head on the block. And since *Julian the Apostate*, as prior discussion has shown, expanded in concrete detail some of Milton's arguments against passive obedience, it is no exaggeration to say that Milton himself must share some of the blame for Lord Russell's fate.

Less than a half-year after the execution of Lord Russell, Algernon Sidney, convicted of high treason on the same grounds, followed him to the scaffold to become the second great martyr to the Whig cause. Unlike his predecessor's, however, the paper he delivered to the sheriffs was not cryptic but crystal clear. He openly proclaimed his political principles, which were Whig to the core; and in a closing prayer he not only called upon God to stir up the faint-hearted, direct the willing, confirm the wavering, and grant wisdom and integrity to all, but also thanked God that he had been singled out as a witness of truth and of the Good Old Cause, with which he had been associated since the time of his youth.[96] But if on the scaffold he spoke more clearly, and more vehemently defended Whig doctrines than his predecessor had done, his trial revealed less evidence of complicity in any conspiracy than even the confused testimony which had convicted Lord Russell. Indeed, the Crown found Sidney guilty of high treason mainly for doctrines he had expressed in an unpublished treatise written in answer to Sir Robert Filmer's *Patriarcha*. At any rate, Sidney said precisely this in the paper he delivered to the sheriffs[97] and the conduct of the trial confirms his contention. For, though the attorney general declared that he would show that Sidney was one of the famous "Six" planning the death of the King, an accusation he later

[95] *Ibid.*, p. 52.

[96] Milton knew Sidney. He praised his illustrious name and agreed with him on the value of Ramus. See *The Works of John Milton*, VIII, 235; XI, 3.

[97] *The Very Copy of a Paper Delivered to the Sheriffs, Upon the Scaffold on Tower-Hill, on Friday Decemb. 7. 1683* [London, 1683].

supported with the doubtful testimony of Lord Howard and others, he claimed that if such testimony were not enough he could present as a prime witness Sidney's answer to Filmer, which would demonstrate that Sidney had given both his head and heart to the service of the conspirators.

To give the jury a notion of how Sidney's answer to Filmer could convict him of treason, the attorney general described it briefly as a treatise whose "whole Design" was to persuade "the People of *England*, that it is lawful, nay, that they have a right to set aside their Prince, in case it appear to them, that he hath broken the Trust laid upon him by the People." Furthermore, he continued, Sidney reasoned with arguments drawn from the Puritan Rebellion "That all the Power of the Prince is originally in the People . . . That tho all the People do rise against their Prince, it is no Rebellion." Indeed, the whole book was "an argument for the People to rise in Arms, and vindicate their wrongs." In short, he concluded, if it could be proved that Sidney actually wrote such sentiments he was sure that the jury would show abhorrence for them, since, were they put into practice, they would destroy not only the King but also "the best Monarchy in the World."[98] Though Sidney denied at the trial that the treatise to which the attorney general referred had been proved his, in his speech on the scaffold he declared that the Prosecution had apparently made use of his answer to Filmer; and the Lord Chief Justice, in his summary of the case, maintained that if the jury believed that the "most Traiterous and Seditious Libel" presented during the trial was "Coll. *Sidney*'s Book, writ by him, no man can doubt but it is a sufficient Evidence, that he is Guilty of Compassing and Imagining the Death of the King."[99] Thus Sidney too, with Lord Russell, went to the block for holding and expressing Whig principles.

Now a contemporary witness of political affairs claimed that Sidney's incriminating answer to Filmer, which appeared in print as *Discourses Concerning Government* at the turn of the century, had been drawn from Buchanan and Milton. Not all the late members of Parliament had been Shaftesburys or Sidneys, he observed; nor had all been "for *Associating* to KILL-KINGS, to KEEP OUT POPES, nor answering of *Filmers* out of *Buchanan's* and *Miltons*, nor seating the GOOD

[98] *The Arraignment, Tryal & Condemnation of Algernon Sidney, Esq; For High-Treason* (London, 1684), pp. 12–13.
[99] *Ibid.*, p. 59.

OLD CAUSE at the *Right Hand of* GOD."[100] Some had been forced out of their wits by these "*Nation-Saviours*," it was clear, thinking that by combating popery they were preserving the king and the kingdom; but not all had been so influenced. Furthermore, Thomas Sprat, in his official account of the conspiracy, stated flatly that Sidney's papers, which contained "rank Treason almost in every Line," had argued "according to the usual false Reasoning of all Republican Writers,"[101] that is, writers of the Puritan Rebellion. Why contemporary witnesses should surmise that Sidney had employed arguments against absolute regal authority taken from earlier authors and should mention Milton as a particular source will become understandable after only a glance at the *Discourses Concerning Government* and *Pro Populo Anglicano Defensio*. Both Sidney and Milton directed their tracts to exponents of absolute monarchy; both twitted their adversaries for inconsistencies in thought, revealed misreadings of authority, and reinterpreted citations from Scripture and the ancients to mean the opposite from what their foes had originally intended. Moreover, both denied the divine right of kings, opposed the concept of hereditary succession, excoriated extravagant courts, argued against passive obedience, and claimed that the analogy between civil government and the family was wholly unsound. In addition to this, they both upheld the theory of compact, placed in Parliament the supreme power, and stressed that the best government was government by law, as revealed in nature and Scripture. In short, both Milton and Sidney saw the king, not as a ruler with absolute power, but as a servant of the people upon whom his tenure depended—not a maker but an executor of laws arrived at by the exercise of right reason and through the revelations of God.[102]

Such observations on the nature of government, however, gave distinction to neither Milton nor Sidney; they sprang from a long Classical-Christian tradition to which both often referred and of whose exponents they availed themselves many times. Any suggestion that Sidney found in Milton his answers to Filmer must therefore be viewed with considerable caution. Nevertheless, in addition to general similarities between the *Discourses Concerning Government* and

[100] *Salus Britannica: Or, The Safety of the Protestant Religion, Against all the present Apprehensions of Popery Fully Discust and Proved* (London, 1685), p. 22.

[101] *A True Account and Declaration of The Horrid Conspiracy Against the Late King, His Present Majesty, and the Government*, p. 131.

[102] See Zera S. Fink, *The Classical Republicans* (Evanston, Ill., 1945), p. 151, for further comparisons between Sidney and Milton.

Pro Populo Anglicano Defensio, several identities of detail indicate that Sidney actually knew Milton's reply to Salmasius and that he called on his memory of it when he set about his refutation of Filmer's positions. When Filmer contended that beasts possess a natural propensity to be governed by one head, for example, by which he thought to establish by reference to natural law the validity of absolute monarchy, Sidney recalled that Salmasius had made the same claim by referring to the government of bees. Then, even as Milton had answered Salmasius' claim by reference to Aristotle and the laws of God, so Sidney replied to Filmer by invoking the same classical and Christian authority.[103] Moreover, when Filmer, in his attempt to invest the king with absolute temporal power, cited in support of his contention Christ's words to the Pharisees to render unto Caesar the things that were Caesar's and unto God the things that were God's, Sidney answered that the passage was difficult, that it was obscure and furthermore had no relation to kings of present-day England, though he hastened to affirm that Christ's injunction did not mean, as Filmer had inferred, that subjects should give as tribute to princes "*all their Coin*, nor a considerable part of it, nor more than what was understood to go for the defraying of the publick Charges." Indeed, Sidney went on to explain, "Christ did not so much say this to determin the questions that might arise concerning *Cesar's* Power; for he plainly says, that was not his work; but to put the *Pharisees* to silence who tempted him."[104] Now Milton said almost the same in reply to Salmasius, who, in arguing for absolute regal supremacy, had employed the same passage from Scripture. "Christ leaves undecided," declared Milton, "what things are God's, and what Caesar's." For "Either Christ gave Caesar nothing but that penny, and declared everything else ours, or else, if he assigned to Caesar all money that has Caesar's name upon it, he gives Caesar nearly all our property, and contradicts himself." "Whence it is clear," Milton concluded, "that Christ in this passage meant not so much to teach us our duty to kings and kesars—so involved and dubious is its doctrine—as he meant to expose the malice and wickedness of the hypocritical Pharisees."[105]

Finally, when Sidney spoke of the primitive Christians, he so

[103] *Discourses Concerning Government* (London, 1698), pp. 94–95; *The Works of John Milton*, VII, 87.

[104] *Discourses Concerning Government*, pp. 283–84.

[105] *The Works of John Milton*, VII, pp. 153–55.

echoed Milton's sentiments that there must have been, to employ Thomas Long's expression, a transmigration of souls. The "primitive Christians used Prayers and Tears only no longer then whilst they had no other arms," Sidney declared,

> knowing that by lifting themselves under the ensigns of Christianity they had not lost the rights belonging to all mankind, when Nations came to be converted, they noway thought themselves obliged to give their Enemies a certain opportunity of destroying them, when God had put means into their hands of defending themselves. . . . They did with the utmost vigour defend both their civil and religious Rights against all the Powers of Earth and Hell, who by force and fraud endeavoured to destroy them.[106]

These and other echoing sentiments, to which may be added Sidney's use of Bracton's *De Legibus* in the manner Milton seems to have established among his disciples, that is, citations from Book I, chapter viii, supported by references[107] to Book III, chapter ix—all strongly suggest that Sidney had in mind *Pro Populo Anglicano Defensio* when he sat down to write his own *Discourses Concerning Government.* At any rate, their replies to proponents of absolute monarchy sufficiently resemble each other for a contemporary to state that Sidney answered Filmer out of Milton, for later pamphleteers to speak of Sidney and Milton together as two champions of the Whig cause, and for Richard Baron, in his mid-eighteenth-century edition of *Eikonoklastes*, to say that "*All Antiquity cannot shew two writers equal to these. They were both great masters of Reason, both great masters of Expression. They had the strongest thoughts, and the boldest images, and are the best models that can be followed.*"[108] Such declarations by men so close in time to the attempted Whig revolution could hardly arise without some foundation.

Milton's revolutionary program, either directly or indirectly, thus made itself felt in the very highest of Whig councils. Perhaps more than Roger L'Estrange realized, Milton's principles lived to influence men of importance and power against the succession of James and for the Bills of Exclusion. But not only this. Lord Russell's execution, with which Gilbert Burnet was so intimately concerned, so moved that divine that he became biased "*rather in favour of resistance than*

106 *Discourses Concerning Government*, p. 282.

107 *Ibid.*, p. 290, for example.

108 London, 1756; p. v. Baron made comparisons between Milton and Sidney all through this edition.

against it";[109] and on the eve of the Glorious Revolution, in a carefully reasoned *Enquiry into the Measures of Submission to the Supream Authority*, he expressed at great length exactly the position for which Lord Russell had gone to the scaffold.[110] Moreover, in the year of the Settlement, Algernon Sidney arose from the block to speak again through pamphleteers of that day.[111] As martyrs in the attempted Whig Revolution, both Lord Russell and Algernon Sidney lived on to stir up the faint-hearted, confirm the wavering, and direct the willing into the paths of the Good Old Cause. Through them, through these disciples whose executions aroused so much comment, Milton marched silently but nonetheless steadily into the minds and hearts of his countrymen.

V

Reports from "Tory-Land," to borrow a phrase from *The True Protestant Mercury*, not only announced Whig adaptations of Milton during the conflict over the Bills of Exclusion and the succession of James but also revealed him to the public as an opponent of such stature that specific steps had to be taken to counter his influence. Except for Thomas Hobbes, who himself commented famously on Milton and Salmasius,[112] saying that he knew not which wrote better Latin, or which reasoned worse, perhaps no one controversial figure aroused among Churchmen more fear and opposition, a reaction which in itself serves to measure Milton's effect on the minds of his countrymen. Tories could quote him, to be sure, when he spoke to their purpose, and unlike Whigs they admitted their source; but few at this time saw fit to have Satan argue their cause.

Nevertheless, Milton could furnish Tories with positions much to their liking, and Matthew Rider, a foe of Whig theories, did not scruple to avail himself of whatever would argue his case. He actually made Milton speak against the Bills of Exclusion in his examination of *The Power of Parliaments in the Case of Succession*, a defense of regal supremacy. Introductory to his defense, Rider claimed that

[109] Clarke and Foxcroft, *op. cit.*, p. 198, as quoted from Burnet's journal.

[110] [London, 1688.] The similarity between Burnet's later views and those expressed by Russell is striking. Note also Doreen J. Milne, "The Results of the Rye House Plot and Their Influence upon the Revolution of 1688," *Transactions of the Royal Historical Society*, 5th Series, I (1951), 91–108.

[111] See *Sidney Redivivus* (London, 1689).

[112] See Masson, *op. cit.*, VI, 636, for Samuel Butler's verse comment on Salmasius and Milton.

present troubles in England had sprung from two errors: belief that the law of nature, by proclaiming equality, freed man from all earthly subjection, and belief that sovereignty was conferred on kings not immediately by God but by the people to be held by them as a trust. This understood—that is, that England's troubles had sprung from such doctrines—Rider went on to develop his case by reference to Scripture, the laws of nature, and civil authority, turning finally to "*political Expedience*" and the Bill of Exclusion. The passage of such a bill would be a remedy worse than the disease, he maintained; such a violent alteration would shake the very foundations of government and lay the nation open to the designs of the factions. The republicans, he went on, could not expect a fitter opportunity to set up their "popular *Idol*, their well-beloved *Common-wealth*," which perforce would "reduce the so much envied greatness of the *Nobility* to that degree, as to be all Fellows at Football." Such should not be allowed to happen. "For, as *Milton* well argueth against *Salmasius: The Peers are ordained by the King, they are his Companions, and Servants, and as it were his Shadows; he therefore being taken away, it's necessary they be reduced to the Commonalty, from whence they had their beginning.*" Rider then recalled that such leveling had occurred within the memory of man and warned that if the republicans came into power the same would happen again, that the two houses of Parliament, which before the Puritan Rebellion had been a bulwark of liberty, keeping the people of England from slavery and arbitrary rule, had "degenerated to that degree of *Wickedness*, that the World could not find their match for *Disloyalty*, *Tyranny*, and *oppression*.[113] In fine, Rider believed that the Bill of Exclusion had been designed not only to reduce regal authority but also to raise parliamentary power to the heights it had enjoyed under the Commonwealth, when both the king and his peers suffered something of a leveling to the "Commonalty." Now, Milton had stated in his *Defensio* that peers, created as they were by the king and hence unrepresentative of the people, should themselves fall if and when the king fell; and Rider took this as an argument against the Bill of Exclusion. But however much Milton would have agreed with Rider on the evils of leveling, he would have felt uneasy over his attempt to make him speak for the hereditary

[113] *The Power of Parliaments in the Case of Succession; Or, A Seasonable Address To The High Court of Parliament, Touching the Present Grievances of the Nation* (London, 1680), pp. 2, 8–9, 39–40.

succession of James and against Whig efforts to exclude him from the throne. Milton's principles, as Rider himself must have realized, ran directly athwart Tory policies; and the High Court of Parliament, to which Rider addressed his contentions, must have realized this also.

But if Matthew Rider twisted Milton from context to argue against the exclusion, Tories made no mistake when they employed him in their attacks on the Presbyterian faction. Milton had, after all, accused the Presbyterians of fomenting the Puritan Rebellion, of undermining the power of Charles I, and of helping bring that unfortunate sovereign to his doom. Such accusations meshed exactly with Tory strategy to discredit a faction which by the time of the attempted Whig revolution was considered more dangerous than Rome. Thus William Denton, though Whiggish in his sympathies for a free press, nevertheless expressed Tory sentiment when he struck against the Presbyterian danger by revealing, on no less an authority than Milton himself, how insolently the faction acted toward their prince, Charles I.[114] The inference was that Presbyterians still so behaved toward their lawful superiors.

William Denton, however, whose main enemy was Rome, made only a passing reference to Milton's appraisal of Presbyterian behavior; it remained for Thomas Wilson, in a memorial sermon on the martyrdom of Charles I, to work out in detail the contribution Milton could make to Tory polemics. Developing the text, "Let every soul be subject to the higher powers," Wilson had occasion to inform his congregation that the doctrine of passive obedience, unless twisted by perverse malice, meant simply obedience to a king who by his coronation oath had promised to govern by law. "And whilst thus he governs," Wilson explained, "even *J. Milton*, our late good King's heavy friend, affirms, That *the Subject, if he hold the thing to be unlawfull which by Law is commanded, ought not to resist, but to submit to the penalty which the Law imposes: and in this case to rise against the King, is to renounce Allegiance to him, and is an actual and total deposing of him.*"[115] Wilson failed to explain, however, that Milton, in speaking thus, was leading up to his argument that the Presbyterians had acted in these ways and hence could be accused of open rebellion.

[114] *Jus Caesaris Et Ecclesiasiæ vere Dictæ*, p. 67. The reference was to *The Tenure*.

[115] *A Sermon on the Martyrdom of King Charles I. Preached January 30. 1681* (London, 1682), p. 16. In a marginal note, Wilson referred specifically to *The Tenure of Kings and Magistrates*, p. 33.

For the time being he allowed these sentiments to stand by themselves, saying only that the design of passive obedience was to prevent the horrid sin of rebellion and the multifarious mischiefs of a civil war. He even went so far as to maintain that, should the King prove himself a tyrant, resistance might be condoned; but he was assured that Charles II, with his gentle nature and great wisdom, would never rule so barbarously or give such provocation to the factious multitude as to expose himself to war and the hazard of his crown and life. And by tyrant, Wilson meant not simply one who had acted once or twice illegally, but one who, as Milton defined him in *The Tenure of Kings and Magistrates*, ruled "either *wholly* or in *great part* contrary to the Laws," and continually oppressed "*grievously*," nor would be "*persuaded* from his frowardness, injustice and cruelty."[116] After these observations, Wilson moved into a short account of how Charles I had been brought to the block, deeds which the raisers and prosecutors of the war could not wash from their hands, though some, like the Presbyterians, recoiled at the execution itself. At this point in his discourse, where he launched into an excoriation of the Presbyterian faction, he found it convenient to continue citing evidence from Milton, picking up the thread at the very sentence he had broken off so abruptly in his first reference. "*The Presbyterians* (says *John Milton*, the defender of the Regicides) *have for these seven years Deposed the King, not only by depriving him of his authority, but by conferring it upon others.*" If then, Thomas Wilson continued from Milton, "*If then the Oaths of Subjection broken, new Supremacy obeyed, new Oaths and Covenants taken, have in plain terms unkinged the King; much more then hath the seven years War, not Deposed him only, but Outlawed him, and defied him as an Alien, a Rebel to Law, an Enemy to the State.*"[117]

Wilson thus revealed to his congregation, through evidence from Milton, that the Presbyterians, far from being guiltless in the tragedy of the King's death, actually drove him by their actions and oaths to his defeat and final doom on the scaffold. Indeed, Wilson found Milton's attack upon the Presbyterians so congenial to his purpose that he paraphrased further. Had not the Presbyterians levied war against their sovereign King?

116 *Idem.* In a footnote, Wilson referred to *The Tenure of Kings and Magistrates*, p. 19, and repeated Milton's definition of a tyrant.

117 *Ibid.*, p. 21. In a marginal note, Wilson referred to *The Tenure*, p. 32.

They certainly who by deposing him have long since taken from him the life of a King, his Office and Dignity, they in the truest sense may be said to have killed the King, not only by deposing, and waging War against him, which set him in the farthest opposite point from any vital function of a King, but by their holding him in Prison, vanquished and yielded into their absolute and despotick power, which brought him to the lowest degradement and incapacity of a Regal name.[118]

Such admissions of Presbyterian defection by a prime enemy of the Church proved to Thomas Wilson, and through them he hoped to convince his congregation, that the faction, even more than the Jesuits, whom he had occasion to mention later in connection with Milton, threatened established religion and government. Satan himself could be quoted to prove the accuracy of Tory contentions.

If Tories could employ parts of *The Tenure of Kings and Magistrates* to strengthen their cause, they found that Milton's *Character of the Long Parliament and Assembly of Divines* spoke even more favorably in support of their current positions. This brief tract, which appeared first in 1681, had been, according to a prefatory comment, expunged from *The History of Britain* "*out of tenderness to a Party*";[119] but now it was to be printed because it was very seasonable to the times. In its attack upon Long Parliament and the Presbyterian divines it was seasonable for the Tories indeed; and just because it was so timely, *Heraclitus Ridens*, in a dialogue between Earnest and Jest, devoted a little less than half the issue for April 4, 1681, to a discussion of its preface and contents. Jest opened the discussion by saying that, in this age of walking ghosts from the Old Rump, he had had the pleasure of meeting John Milton, an observation which compelled Earnest to ask whether he was "going to look out his Old Enemy *Salmasius*, and have the other crash with him in justification of the Kings Murder." Jest's reply was that Milton was not, that he had with him a dog and a bell and went about crying, "*Pray pity the poor Blind, one peny for the poor Blind.*" Jest then explained that Milton walked about thus because, during the "late times," he had "adventured his stock in the bottom of the Public Faith" and had lost all—information which Jest gleaned from comments introducing the tract.

[118] *A Sermon on the Martyrdom of King Charles I.*, p. 21. For the originals of these paraphrases, see *The Works of John Milton*, V, 32–37.

[119] *Mr John Miltons Character of the Long Parliament and Assembly of Divines in MDCXLI* (London, 1681), "To the Reader."

Thus in view of Milton's loss, Earnest asked, would the "well-disposed of the Party" make a purse for him now? Jest answered no. Moreover, he believed that they would not inasmuch as Milton railed at the owners of the public faith and their partners in the Synod at a most fearful rate. Indeed, Jest went on, Milton said that they had set a padlock on the press and had stopped his mouth with an Index Purgatorious, but that now the press was free he would tell all their tricks to the world.

Earnest knew, of course, that Jest referred to Milton's newly published *Character of the Long Parliament and Assembly of Divines*, which had been deleted from *The History of Britain*—a tract whose every line could be turned to the discredit of the Whig Party. Jest's strategy was simply to summarize what Milton had said. "*The greatest part of the Parliament were such whom bold and active Ambition, rather than merit, had commended to the place*," Jest began; "*Justice was delayed and denied, Spight and Favour determined all; Faction and Treachery, Wrong and Oppression ruled all.*" Furthermore, Jest continued, "Their Votes and Ordinances, instead of repealing old Grievances, laid on new Taxes; they who aided them most faithfully, were slighted and forced to dance attendance with Petitions after Committees, whom . . . [Milton called] *an innumerable company of Thieves in Office;* who for fear of an account, and laying down their Authority, for want of new business, wire-drew all affairs to the ruin of a whole Nation.[120] To this summary of the first part of Milton's tract, Earnest declared: "A very fair Character of the state of the Common-wealth: And what says he of Religion?" In answer to this query, Jest condensed the last part of the pamphlet. "*The Assembly of Divines were neither eminent for piety or knowledge, but for crying down Pluralities and Prelates*," Jest declared, employing many of Milton's own terms; "*and yet the Conscientious men, before they had done their work, took their wages, some two or more of the best Livings, besides Lecture-ships, and Master-ships of Colleges; and were the greatest Pluralists and Nonresidents that ever were in* England." Besides all this, Jest went on, "*they sailed by every wind of profit, and at last came to an Anchor in the Road of Persecution, against which they had so declaimed in the Bishops, persuading the Magistrates to use bodily compulsion as a stronger means to subdue that*

120 *Heraclitus Ridens* (April 4, 1681), No. 10.

Rebel Conscience *of* Malignant Dissenters *than their Evangelical persuasion.*" Finally, Jest brought his précis to a close with a ringing indictment of the Assembly of Divines, together with their disciples: "*they were* Trim tram, like Master like Man, *commended by Committees for Zealous Godly men, but acted like Children of the Devil, unfaithfully, unjustly, unmercifully, corruptly and stupidly, that between the Teachers and Disciples, a more ignominious and mortal wound was never given to Faith, Piety, and the Reformation.*"[121]

Thus Jest, with all the vigor of Milton's own phrases, struck against the Whig party through the vulnerable sides of the Long Parliament and the Assembly of Divines. It was perhaps a happy circumstance, as Earnest jocularly concluded, that Milton was at this time a mere shade; for had a *living* man said as much against the Dissenters he would have been teased as a "*Jesuit, Tory, Tantivy,*" and what not. Now Milton did, as will shortly be seen, achieve a reputation as a Jesuit in disguise; but this was the only time that "Tory" was ever pinned to his memory, even facetiously. His disinterested account of Presbyterian depravity in office accorded him this anomalous distinction.

Tories must have realized, however, that they could use only a small part of Milton's works to argue their cause. After all, they knew that the main part of his revolutionary program spoke effectively against their fundamental positions. They therefore openly recognized his stature as a political antagonist and signified in various ways their fear of his power and influence. Thomas Flatman, for example, ironically called him "that grand Whig *Milton*,"[122] and declared that the party prized the "Whig stuff" of John Phillips because he had been brought up at the feet of "that great *Gamaliel*," his uncle.[123] Moreover, Edward Pelling, whose memorial sermons on Charles I became famous, deemed Milton a "great *Oracle*";[124] and Roger L'Estrange named him one of the "*Classical Authors*"[125] of the Whig party, as well as one of the most dangerous.[126] Furthermore, through *The Observator* L'Estrange kept the public aware of this man he considered so important in Whig councils, particularly in the year preceding the Rye House conspiracy, when political passions flamed

121 *Heraclitus Ridens* (April 4, 1681), No. 10.
122 *Ibid.* (May 9, 1682), No. 67.
123 *Ibid.* (April 18, 1682), No. 64.
124 *The Good Old Way* (London, 1680), p. 115.
125 *The Observator* (February 3, 1682), No. 283.
126 *Ibid.* (August 16, 1682), No. 190.

at a white heat. He called attention to the libelous *Eikonoklastes*,[127] for example, announced the translation of Milton's "*Republican Letters*,"[128] designated him an "*Observator*" upon the "*Portraiture of his Late Majesty*,"[129] and named him with many others in a discussion of the martyrdom of Charles I.[130] It is thus little wonder that the Oxford University Convocation, in its attempt to lay open the writers and principles responsible for the Rye House conspiracy, should name Milton twice: once as the joint author of the multiple proposition that "All Civil Autority is derived originally from the People," that "there is a mutual compact, tacit or express, between a Prince and his Subjects," "that if he perform not his duty, they are discharg'd from theirs," and "That if lawful Governors become Tyrants, or govern otherwise then by the laws of God and man they ought to do, they forfeit the right they had unto their Government"; and once as an asserter that "King Charles the first was lawfully put to death, and his murtherers were the blessed instruments of Gods glory in their Generation."[131] Events immediately following this official recognition of the part Milton played in the attempted Whig revolution bear further witness to his importance and influence. Roger L'Estrange, naturally enough, spread the Oxford decree abroad through *The Observator*, naming Milton, along with other culprits, in his story of this solemn affair;[132] and a Latin poem celebrating the immolation of subversive books on the quadrangles of Oxford accorded Milton special attention:

> In mediâ videas flammâ crepitante cremari
> MILTONUM, coêlo terrisque inamabile nomen.[133]

Only a man of recognized leadership in political controversy would be likely to merit such remarks of opprobrium.

But the most significant sequel to the Rye House conspiracy and the Oxford decree revealing how Tories both recognized and feared Milton's power and influence was the sudden expulsion of James Parkinson, a Fellow of Lincoln College, for "whiggisme." Parkinson

127 *Ibid.* (February 19, 1682), No. 292.
128 *Ibid.* (May 6, 1682), No. 133.
129 *Ibid.* (September 20, 1682), No. 208.
130 *Ibid.* (April 11, 1683), No. 317.
131 *The Judgment and Decree Of The University of Oxford Past in Their Convocation July 21. 1683*, pp. 2–3, 7, Propositions 1 and 26.
132 August 1, 1683, No. 382.
133 Quoted from Masson, *op. cit.*, VI, 814.

had, according to an unofficial University report, approved the sentiments of *Julian the Apostate* and had openly defended some of the propositions which University officials had found so offensive to the government of Charles II. He had, furthermore, specifically recommended that his students read Milton as an antidote against Sir Robert Filmer, whom he considered too high a Tory. Charged with these and similar crimes, the last of which mentioned here compelled Anthony Wood to comment marginally on his record of the expulsion proceedings, "John Milton, who wrot a vindication of the murder of King Charles I," James Parkinson was let out of his college, a victim of Tory fear of Whiggish counsels.[134] In view of this and other events, coupled with Tory affirmations of Milton's political significance, Francis Turner made no mistake when, in a sermon before Charles II in the last year of that monarch's reign, he charged that Milton was a leader of rebellion, one who, along with Knox, Buchanan, and later patrons of the Good Old Cause, would some "day be star'd in the face by all that pretious *Blood* which *their Writings* encourag'd *others* to shed so prodigally."[135] Milton's principles had indeed caused the shedding of blood, the most noble of which, perhaps, had been that of Lord Russell.

Recognition of Milton's political stature and of his influence on the minds of his countrymen forced Tories to expose and refute his dangerous principles. Thomas Long, as previous analysis has shown, not only revealed the extent to which Johnson and Hunt drew from Milton but also pointed out the danger of the principles they borrowed. Moreover, Sir George Mackenzie, in *Jus Regium*, defended the Anglican story of the primitive Christians even as he opposed the one told by Milton.[136] Roger L'Estrange, however, inclined as he was to stress the power of print, conducted the most vigorous campaign of disclosing what he considered to be Milton's false political principles. In *The Reformed Catholique*, for example, he recalled how the enemies of the established Church and State still fished in troubled waters, even as their predecessors had done—how in that earlier time people's

134 *The Life and Times of Anthony Wood, Antiquary, of Oxford, 1632–1695, described by Himself*, compiled by Andrew Clark (Oxford, 1894), III, 68–71.

135 *A Sermon Preached before the King on The 30th of January, 1684/5* (London, 1685), p. 16.

136 *Jus Regium: or, The Just and Solid Foundations of Monarchy in General; and More Especially of the Monarchy of Scotland: Maintain'd against Buchannan, Naphtali, Dolman, Milton, &c.* (London, 1684), p. 116. See also "To the Reader" for mention of Milton.

minds had been prepared for rebellion through the dissemination of pestilent principles, such as the supremacy of Lords and Commons and the right to depose and to put a king to death. As then, so now. Hence L'Estrange considered it important to remind the public, in the same terms he had employed in 1663, that these principles so dangerous to established authority had sprung from "*Milton*, *Goodwin*, *Rutherford*, and a hundred more."[137] But his most concerted attempt to put the people of England on guard came with the publication of *The Dissenter's Sayings*, a sort of handbook of rebellion containing all possible maxims inimical to Church and State, together with the authors and books from which they were gleaned. In this volume Milton appeared as the author of the principle that it was lawful for any who had the power to call a wicked king to account and after due conviction to depose him and put him to death, if the ordinary magistrate had neglected or denied to do it—a sentiment L'Estrange rightly attributed to *The Tenure of Kings and Magistrates*.[138] This handbook of sedition, disclosing so many partners in crime, apparently proved so successful that L'Estrange followed it with an enlarged *Second Part*, in which Milton figured more prominently. Under section 9, for example, entitled "Principles and Positions," he cited from *Eikonoklastes* Milton's principle of the supremacy of Parliament; and under section 14, called "The Kings Murder Justifi'd," he quoted five selections from the same tract in support of the heading.[139] These volumes attracted a good deal of attention. Indeed, Samuel Johnson intimated that his enemies found their information about Whigs in the excerpts L'Estrange had collected rather than in the original authors themselves, an implication which George Hickes felt called on to answer in *Jovian*, declaring that at least Edward Pelling was well versed in "the Fanatical Originals," since he made one sermon which Johnson had questioned before L'Estrange had printed the first of these books and, moreover, had in his library "*Junius Brutus*, *Lex Rex*, *Prynns* Soveraign Power of Parliaments, *Naphthali*, *Jus Populi Vindicatum*, *Miltons Apology*, *Plato Redivivus*, with very many others, and *Julian the Apostate* among the rest."[140] If L'Estrange failed to turn the

137 *The Reformed Catholique: Or, The True Protestant* (London, 1679), pp. 16–17.

138 *The Dissenter's Sayings* (London, 1681), p. 31.

139 *Dissenters Sayings. The Second Part* (London, 1681), pp. 47, 74–75. See also *Le Non-Conformiste Anglois Dans ses Ecris, dans ses Sentimens, & dans sa Pratique* (Londres, 1683), pp. 44, 45, 74; and *The Dissenters Sayings. Two Parts in One* (London, 1685), pp. 25, 35, 38, 53.

140 *Jovian*, pp. 237–38.

people of England against the doctrines and men he believed were so dangerous, he at least exposed both to public review; and the very fact that in *The Reformed Catholique* he named Milton with two others from the hundred or more he later collected indicates the value he placed on his head.

Tories considered Milton an antagonist of such stature during the attempted Whig revolution that they felt it necessary to counter his influence with a concerted campaign of vilification and falsehood. Some carried on this campaign with tactics inherited from an earlier day. Francis Turner, for example, in a memorial sermon preached before the King, proclaimed Milton a "vile mercenary" satirist, one who dipped his pen in the poison of asps and overflowed with venom and gall in his justification of regicide and in his attack upon the memory of Charles I. Milton was "worse than an Atheist," if such were possible, Turner informed Charles II and the congregation gathered before him; he wrote upon divorce to make "Adultery as well as Murder as lawful in themselves, as they were delightful to him." Then calling upon the old saw of the Restoration, Turner declared that it pleased God to strike Milton blind, as He struck "those *Sodomites* that durst attempt to violate even Angelical Purity."[141] What Turner embroidered with such emotion, William Dugdale intimated in the dignity of his *Short View of the Late Troubles in England.* The Commonwealth "encouraged a needy Pedagogue," he said, and preferred him to the office of Secretary "to write that Scandalous Book called Εἰκονοκλάστης, being a bitter invective" against the King's "*Divine Meditations.*"[142] But such charges of venality, which early in the Restoration apparently proved quite effective, no longer seemed to capture attention and hence were seldom recalled. What Tories needed at this time to counter Milton's growing power and influence was a story at once plausible and capable of stirring emotion, a strange yet believable tale which would discredit in the eyes of the people both the man and his doctrines. What would be more logical, in view of similarities in Presbyterian and Catholic political theory, than to identify Milton's positions with those of the Jesuits? What would be more emotionally startling than to call him a Jesuit in disguise? Such a story

141 *A Sermon Preached before the King On the 30/1 of January 1680/1* (London, 1681), pp. 40–41.

142 *A Short View of the Late Troubles in England* (Oxford, 1681), p. 380. For a further reference to *Eikonoklastes*, see David Jenner, *Beaufrons* (London, 1685), p. 24.

would make him appear even more reprehensible than before and would help turn public opinion against both him and the Whig cause which his principles so ably defended.

No less a person than the notorious Titus Oates furnished the basis upon which Tories could build such a story. In the introduction to his *True Narrative of the Horrid Plot and Conspiracy*, which he addressed to Charles II himself, Oates exercised his lively political imagination and came up with the statement that "*Milton* was a known frequenter of a Popish Club." Since this statement, as well as others surrounding it, struck Tory fire, it is important to see the accusation in context:

> The Popish Lord is not forgotten, or unknown, who brought a Petition to the late Regicides and Usurpers, signed by about Five hundred principal Papists in *England*; wherein was promised upon condition of a Toleration of the Popish Religion here by a Law, their joint resolution to abjure and exclude the Family of the *Stuarts* for ever, from their undoubted right to the Crown. Who more disheartned the Loyalty and patience of your best Subjects, then their confident Scriblers, *White* and others? And *Milton* was a known frequenter of a Popish Club. Who more forward to set up *Cromwell*, and to put the Crown of our Kings upon his head, than they? Give me leave to tell Your Majesty, that his new-fangled Government was contrived by a Popish Priest, and *Lambert*, a Papist for above these Thirty years.[143]

Now such a passage could not have suited Tory designs better had it been conceived, after long consultation, by party members responsible for mapping high strategy. It made the late regicides exclusionists and hence by implication made the exclusionists of 1679 no better than regicides. It attributed the defection of good subjects in Civil War days to the efforts of "confident Scriblers." But best of all, it intimated that one of those scribblers—that is, Milton himself—wrote what he did in collusion with Rome. At a time when fears of a Catholic invasion gripped a good part of the nation, such allegations, supposedly dug up from secret files of the Jesuits, could spell disaster for the Whig cause.

143 *A True Narrative of the Horrid Plot and Conspiracy of the Popish Party Against the Life of His Sacred Majesty, the Government, and the Protestant Religion* (London, 1679), sigs. [Bv–B2]. A[uguste] Geffroy, in his *Étude sur Les Pamphlets Politiques et Religieux de Milton* (Paris, 1848), was puzzled by this statement of Oates. "On ne peut comprendre l'absurde calomnie de TITUS OATES, qui accusait Milton de fréquenter à cette époque un club-papiste," Geffroy said. See p. 214, note. For commentary on the legend which stemmed from this assertion of Oates, see Carolus, "Milton An Alleged Papist," *Notes & Queries*, 7th Series, XI (1891), 306; and John Walter Good, *Studies in the Milton Tradition*, Appendix E.

For this reason it is not surprising to find Roger L'Estrange exploiting the information for all it was worth, despite his altercations with Oates on other political matters. He found Oates's assertions concerning the Faction to be "punctually true"; its members had indeed, L'Estrange stated, preached and written sedition, instructing themselves and others in "the Methods and Principles of Rebellion." What Oates had to say about the present state of affairs thus looked to L'Estrange "liker a *Revelation*, then a *Conjecture*." With this assuring comment as to the veracity of Oates, L'Estrange turned his attention to the startling passage about the Civil War and the Papists, in which Milton had appeared as a frequenter of a popish club. Repeating a good part of the passage verbatim, he nevertheless significantly omitted the Papist White from the list of seditious scribblers, thus focusing attention on Milton alone:

> *What broke the* Uxbridge Treaty, *but the* Romish Interest, *and* Policy? *Who continu'd to baffle all designs of Peace, and Settlement to this Nation, and Prosperity to his Majesties Family, but* those Incendiaries, Milton *was a known frequenter of a* Popish Club; *who more forward to set up* Cromwell, *and to put the Crown of our Kings upon his Head, then* Papists? *And his new fangled Government was contriv'd by a* Popish Priest; *and* Lambert *a* Papist, *for above these* Thirty years.[144]

L'Estrange admitted, to be sure, that he had inserted this passage as a curiosity in the history of earlier times; he had done so, moreover, because the information it contained might have escaped other men, as it had himself. Yet he was of the opinion that, although the Church of England was ever an eyesore to Rome, ambition and schism among themselves had carried a great "stroke" in "that *Fatal Revolution*." Despite his disagreement with Oates on this particular position, however, he made it a point to repeat Oates's original assertions, including the damaging allegation that Milton had had popish connections. Even if he privately believed the whole passage false, he unhesitatingly spread the information it disclosed, apparently believing, like politicians in all ages, that party interests transcend those of truth. He was well aware that if politicians repeated the story often enough, people might begin to believe it; and belief at this time that Milton had consulted with Papists could turn many against him and hence against the Whig party.

144 *A Further Discovery of the Plot: Dedicated to Dr. Titus Oates* (London, 1680), pp. 26–27.

L'Estrange's political instinct proved sound. Tories picked up the passage he so consciously called to public attention and developed from it a legend that Milton had been a Jesuit in disguise, living and dying in the Roman communion. Indeed, L'Estrange himself contributed further to this development inasmuch as his comment that he could not agree with Oates on Rome's responsibility for the Puritan Rebellion brought an immediate reply, which repeated the passage in question and allowed L'Estrange to refer to it again. The author of this reply, who called himself simply "B. W.," challenged L'Estrange's concession that others besides Jesuits should share the blame for fomenting the Puritan Rebellion. Leading up to his point, B. W. recalled how L'Estrange had repeated from Oates that "*the Jesuitical Party were the Contrivers of the last War*," that the Romish Interest had broken the Uxbridge Treaty, that "Milton *was a known Frequenter of a Popish Club*," that Papists had been forward to set up Cromwell and crown him king, and that his government had been contrived by a priest and Lambert had been a Papist for above thirty years.[145] Now B. W. wanted to know why L'Estrange cast a shadow on these assertions by saying that others should share some responsibility for contriving the late wars, why he should intimate that, concerning some of these allegations, Oates might be mistaken. Such queries went unanswered. But, conceding that many of the events to which Oates referred had occurred before Oates had been born, or at least able to judge of things, B. W. claimed that Oates should be believed because he had had access to "the Jesuits Memoirs," that he had found here, except for the Addresses to the King, all the information needed to make good his assertions.[146] The Jesuits themselves, according to B. W., had recorded that Milton had worked in collusion with Rome and Oates had merely revealed that fact to the people of England.

Such a position L'Estrange saw no reason to deny; indeed, he supported it. Addressing himself to the common objection that Oates was too young to speak of the things he discovered to the King upon "*Knowledge*," that it would have been well had he "produced some *Historical Authority* in *Confirmation* of the Reports, that *Lambert* was a *Papist*, and *Milton* a *Frequenter of a Popish Club*," L'Estrange resolved all doubts easily by simply stating that such information was private, that it "was only *Proper* for the *Registries* of the *Society*, and

[145] *An Additional Discovery of Mr. Roger L'Estrange His Further Discovery of the Popish Plot* (London, 1680), p. 15. [146] *Idem.*

not of a quality to be Inserted into Our *Publique Annals*."[147] Whether L'Estrange convinced anyone by this ingenious and perhaps ironical argument is unknown; but it is certain that from the allegation that Milton was a frequenter of a popish club arose the story that he was a Jesuit in disguise.

Edward Pelling, in *The Good Old Way*, first gave Oates's discovery this particular twist. In his sermons and pamphlets, Pelling had often turned his attention to the struggle over the succession of York; no Tory upheld more vigorously the doctrines of passive obedience and divine right, or attacked more vehemently Whig principles of government. In this particular work, he turned to the attack by associating, as common Tory practice now dictated, Jesuit positions with those of the Dissent; and this reminded him of the particular position Milton had taken in *The Tenure of Kings and Magistrates*, that every worthy man in Parliament might, for the public good, be thought a fit peer and judge of the king. This in turn brought to Pelling's mind what Titus Oates had "discovered of that great *Oracle*, Mr. *Milton*; namely, that he was a member of a *Popish* Clubb." "The thing is credible enough," Pelling declared, "that he was a *Jesuit in disguise*."[148] And, in further support of what Oates had claimed, Pelling maintained that it was "manifest, that they were *Jesuitical* Doctrines which in 48 did pass in the *Pulpits* for *Divinity*, and in *Westminster-hall* for *Law*; and that the *infamous Court* of Justice did consist of men, who were the *Sons* of the *Jesuit*, who was the *Son* of the *Devil*."

The story that Milton was a Jesuit in disguise seemed indeed so credible that Edward Pettit developed it further in *The Vision of Purgatory*, a satire on political events attending the debates over the succession. Pettit began by relating how, during Roman solemnities in 1679, he had fallen asleep on the banks of the Tiber and had had a dream. In this dream he walked among the shades of the dead, guided by an honest Capuchin. Much to his surprise, they came upon Milton addressing a provincial of the Jesuits, and because Milton was, as Pettit recalled, a man of "singular Eloquence," he took pains to hear what he said. The gist of Milton's address was that he had been injured, that he had been denied the honors which had been granted to others, who were vastly beneath his merits and deserts. For the bene-

[147] *L'Estrange's Narrative of the Plot* (2d ed., London, 1680), p. 7.

[148] *The Good Old Way*, pp. 114–15. See also George W. Whiting, "Milton a Jesuit," *Notes & Queries*, CLXVIII (1935), 150–51.

of the provincial, Milton listed his solid accomplishments. Had he not constantly attended Jesuit "Consults" and observed Jesuit "Orders"? Had he not promoted "the late Rebellion in *England* by all the Artifices Imaginable"? Had he not sided with the "Malcontents and seditious Rabble," who had wanted a man of his parts and learning "to Gild their Treasons, with pompous pretences of Justice, and Reformation; and to urge them to greater Excesses"? Had he not bestowed "the best Flowers of Rhetorick for garlands to adorn the heads of victorious Traytors, and triumphant Usurpers"? Had he not given "them a Counterfeit Majesty with the Roabs of Eloquence"? Finally, had he not gulled the people "to part with their religion, and Property," to give them to those whom he had given the "Glorious Titles of *Preservers of the Commonwealth, and Redeemers of their* Liberty"? Had he not shaken the crowns of princes in his "unparallel'd Book" against Salmasius? Now Milton would have gone on, Pettit reported, but the Jesuit interrupted Milton to say that he should not, for the welfare of the Order, desire unreasonable honors. What if the Jesuits were to declare to the world that Milton and his companions had been instrumental in carrying out the designs of the Order under the "Notion of Commonwealthsmen, Nonconformists, &c"? Why, were this to happen, the old Jesuit game would be at an end. Milton was therefore advised to rest content for a while; but he was promised that, if ever the universal order of things came under the Jesuit's disposal, he would not be forgotten.[149] In Pettit's dream, Milton actually became a Jesuit in disguise, carrying out under the pose of a Commonwealth's man or a Nonconformist the plans of the Order to conquer the world. Even as satire, the tale could turn people against Milton and his political principles; and this, of course, is exactly what Pettit designed it to do.

While Pelling and Pettit told their stories of Milton's actual affiliation with the Society of Jesus, other Tories pointed out their identity of thought. Robert Hancock, for example, in *The Loyalty of Popish Principles Examin'd*, began with the claim that the Bishops of Rome first enunciated antimonarchical doctrines, though he admitted that whether the ringleaders of sedition in England poisoned the Jesuits, or the Jesuits the ringleaders, was still a matter of dispute. Perhaps the bishops of Rome had the honor of poisoning them

149 *The Vision of Purgatory, Anno 1680* (London, 1680), pp. 98–102.

both. In view of this, Hancock declared, "If *Milton* (the great Oracle of one of the Factions) had owned himself to be a Papist, there had been no reason to wonder at the Impiety of his Doctrines, which he either did, or might have learned from the Popes and greatest Divines of the *Roman* Church."[150] But instead of owning this affiliation, Hancock continued, instead of agreeing with Salmasius that the doctrine of "Sacred and inviolable Authority of Princes was preserved pure and uncorrupt in the Church, till the Bishops of *Rome* attempted to set up a Kingdom in this World paramount to all Kings and Emperours," Milton, "with his usual confidence," acquitted the popes and traced his antimonarchical principles to Luther, Calvin, and other reformed divines.

Hancock decidedly could not believe that the popes should be thus acquitted and hence opposed "the authority of *Milton*" with a late author of the Roman Church, who was well acquainted with its doctrines. To the charge that the Jesuits had articulated the principle that government was originally in the people and that their representatives could call their sovereign to account and alter the form of government, this author replied that such doctrine, however much speculative truth it might contain, should by no means be preached to the people, who might stretch cases and pick quarrels with their best governors, and that furthermore it had been taught many ages before the Jesuits were thought of. It indeed had not only been taught but practiced, at least so far as the right to put a king from his throne was concerned, as witness Pope Zachary, who deposed Childeric the French king and then absolved his subjects from their allegiance. This should prove, Hancock went on, that popes were authors of antimonarchical doctrines, despite Milton's pretention that the Pope's act was unnecessary, Childeric by his own perfidiousness having discharged the people from their oaths of allegiance. Yet, though Hancock purposed chiefly to pin the origin of antiregal sentiment on the popes themselves, he freely admitted that Doleman and Suarez, Mariana and Molina, as well as Knox and Buchanan and others, furnished the leading faction with "Principles and Precedents, with Arguments and Texts of Scripture" for all it did against Charles I. From these authors could be deduced "all the Materials of that Bloody Ordinance, to

[150] *The Loyalty of Popish Principles Examin'd* (London, 1682). See particularly pp. 32–50 for Hancock's analysis of Milton's positions as presented in *Pro Populo Anglicano Defensio* and in *Eikonoklastes.*

erect an High Court of Justice for the Trial of the King; the Impeachment against his Majesty in the name of the Commons of *England*; the Speech of *Bradshaw*, President of that Mock-Court of Justice; and *Milton's* Vindication of the Proceedings against the King." Whether Milton owned himself to be a papist or not was immaterial to Hancock; it was important, however, to see his sympathy for popes and to note the identity of their political doctrines.

Other Tories pointed out this identity in even greater detail. George Hickes, in a sermon preached before the Lord Mayor of London, claimed that those who had "imbibed the Popish Principles of Rebellion," like Knox, Buchanan, Goodman, and Milton, had proved to be, both in principle and practice, a "pestilent sort of people, and movers of Sedition, enemies from their first Original unto *Cæsar*, haters of His Royal Prerogative, and Actors against his Interests and Decrees"; and he later reminded his congregation of the "Popish" belief that a tyrant might be either killed or deposed, referring as he did so to *The Tenure of Kings and Magistrates* and to *Eikonoklastes*.[151] But it remained for Thomas Wilson, who in his sermon on the martyrdom of Charles I had spoken of Milton as the late king's heavy friend, to draw specific parallels between the Jesuits and Milton with citations of chapter and page. Thus when Wilson referred to *Pro Populo Anglicano Defensio*, chapter iii, page 64, wherein Milton, in refuting Salmasius on the issue of rebellion, had declared that it was not forbidden to resist tyrannical magistrates, he marked his citation and referred to it in a note which reads: "Just so says the Papist *Suarez*, *Adv. Sec. Ang.* l.6.c.6.¶24"; and when he called attention to page 70, where Milton had implied that early Christians, in their obedience to pagan kings, were not, as Salmasius had contended, therefore better than rebellious Englishmen but merely prudent, these early Christians being private persons and inferior in strength, he starred his reference and remarked in a footnote, "This is just *Bellarmine's* doctrine, *De Rom. Pontif.* l.5.c.7."[152] Again, when Wilson quoted from page 14 of the 1649 edition of *The Tenure of Kings and Magistrates*, "*The people may, as oft as they shall judge it for the best, depose the King, though no Tyrant*," he marked the quotation

151 *A Sermon Preached before the Lord Mayor, Alderman, And Citizens of London, At Bow Church, on the 30th of January, 1681/2* (London, 1682), pp. 17, 18–19, 23.

152 *A Sermon on the Martyrdom of King Charles I*, p. 32. Wilson's references were to Suarez, *Defensio Fidei Catholicae Adversus Anglicanæ Sectæ Errores*, Liber Sextus, caput vi, paragraph 24; and Bellarmine, *De Romani Pontificis*, Liber Quintus, caput vii. The similarities are striking.

and explained at the foot of the page, "The like, but somewhat better, says *Bellarmine, De Rom.* l.5.c.6."[153] Such exactitude indicates that Thomas Wilson intended to verify the generally accepted report of the similarity between Milton and the Jesuits by placing their identity of thought on political matters in the realms of demonstrable fact, though it is only fair to add that he did not believe that Protestants who acted like Catholics were therefore papists in disguise. Nevertheless, a demonstration like this would lend support to the story that Milton himself was a Jesuit in Puritan clothing, which in turn would further Tory designs.

Thomas Long, at any rate, carried on the story in *A Vindication of the Primitive Christians*, arguing that Milton's sympathy for popes and their doctrines, as well as events in the poet's life, should substantiate the report of his allegiance to the Roman communion. "And because it hath been creditably reported that *Milton* died a *Papist*," Long began, "and it is certain that he had been at *Rome*, and was there caressed by some great men, (Cardinals and others) I shall desire the Reader to consider with me, whether that *defence* which he makes of the *Popish Doctrine* for *deposing of Kings*, in the same Chapter, be not a probable Argument of the truth of that Report." Long then translated from chapter iv of *Pro Populo Anglicano Defensio*, where Milton, as has already been seen, stated that the French had deposed Childeric and had placed Pepin on the Frankish throne not by the decree of Pope Zachary, as had been claimed, but by ancient French laws, which allowed the deposition of a king should he misgovern or prove perfidious. Such an interpretation of this event in medieval history Long described as an "Invention of *Milton's Own*" to clear the Pope; and he went ahead to say, as Robert Hancock had claimed earlier, that Pope Zachary did have a hand in deposing Childerick and raising Pepin to power. In support of this contention, Long called upon Bishop Bilson, whose *Christian Subjection* had also touched on this event in medieval history. Long made it clear that Bishop Bilson had abundantly proved that the authority of Pope Zachary had deposed Childeric and had given the kingdom of France to Pepin. He conceded, to be sure, that, so far as the annals of France disclosed, the Pope had "not intirely grasped the power of deposing Princes in those days," a concession which invalidated much of his argument; but he stressed that the Pope worked through other instruments to

153 *A Sermon on the Martyrdom of King Charles I*, p. 32. For the comparison, see *De Romani Pontificis*, Liber Quintus, caput vi.

achieve his power. And the true reason, Long explained, for the Pope's interest in the matter of the French succession was that the Pope relied on Pepin to quell the Lombards and defeat the Grecians, so "that he and Pepin might divide the Spoils of the West." After this excursion into medieval history, the purpose of which was to disprove Milton's reading of it in connection with the succession of kings, Long finally came back to his original proposition. "Now let the Reader judge how diligent an Advocate *Milton* was for the Pope," he concluded. "And is this a fit *Guide* for our *Modern Writers*? Is it not possible (as our Author says) but to *take many things from* Doleman *in the case of Succession*? and many more from *Milton*, when you would irritate or *defend* the People of *England* in case of *Resistance* and *Regicide*?"[154] Long here not only reaffirmed the story that Milton was a papist in disguise; as a good Tory, he naturally questioned whether such a man was a fit mentor for current political writers, since he had shown such sympathy for popes and their principles.

Milton merited Long's query inasmuch as his principles did work themselves out through Whigs like Samuel Johnson and Lord Russell and in events like the Rye House Plot. Could it be, Roger L'Estrange implied in an issue of *The Observator* devoted to reports on Lord Russell and Algernon Sidney—could it be that recent threats to the Crown materialized because the bishops had not listened when Titus Oates revealed to the country, among other things, that the Catholics had poisoned James I, had fomented the Rebellion of '41, and had "*Discover'd to the* King *that* Milton, *and* Lambert *were* Papists"?[155] "*Ay! if they would have Hearken'd to the* Doctor," the nation "*should have had Clear Work made of all the* Papists, *and their* Adherents, *i'faith, long ere This time*." L'Estrange must have had his tongue in his cheek when he said this, but it made good political copy.

After the rout of the Whigs following the discovery of the Rye House conspiracy Milton's role as a papist appears to have aroused less interest, but it was not forgotten. Richard Forster, for instance, associated Milton with Jesuits and their schemes; indeed, he suggested that the disciples of Loyola, by whom he meant the Protestant revolutionaries in England, had excelled their political and spiritual

[154] *A Vindication of the Primitive Christians*, pp. 192–96. For the substance of Milton's reading of the deposition of Childeric, see *The Works of John Milton*, VII, 263–67.

[155] December 17, 1683, No. 457.

mentors, "since they have been transplanted into a ranker Soil, and being water'd with Bloud, are render'd if possible more prolifick at home, by an OWEN, a BAXTER, and a GOODWIN: by a RUTHERFORD and a FERGUSON: by a MILTON and a MARVEL."[156] In addition to this, John Moore, in a sermon on submission to authority, associated the republican principles of Hildebrand with those of "*Knox, Milton, Rutherford, Goodwin,* or any *Commonwealth's Man*";[157] Edward Pettit, in another political vision, saw, with some surprise, "*Hobbs* and *Baxter, Knox* and *Buchanan, Hunt* and *Gilby, Milton* and the *Jesuits,* sitting all together like friends, but in a very disconsolate posture," since they were witnessing the immolation of their books on the quadrangles of Oxford;[158] and Robert Brady, in a political history, declared that Bradshawe's speech was borrowed from the Presbyterians and Jesuits, "as likewise was much of the most Seditious part of *Miltons* Book, Entituled, *The Defence for the People of* England."[159] Finally, Thomas Long brought the whole matter to a proper conclusion in *A Compendious History of All the Popish & Fanatical Plots and Conspiracies Against the Established Government.* Linking early rebels like Prynne, Milton, White, Bradshawe, and the Jesuits with Shaftesbury, Hunt, Johnson, Sidney, and Lord Russell, he stressed the Catholic origin of the Puritan Rebellion and the continuity of revolutionary thought from that time to his. The claim that Catholics had fomented the civil wars reminded him that White had written a Jesuitical book, and that Milton had seconded him; and this in turn inspired him to speak further of "that wretched *Milton, Cromwel's* Secretary," who had been at Rome and had been received with great kindness there. This man had printed books on divorce, against tithes, and in justification of the regicides to bring the nation to atheism first and then to confusion, Long declared; and "He was by very many suspected to be a *Papist.*" Indeed, "if Dr. *Oates* may be believed," he "was a known frequenter of the *Popish Club,* though he were *Cromwel's* Latine Secretary."[160] Long himself was inclined to believe Oates, and no reason exists to doubt that many people in England suspected that Milton was a Jesuit in disguise.

156 *Prerogative and Privilege Represented in a Sermon in The Cathedral Church of Rochester in Kent, March 18. 1683/4* (London, 1684), p. 32.

157 *Of Patience and submission to Authority* (London, 1684), p. 40.

158 *The Visions of Government, Wherein The Antimonarchical Principles and Practices of all Fanatical Commonwealths-men, and Jesuitical Politicians are discovered, confuted, and exposed* (London, 1684), pp. 148–49.

159 *An Introduction to the Old English History, Comprehended in Three Several Tracts* (London, 1684), p. 355.

With the succession of James, the Catholic Duke of York, the story lost its political significance, since Tories could profit little by pointing out that Milton adhered to the religion of the reigning king. It lived on, however, in oral tradition to bob up in an early eighteenth-century sermon by William Binckes and in the recollections of Thomas Hearne,[161] becoming at this time simply an oddity of an earlier day. But during the hectic aftermath of the Popish Plot, as Whigs made their first real thrust for power, it apparently served the Crown well. The very enthusiasm with which Tories embraced Oates's allegation and developed it into a story at once so plausible and startling indicates not only the effectiveness of the tale as a weapon of propaganda but also the stature of the enemy whose influence they hoped to diminish by spreading it abroad among the people of England.

Milton thus achieved during the attempted Whig revolution a stature commensurate with that for which he had struggled in the days of the Puritan Rebellion. Disciples adapted his tracts and employed some of his best arguments, and these disciples in turn moved others to adopt Milton's positions, some of which became fixed planks in the platform of the Whig party. Though at this time, for political reasons, these disciples refrained from disclosing the source of their power, Tories, for the same reasons, revealed the extent of Whig debt and in addition admitted, tacitly in their campaign against him and openly in their pronouncements, that Milton was an antagonist not to be reckoned with lightly. Nathaniel Lee, in praise of Dryden, spoke a good deal of truth when he said that *Absalom and Achitophel* forced admissions of worth from even Fanatics,

> As if a *Milton* from the dead arose
> Fil'd off his Rust, and the right Party chose.

But he might also have observed, less metaphorically, that Milton himself, through his disciples, had arisen from the grave to speak to his countrymen, that he had become, by Tory admission, an oracle and a classic of the opposition, a most dangerous antagonist, a grand Whig. The party which owed Milton so much would not accord him these honors for more than a decade.

[160] London, 1684; pp. 92–93.

[161] See William Binckes, *A Sermon Preach'd before the Honourable House of Commons at St. Margaret's Church in Westminster, Novemb. 5. 1704* (London, 1705), p. 16; and Thomas Hearne, *Remarks and Collections of Thomas Hearne*, I (ed. C. E. Doble, Oxford, 1885), p. [1]; pp. 288–89. For other references, see *Matchiavel Junior* (London, 1683), p. 23; and Edward Cooke, *Certain Passages Which happened at Newport* (London, 1690), sigs. [A3v-A4r.].

Chapter Four

THE REVOLUTIONARY SETTLEMENT

THE REVOLUTIONARY SETTLEMENT, which deposed James II and placed the Crown on William and Mary, brought some unity to a nation long divided in mind over the power of kings and liberty of conscience. The Settlement itself testified to the supremacy of Parliament; the Bill of Rights which accompanied it secured a considerable measure of toleration, and within a few years England enjoyed a free press. James II himself precipitated these logical conclusions to a century of conflict and debate. He ruthlessly punished the misguided followers of the Duke of Monmouth after their rebellion in the West. He prorogued Parliament in 1685 and initiated a rule by royal prerogative and by a Court of High Commission, which he invested with illegal authority. He turned the dispensing power, a legal right of the Crown reserved for operation in particular cases, into a suspending power, which rendered all laws subservient to his will. He appointed those of his faith to the judiciary and to high office at Oxford. He encamped a large number of troops on Hounslow Heath to awe the people of London and began to raise a really Catholic army in Ireland. He issued two declarations of indulgence, not out of sympathy for the ideal of toleration but for the purpose of securing Catholics in positions of power. He brought to trial William Sancroft of Canterbury and six Anglican bishops because they refused to read from their pulpits his second order granting indulgence. Such arbitrary acts revealed the doctrines of divine right and of passive obedience, which logically supported the King, simply as instruments of naked aggression against the rights and liberties of the people of England; and in consequence, since James II had invaded their privileges also, Tories joined with Whigs in asking William of Orange to cross the Channel for the purpose of defending the Protestant faith. With his arrival came the Glorious Revolution, followed by the deliberations of the Convention Parliament and the Settlement itself, which through its Bill of Rights assured for many outside the Church legal equality with Anglicans and secured them as citizens of the English State.

Such momentous events created new party alignments. Most

Whigs and many Tories supported the Settlement and hence became known as Williamites. A few Whigs and more Tories supported the heredity claim of James II to the English throne and hence became known as Jacobites. Jacobites themselves split into two camps: the Jurors, or those who swore allegiance to William of Orange as King *de facto* but considered James II as Monarch *de jure*; and the Nonjurors, or those who held faith with James II and refused to recognize the legality of either the Revolution or the Settlement, for which some four hundred in the Church lost their livings and sees. The old Tory party, split asunder and bereft of its most loyal members, began to disappear as a power in national affairs, while at the same time the Whigs, supported by Williamite Tories and equivocating Jurors, waxed in strength.

Milton contributed to this growing Whig power by lending his voice in support of the Williamite cause. *The Tenure of Kings and Magistrates* appeared in 1689 as *Pro Populo Adversus Tyrannos*, an adaptation tailored to uphold the rationale of the Settlement. A reprint of *Eikonoklastes*, to which was attached the famous "Anglesey Memorandum," came from the press in 1690 to argue against the Jacobite cause by recalling the tyrannies of Charles I, as well as alleged dishonesty among Royalists for foisting off on the nation *Eikon Basilike*, which Whigs now claimed was the work not of the martyred king but of Bishop Gauden. Moreover, an anonymous "General Ludlow" freely paraphrased from *Eikonoklastes* in a series of pamphlets attacking Jacobite positions concerning the authorship of *Eikon Basilike* and the character of Charles I; and in 1692 *Pro Populo Anglicano Defensio* appeared in translation, with a prefatory note indicating its appropriateness to the times.[1] Finally, Charles Blount issued in 1693 a new adaptation of *Areopagitica* for the specific purpose of convincing Parliament and the nation that the incumbent Surveyor of the Imprimery, Edmund Bohun, was a fool and that the Licensing Act, which was up for renewal, should be allowed to lapse. Milton thus continued to support Whig principles and policies, many of which had now received official recognition in the Revolutionary Settlement; and for this reason Tories, both Jurors and Nonjurors, fired salvos against him. The very fact that the Settlement

[1] In the same year Milton's edition of Sir Walter Raleigh's *The Arts of Empire* appeared with no critical comment.

recognized Whig doctrines and repudiated divine right and passive obedience perhaps spurred Tories to find new epithets and devices to counter his influence.

I

That the Revolutionary Settlement repudiated in fact the old Tory doctrines and found its rationale largely in theories for which Whigs had long argued hardly meant, however, that the debate of the century had come to a close. Even during the period of coalition, when Tories and Whigs alike recoiled at growing Catholic power in James II at home and in Louis XIV abroad,[2] when many people suspected that the Stuart line had leagued with the French for the purpose of subverting Protestant England,[3] and when cries to bring both Church and Dissent under one communion rang through the nation[4]—even during this time of coherence and understanding in the face of a common enemy, it was evident that the old Tory doctrines would be long a-dying; and with the advent of the Revolution and the deposition of the hereditary king conflict broke out anew. Any understanding of how much and in what way Milton contributed to the Whig cause in the Revolutionary Settlement therefore requires a glance at this old conflict in its new setting.

Though in 1688 the tyrannies of James II became more apparent and the bishops themselves prepared to stand against the Declarations of Indulgence, Jacob Bury could argue in the old Tory way that "perfect Harmony, Consent and Agreement" exist between "Divinity and Law" and that "Kingly Government is by Divine Right."[5] Moreover, the anonymous author of *Melius Inquirendum*, a pamphlet reviewing the famous trial of the bishops, could refer to the people as rabble, to the bishops as traitors, and to the King as the absolute head of both Church and State, whose rights and privileges should not even be questioned.[6] Furthermore, while the Convention Parliament deliberated the fate of the nation, pamphlets addressed to its

[2] See, for example, Jean Claude, *An Account of the Persecutions and Oppressions of the Protestants in France* (London, 1686).

[3] *An Account of the Private League Betwixt the Late King James the Second, and the French King* (London, 1689).

[4] N. N., *A Letter from a Dissenter to His Friend of the Same Perswasion* (London, 1689).

[5] *Advice to the Commons Within All His Majesties Realms and Dominions* (London, 1688). See the title page.

[6] W. E., *Melius Inquirendum: Or, An Impartial Enquiry into the late Proceedings against the Bishops* (London, 1688), *passim.*

representatives and to the people at large warned of the danger of treating lightly the sacred person of James II;[7] and George Hickes arose from the ashes of his party to express what he and perhaps many others believed: the King's person was sacred and holy and therefore not to be touched.[8] As the theory of divine right still found exponents, so also the doctrine of passive obedience. Abednego Seller, for example, published in the year of the Settlement *The History of Passive Obedience Since the Reformation*, a lengthy pamphlet in which he pointed out the importance of passive obedience to the Anglican Church, the consistency with which its divines had adhered to it, and the validity of the doctrine in spite of the fact that many Churchmen, as James II came to the end of his reign, had turned against it. To Seller, belief in passive obedience still distinguished the Church of England from Rome and the Dissent, and despite the Settlement he considered the doctrine still seasonable. Indeed, in this volume as well as in its *Continuation*, which appeared the next year, Seller reiterated the position that it was "*the duty of every Christian, in things lawful*, actively *to obey his Superior; in things unlawful, to* suffer *rather than obey, and in any case, or upon any pretence whatsoever not to resist, because whoever does so*, shall receive to themselves Damnation."[9] To such defenders of divine right and passive obedience the Settlement had been a betrayal, and the men responsible for it contemptible villains—nay, even worse, Commonwealth men and republicans who disguised their perfidious acts under the cloak of defending the Crown. To men like George Hickes and Abednego Seller, support of the Revolution was the worst of all treasons because it denied James II a throne which was his by the direct appointment of God.

Such cries in support of the old doctrines, however, signified weakness rather than strength; they tokened apparent coherence but spelled final defeat. For aside from this one point of unity the old Tory party possessed no clear plan of attack or defense and was split by internal broils and confusions. The some four hundred beneficed clergymen, including five bishops, who persisted in holding these doctrines and hence lost, as Nonjurors, their livings and sees, accused

[7] Elinor James, *To the Honourable Convention* [London, 1688]. A broadside.

[8] *A Word to the Wavering: Or An Answer to the Enquiry Into The Present State of Affairs* (London, 1689).

[9] *The History of Passive Obedience since the Reformation* (Amsterdam, 1689), Preface. See also *A Continuation of the History of Passive Obedience since the Reformation* (Amsterdam, 1690). The second volume appeared anonymously.

Tory Jurors of treason and, as an extremely articulate group, embarrassed their own party by constantly pointing out the inconsistency of the Revolution with the beliefs which had been formerly held as the unique possessions of the Anglican Church. Tory Jurors, on the other hand, seeing themselves caught in a genuine dilemma, attempted to square their own consciences and justify themselves to the world by presenting reasons for swearing allegiance to William and Mary in the face of their former professions of faith. A Williamite of the time summarized succinctly their dilemma, as well as their attempts to extricate themselves from it. "The Revolution being thorowly wrought," he began, "they were glad to find themselves in the Condition they were in; and as the Wit of Man is fruitful of Inventions, they cast about how to come in to the Interest of this present Government, without renouncing what they had formerly so openly avow'd to be the Law of God." Hence, he continued, "according to their several Judgments, Wits, Apprehensions, Fancies, Whimsies, Fooleries, &c. one submits to Providence, another to an Usurper, another to a King *de facto*, another to a Conqueror: one says, King *James* left us; another, we turn'd him out; another, *Gallio*-like, cares for none of these things, but submits to the Powers that are."[10]

Among Nonjurors arousing widespread comment for such attempts to explain their defection was William Sherlock, a passionate defender of divine right and passive obedience before the Revolution, but no less an advocate for the new government established by King William and Queen Mary. Through numerous sermons and pamphlets he argued that the Glorious Revolution had been an act of Providence, that obedience to the newly established sovereigns was in accordance with the will of God, that James II might hold his allegiance *de jure* but that William and Mary held it *de facto*. He was chastened enough by events to declare in *A Sermon Preach'd before the Honourable House of Commons* that he would "not dispute the Lawfulness of Resisting the King's Authority," but was loath to admit that such resistance in the Glorious Revolution repudiated the doctrine of passive obedience. This event, he claimed, had "made no alteration at all in the Principles of Government and Obedience"; it had not obliged the people of England "to own the Superior

[10] N. N., *A Letter From Oxford, Concerning Mr. Samuel Johnson's Late Book* (Oxford, 1693), pp. 9–10.

Power of the People over the King, which would be a very tottering Foundation for Monarchy, and could never support it long." Therefore, he went on, "Those who believed the Doctrine of Non-Resistance and Passive Obedience to be a good Doctrine before may think so still, and be never the less Friends of the Present Government." Then, in a masterly exercise of equivocation, he observed that he had often thought it "a wonderful Providence of God, that in an Age, wherein the strictest Loyalty and Obedience had been so earnestly pressed on Men, so great a Revolution should be brought about, while the generality of Subjects were meerly passive, and surprized into a Deliverance."[11] Such tenuous arguments, though they failed to satisfy either Nonjurors or Williamites, apparently struck the imagination of a considerable body of Anglican clergymen, who grasped at the chance of having their Revolution and their doctrines, too;[12] but it was obvious that such a flimsy justification could not long support an official position. Sooner or later the actions of William Sherlock, as well as those of men who thought as he did, would be recognized as a repudiation of the doctrines of divine right and passive obedience by a sufficiently large number of people to discredit the equivocal positions they took.

Supporters of the old Tory doctrines, whether Jurors or Nonjurors, indeed fought in a lost cause. Split by defection and internal dissension, and faced with the immovable fact of the Revolution itself, they dissipated their strength and fell easy prey to Whig logic and ridicule. *A Dialogue Between Dr. Sherlock, the King of France, the Great Turk, and Dr. Oates*, for example, showed that the doctrines of divine right and passive obedience would give to Turkish monarchs and Louis XIV the same claim to absolute power as these Anglican beliefs had allowed James II—a proposition most Jacobites would be quick to deny.[13] Moreover, the *Dialogue* revealed that even Dr. Oates, who spoke of government by compact and law, uttered more sense than William Sherlock could ever dream up about *divino jure* and oaths of allegiance. At any rate, Whig appeals to consider

[11] *A Sermon Preach'd before the Honourable House of Commons, at St. Margaret's Westminster, January the XXXth, 1691/2* (London, 1692), pp. 6, 22–23.

[12] See, for example, *Allegiance Vindicated: or, the Takers of the New Oath of Allegiance to K. William & Q. Mary Justified: and the Lawfulness of taking it Asserted, in its Consistency with our Former Oaths; and also with the Doctrine of the Reformed Church of England, Concerning Non-Resistance & Passive Obedience* (London, 1690).

[13] *A Dialogue Between Dr. Sherlock, the King of France, the Great Turk, and Dr. Oates* ([London], 1691). A broadside.

government in terms of agreement and law seemed more reasonable than Juror attempts to reconcile the irreconcilable. "*Who shall set Bounds to a Divine Authority?*" asked Samuel Johnson; and no Jacobite could give him a logical answer. If the King is divine, he continued, then "*Humane Laws are Sacrilegious waste Paper*" and the whole nation is at the monarch's discretion. Furthermore, what profit is it to a people to have a king "*Accountable to God*" if for all that he bathes the nation in blood? To answer this question, Johnson pointed his finger at England's Catholic enemy across the Channel, Louis XIV: "*Is not the French King accountable to God? And yet what Reparation is that to the many millions of Souls which he had destroyed, or what Remedy against the Destruction of as many more?*"[14] Then, with evident irony, Johnson recalled how an earlier King of England had claimed to be accountable to God only and therefore had been sent, though with the regret of a great part of the nation, to God so that he could give his account. Bitter experience, as well as logic, militated against the old Tory doctrines—so much so that to some it appeared criminal for a sovereign, in view of his duty, to act in his kingly office as if he were "accountable to none but God, and Subjects must not rebel, nor resist, but suffer and pray."[15] The actions of James II at home and Louis XIV abroad could lead to no other conclusion.

Whigs not only made Tory doctrines appear ridiculous and unsound but also wholeheartedly supported the Revolutionary Settlement with arguments proclaiming its legality and justness. "Either the People to be governed have a Right and Power to chuse their own Governor, or they have not," declared William Denton;[16] and in answer to this succinct statement, Whigs replied: They possess both the power and right. But not only this. In contrast to Tory shifts and dissensions, Whigs unanimously agreed that the people possessed not simply the power and right to choose kings but to hedge them with laws and restrictions. Moreover, they agreed further that, since the people made kings, the people themselves stood above them in

[14] *An Argument Proving, That the Abrogation of King James by the People of England from the Regal Throne, and the Promotion of the Prince of Orange, one of the Royal Family, to the Throne of the Kingdome in his stead, was according to the Constitution of the English Government, and Prescribed by it* (London, 1692), pp. 29–30.

[15] *Four Questions Debated* (London, 1689), pp. 4–5.

[16] *Jus Regiminis: Being a Justification Of Defensive Arms In General And consequently of Our Late Revolutions And Transactions To Be The Just Right Of The Kingdom* (London, 1689), p. 91.

power; indeed, they themselves were the sole legislators, and the safety of the people became the supreme law: *Salus populi, suprema lex.* Now it was conceded that when a king kept his compact, his subjects were obliged to obey; but it was claimed that if a king purposely ruined the nation, or set up his personal interests above those of the people, he could be legally deposed and another put in his place.[17] The rationale of the Glorious Revolution, then, as well as of the Settlement which followed, sprang fundamentally from the theory of compact, from the concept that human society is essentially an agreement between the governors and those governed—a view of civil society for which Whigs had long argued and which they now unanimously presented to justify the deposition of James II and the ascension of William and Mary. The nation's experience with a tyrannical king made this concept take on the appearance of a self-evident truth.

Whigs thus directed their efforts in the years immediately following the Revolution toward revealing the dangers of old Tory doctrines, the evasions of Jurors, and the power and right of the Convention Parliament to depose James II and to place William and Mary on the English throne. Though it would be unwise to say that Whig polemics on these matters succeeded in convincing the greater part of England that kings received their power from Parliament rather than directly from God, the fact remains that the Revolutionary Settlement and the Bill of Rights stood firm, despite constant Jacobite agitation. The balance of opinion had apparently turned in favor of Whig doctrines; and to the tipping of the scales in this direction, Milton's disciples had and still made notable contributions. The martyred spirits of Algernon Sidney and Lord Russell still walked abroad as symbols of unjust regal power, as proper reasons for the people's revolt from the Crown.[18] William Denton, moreover, further argued against absolute regal authority and for the supremacy of Parliament and laws in ways reminiscent of Milton. Indeed, in his new lucubration, which he addressed to the Revolution itself and to the argument over the terms of the Settlement, Denton employed

[17] These notions appeared in countless Whig pamphlets. See particularly *Vindiciæ Contra Tyrannos*, the earlier Huguenot tract which became so popular during the Glorious Revolution. Note also the 1689 reprint of Edward Sexby's *Killing no Murder* (p. 19) for a specific reference to Milton.

[18] See *A Letter to a Gentleman at Brussels, Containing An Account of the Causes of the Peoples Revolt from the Crown* (London, 1689), p. 11.

quotations from Bracton's *De Legibus* in precisely the order and wording Milton had made familiar in *Pro Populo Anglicano Defensio.*[19] And Samuel Johnson, because of his earlier tracts as well as current ones in defense of the Settlement, became generally recognized as one of the most powerful forces responsible for preparing the people of England for the Glorious Revolution and for maintaining the real principles which directed its course, particularly in connection with his long fight against passive obedience.[20] Old disciples continued to speak, some of them, as later analysis will show, in even greater detail; but new ones also arose to carry Milton's political principles into the very heart of the Revolutionary Settlement.

II

Milton contributed most ingeniously to the defense of the Settlement through *Pro Populo Adversus Tyrannos*, an anonymous adaptation of *The Tenure of Kings and Magistrates.* Addressed to the debates of 1689, this adaptation scorned Jacobite loyalty to James II, called for a union of Protestants, and revealed the threat of Rome through the activities of Catholic kings, both at home and abroad. Moreover, it defended the decisions of the Convention Parliament and cogently stated the rationale of the Settlement. No other tract of the time covered current issues more concisely or argued more forcefully for Williamite principles of government.

Such a metamorphosis of *The Tenure* into a Williamite tract was an achievement of imagination and skill. *Pro Populo Adversus Tyrannos* began with Milton's opening pronouncement on the nature and causes of tyranny: "If Men within themselves would be govern'd by Reason, and not generally give up their Understandings to a double *Tyranny*, of Custom from without, and blind Affections within, they would discern better what it is to favour and uphold the *Tyrant* of a Nation."[21] This and the immediately following comment

[19] *Jus Regiminis*, p. 91.

[20] See Sir Robert Howard, *A Letter to Mr. Samuel Johnson* (London, 1692), pp. 39–40, and *A Memorial of God's Last Twenty Nine Years Wonders in England, for its Preservation and Deliverance from Popery and Slavery* (London, 1689), p. 99. See also *DNB*, under "Samuel Johnson."

[21] *Pro Populo Adversus Tyrannos: Or the Sovereign Right and Power of the People over Tyrants, Clearly Stated, and Plainly Proved* (London, 1689). See William Riley Parker, "Milton on King James the Second," *Modern Language Quarterly*, III (1942), 41–44, for the first modern notice of this pamphlet.

It is possible, in view of some omissions, that the anonymous author made use of the first edition of *The Tenure.*

applied with equal appropriateness to the Puritan Rebellion or to the Revolutionary Settlement and hence necessitated no change. Indeed, from this philosophic introduction, which forcefully opened both essays, to the section in *The Tenure* giving advice to the clergy, with which *Pro Populo* closed, the adaptation followed its original with considerable fidelity, except where new events and conditions dictated changes in detail and necessitated several additions and deletions, the greatest of which was the excision of Milton's long list of Protestant clergymen. Differences in the lives of Charles I and James II, for example, required shifts in detail to make *Pro Populo* apply to its time. Thus in *The Tenure*, Charles I was imprisoned, "disannointed," and cursed in sermons and pamphlets; in *Pro Populo*, James II was "cursed" all over the land and then "forc'd" to fly. But the most important and skillful changes came with the metamorphosis of Presbyterians into Jacobites. In *The Tenure of Kings and Magistrates*, Milton had attacked the Presbyterian faction for its about face during the last days of Charles I by reminding them, and the people of England, that this very group, early in the Puritan Rebellion, had vigorously assaulted the monarchy and Episcopal establishment. That the party responsible for bringing Archbishop Laud to the block and Charles I to his doom should at this late date, in a new burst of allegiance, extol the principles they formerly condemned and speak of the King as the anointed of God, not to be touched, appeared strange to Milton indeed.

Now the author of *Pro Populo*, focusing his eyes on current events, saw that this attack on Presbyterians applied precisely to Jacobites of 1689. For many Tories, in the turbulent summer of 1688, had cried out against the tyrannies of James II, claiming that he had encroached upon the rights of the people and had, by his declarations of indulgence, dispensed with the laws. Moreover, they had joined with Whigs in inviting Prince William to England for the purpose of saving the nation from popery and arbitrary power; but now, with James actually deposed and in France, these same Tories who a few months before had been so eager to get rid of the King began to call him the Lord's anointed and the rightful heir to the throne. A few changes in wording allowed *The Tenure* to speak directly against this sudden change of allegiance so dangerous to the security of the Revolutionary Settlement:

Pro Populo	The Tenure
Others there are too, who not long ago seem'd fierce against their *King*, under the just Notions of a *Tyrant*, an INCROACHER *on the Rights of the People, a Dispencer with the Laws, and a Promoter of all Arbitrary and Illegal Actions*; Yet when *God*, out of his merciful Providence, and singular Love, hath deliver'd him over to follow such *Councils* and Methods, as have induc'd him to rid us of such an *Enemy* to the *Publick Good* as himself was, on a sudden, and in a new Garb of *Allegiance* (which their late doings seem'd to have cancel'd) plead for him, pitty him, extol him, and protest against those that talk of *Excluding* him from the *Government* of these *Nations*, which by his *Arbitrary* Actings he has justly *Forfeited*. (p. 4.)	Others who have beene fiercest against thir Prince, under the notion of a Tyrant, and no mean incendiaries of the Warr against him, when God out of his providence and high disposal hath deliver'd him into the hand of thir brethren, on a suddain and in a new garbe of Allegiance, which thir doings have long since cancell'd; they plead for him, pity him, extoll him, protest against those that talk of bringing him to the tryal of Justice, which is the Sword of God, superior to all mortal things, in whose hand soever by apparent signes his testified will is to put it. (*Works*, V. 3.)

This Jacobite threat to the government of William and Mary, this about face among Tories, spurred the author of *Pro Populo Adversus Tyrannos* to heights of scorn not found in Milton's attack on the Presbyterian party. "Good God!" he exclaimed, "what Inconstancy, what Folly and Madness possesses the Breasts of this People, to what a miserable Slavery would they lead us, and how fond and eager do they seem, to have him rule over us, who (like the Stork in the Fable) has, and would make it his greatest delight, to devour the best of Free-born Subjects?"[22]

This shift of allegiance among Tories, which for a while threatened the government, compelled the author of *Pro Populo* to remind the people of England that both reason and precedent supported the Williamite cause. The reasoning he took from *The Tenure* will be analyzed later; at the present, attention will be turned to the list of examples he found in Milton to support both the Glorious Revolution and the terms of the Settlement. With little change in Milton's

[22] *Pro Populo Adversus Tyrannos*, p. 6.

account, he told how men in Jewish and Christian times had not been averse to getting rid of their kings; but what struck him particularly was Milton's story of Queen Mary, whose deposition had allowed Milton to refute Presbyterian claims that no Protestant country had ever put a prince off the throne.[23] The author of *Pro Populo* retold Milton's story of Queen Mary almost verbatim, making it serve as an example to the "Passive Obedience Men" of 1689 that the decision of the Convention Parliament to depose James II was not without precedent among Protestant nations; and, as further evidence, he paraphrased a long passage from the journal of Sir Simonds D'Ewes, the gist of which was that Queen Mary had been justly put to death because she was a Catholic and therefore an enemy of God. In fact, D'Ewes had reported that it was incumbent upon the people of England to cut off her head so that the country might not incur the displeasure of God. The message to the men of passive obedience was clear: James II, an avowed Catholic like Mary, was an enemy of God and hence had to be removed from the throne. The Convention Parliament, indeed, not only followed sound precedent but also was the instrument through which the divine will of God had been made to prevail.

Such examples from history, as well as Catholic dangers just passed and present Jacobite threats, inspired the author of *Pro Populo* to call for a cessation of faction. Here, too, Milton argued his case. For Milton, cognizant of divisions over the execution of Charles I, not only asked that the people of England honor the judgment of Parliament and the Military Council but also claimed that what these bodies had done would serve as precedents for future ages to follow. Such words, with slight alterations, spoke directly to Protestant disunity in 1689 and to the cry, in some quarters at least, for a union of Church and Dissent in the face of the common enemy, Rome. By changing "Military Councel" into "Convention" and by omitting references to the death of the king, the author of *Pro Populo* changed Milton's general plea into a specific request that Jacobites cease their cries against the terms of the Settlement and at the same time predicted, with an accuracy supported by later events, that future ages

[23] For an account of how accurately Milton handled some of his sources, see Merritt Y. Hughes, "Milton's Treatment of Reformation History in *The Tenure of Kings and Magistrates*," in *The Seventeenth Century* (Stanford, Calif., 1951), pp. 247–63.

would look with honor upon the decisions of that body—both those already enacted and those to come:

PRO POPULO	THE TENURE
Let Men therefore cease out of Faction and Malice to make Out-cries and report horrid things of things so just and honourable as our most Renowned Convention hath acted hitherto against our common Adversary, and we hope they will go on, to act upon him such Justice as may be a President to future Ages to imitate, who if they prove not too degenerate, shall look up with Honour, and aspire towards those exemplary deeds of their Ancestors, as the highest top of their Glory and emulation . . . (p. 24.)	Let men cease therfore out of faction & hypocrisie to make out-cries and horrid things of things so just and honorable. . . . And if the Parlament and Military Councel doe what they doe without precedent, if it appeare thir duty, it argues the more wisdom, vertue, and magnanimity, that they know themselves able to be a precedent to others. Who perhaps in future ages, if they prove not too degenerat, will look up with honour, and aspire toward these exemplary, and matchless deeds of thir Ancestors, as to the highest top of thir civil glory and emulation. (V, 41.)

In conclusion, the author of *Pro Populo* uttered a word of advice for the "Prelatical," or Jacobite, party by recalling how the old implacable enemy, the Catholic Church, constantly stirred up discords to achieve its ends, and how, as examples from history made clear, overthrown Catholic kings, if returned to power, took revenge on their Protestant subjects with fire and sword. Most of these examples, as well as the sentiment, came from *The Tenure.* But discordant Jacobite notes at home and threats from James II and Louis XIV abroad demanded evidence that Milton could hardly supply. What could be a more appropriate warning than to recall, with other pamphleteers, the continued perfidy of France and England's recent escape from Roman destruction?

And further they may remember, how the present *Tyrant* of *France*, has, after all his many Edicts, Oaths and Grants, to maintain the Protestants in all their Priviledges, besides the Obligations they have laid on him, most inhumanly and perfidiously Banish'd, Dragoon'd, Murther'd and made away most, if not all his Protestant Subjects; nay, what might be more convincing, would they but lay it to Heart, how our late *Tyrant*, notwithstanding the manifold Obligations they heaped upon him, and Oaths he laid himself under, to maintain them and their Grandeur, has nevertheless violated all, and with all his Power (as if Ingratitude was his chiefest Delight) endeavoured their Extirpation and Ruine, as well as other his Protestant Subjects.[24]

Such recollections not only played on deep-seated English fears of Roman dominion but also reminded Jacobites that just a short time before the summer of 1689 James II had "endeavored their Extirpation and Ruine." Few arguments calling for a cessation of faction and hence for support of the Settlement could have been stronger than these.

The author of *Pro Populo Adversus Tyrannos*, by making a few changes and several additions, thus turned *The Tenure of Kings and Magistrates* into an argument against Jacobite claims and activity. At the same time he supported the acts of the Convention Parliament and presented, with all the vigor of Milton's original phrasing, the Williamite rationale of the Settlement. Indeed, with hardly a change of a word he cut out the heart of Milton's philosophical discussion of the origin and nature of government and made it an integral part of his tract. It will be remembered that Milton had traced the origin of society to the chaos which followed the Fall, when it became necessary, in the interests of mutual protection, for men to bind themselves by a common league into cities, towns, and commonwealths. It also became necessary, Milton went on, to delegate proper power and authority to restrain by force and punishment whatever was violated against peace and the common good. To kings and magistrates went such power and authority. But, Milton continued, the very nature of the compact binding men together made it manifest that kings held their power and authority in trust from the people, and that, in view of this, to make rulers accountable to God only would be an abrogation of the compact and an overturning of all law and government. From this it logically followed, since power and authority still lay fundamentally in the people, that the people might, as often as they thought it for the best, exercise their right as freeborn men and depose their kings.

Such sentiments, of course, supported the Glorious Revolution itself, as well as the decisions of the Convention Parliament; such reasoning indeed allowed responsible men to depose James II and argue

[24] *Pro Populo Adversus Tyrannos*, pp. 25–26.

for the settlement of the Crown on William and Mary. As a good Williamite, the author of *Pro Populo Adversus Tyrannos* realized that he could do no better than to repeat almost exactly what Milton had said:

PRO POPULO	THE TENURE
No man that knows any thing, can be so stupid to deny, that all men naturally were born Free, being the Image and resemblance of *God* himself, and were by Priviledge above all the Creatures, born to command, and not to obey; and that they lived so, till from the root of *Adam's* Transgression, falling among themselves to do Wrong and Violence, and foreseeing that such courses must needs tend to the destruction of them all, they agreed by *common League*, to bind each other from mutual Injury, and joyntly to defend themselves against any that gave disturbance or opposition to such agreement: Hence come Cities, Towns and Commonwealths. (p. 7.)	No man who knows ought, can be so stupid to deny that all men naturally were borne free, being the image and resemblance of God himself, and were by privilege above all the creatures, born to command and not to obey: and that they liv'd so. Till from the root of *Adams* transgression, falling among themselves to doe wrong and violence, and foreseeing that such courses must needs tend to the destruction of them all, they agreed by common league to bind each other from mutual injury, and joyntly to defend themselves against any that gave disturbance or opposition to such agreement. Hence came Citties, Townes and Commonwealths. (V, 8.)
First, It being thus manifest that the Power of Kings and Magistrates is nothing else, but what is only derivative, transferr'd and committed to them in trust from the People to the common good of them all, in whom the Power yet remains Fundamentally, and canot be taken from them, without a violation of their natural Birth-right . . . (p. 8.)	It being thus manifest that the power of Kings and Magistrates is nothing else, but what is only derivative, transferr'd and committed to them in trust from the People, to the common good of them all, in whom the power yet remaines fundamentally, and cannot be tak'n from them, without a violation of thir natural birthright . . . (V, 10.)
Thirdly, It follows, that to say Kings are accountable to none but God, is the overturning of all Law and Government. For if they may	Thirdly it follows, that to say Kings are accountable to none but God, is the ouerturning of all Law and government. For if they may

refuse to give account, then all Covenants made with them at Coronation; all Oaths are in vain, and meer Mockeries; all Laws which they swear to keep, made to no purpose; for if the King fear not God, (as how many of them do not?) We hold then our Lives and Estates, by the tenure of his meer Grace and Mercy, as from a God, not a mortal Magistrate; a position that none but Court Parasites or Men Besotted would maintain. (p. 9.)	refuse to give account, then all cov'nants made with them at Coronation; all Oathes are in vaine, and meer mockeries, all Lawes which they sweare to keep, made to no purpose; for if the King feare not God, as how many of them doe not? we hold then our lives and estates, by the tenure of his meer grace and mercy, as from a God, not a mortal Magistrate, a position that none but Court Parasites or men besotted would maintain. (V, 11–12.)
It follows lastly, That the King or Magistrate holds his Authority of the People, both Originally and Naturally, for their good in the first Place, and not his own; then may the People as oft as they shall judge it for the best, either chuse him, or reject him, retain him, or depose him, though no *Tyrant*, meerly by the Liberty and Right of free-born Men, to be Govern'd as seems to them best. (p. 10.)	It follows lastly, that since the King or Magistrate holds his autoritie of the people, both originaly and naturally for their good in the first place, and not his own, then may the people as oft as they shall judge it for the best, either choose him or reject him, retaine him or depose him though no Tyrant, meerly by the liberty and right of free born Men, to be govern'd as seems to them best. (V, 14.)

The author of *Pro Populo* thus allowed the philosophical heart of *The Tenure* to remain virtually unchanged—a testament to his good judgment as well as to the universality of Milton's positions and the skill with which he expressed them. Lifted from the deadening level of local and temporal detail and clothed in memorable language, these and other striking passages from *The Tenure of Kings and Magistrates* still lived to capture the imagination of man—still lived to convince a new disciple, as *Pro Populo* testifies, that the principles they expressed could best be spread abroad in defense of the Glorious Revolution and the Revolutionary Settlement by allowing Milton to speak his own words. Like Charles Blount, who twice copied parts of *Areopagitica* verbatim, he realized that to change such passages would do violence to Milton's thought and detract from the magic of the rhetoric which Royalists of the Restoration so rightly feared.

Whoever this new disciple was, it is evident that he was a man of some judgment and skill. Cutting here and adding there, changing details but leaving the great passages unspoiled, he turned *The Tenure of Kings and Magistrates* into an effective instrument of Williamite propaganda. He even deleted many references to heresies, tithes, sects, and pluralities in view of the widening gap between Church and State and the growing conviction that government was an institution contrived by the reason of man. So secularized and changed, *The Tenure of Kings and Magistrates* in its new garb of *Pro Populo Adversus Tyrannos* spoke so pertinently to the issues confronting the Convention Parliament and defended so forcefully the rationale of the Glorious Revolution and the terms of the Settlement that, as later discussion will show, it attracted attention and merited an angry reprisal.

III

Williamites soon discovered that other parts of Milton's program for man and society could be employed in support of their cause. Indeed, *Eikonoklastes* served their purpose so well that they reprinted it in 1690,[25] and with this as an inspiration another disciple arose under the nom de plume of "Major General Ludlow" to employ its arguments in a series of Williamite pamphlets. The pertinence of *Eikonoklastes* to party struggles consequent to the Revolutionary Settlement may be quickly told. Jacobites, in their efforts to convince the people of England that James II should return to the throne, realized that neither logic nor the national experience stood on their side and hence appealed, particularly in memorial sermons, to old Stuart loyalties by recalling the martyrdom of Charles I and the cruelties of the Commonwealth Parliament. Such appeals, it was their hope, would turn people against the terms of the Settlement and arouse sentiment in favor of hereditary succession. In retaliation to these emotional appeals, Williamites attacked the character of Charles I and extolled the Commonwealth Parliament, aiming thereby to undermine old loyalties to the House of Stuart and at the same time to inspire public con-

[25] For a recent discussion of pen-and-ink corrections in the second edition of *Eikonoklastes*, some of which sharpen political meanings, see *The Times* [London] *Literary Supplement* for June 15, 1951, p. 380, and for June 22, 1951, p. 396.

fidence in the concept of parliamentary supremacy. For information to carry out such a counter campaign, Williamites turned to *Eikonoklastes.*

The publication of *Eikonoklastes* in 1690 threw a bombshell into the Jacobite camp not simply because it reviewed, much to the detriment of the Stuart succession, the arbitrariness of Charles I, but because some copies contained, in a leaf attached either at the beginning or the end, the famous "Anglesey Memorandum" which purportedly proved that Bishop Gauden, not Charles I, had been the author of *Eikon Basilike.*[26] Milton himself had suggested in his attack on this book that it was not by the King's hand, an implication which had perhaps inspired Edward Hyde to remark in his reply to the importunate Bishop Gauden in 1661 that if, as prior discussion has shown, the secret of authorship, which had been imparted to him in confidence, were revealed, he knew of no one who would be pleased except Mr. Milton. The secret of which Edward Hyde spoke, if it did refer to the authorship of *Eikon Basilike,* had been well kept and Milton had not been cheered in his old age with the knowledge that his suspicions were at least partially true. But now, in the heat of the conflict over the Stuart line and the terms of the Settlement, Williamites announced with obvious political intent that the King's Book, long a Royalist Bible and a present Jacobite comfort, was not the issue of a suffering and finally martyred Charles I.

Such an announcement in itself was enough to damage irreparably the Jacobite cause; but to make matters worse, Williamites published with the Anglesey Memorandum an advertisement disclosing the significance of the revelation, as well as the circumstances which brought the secret to light. The advertisement claimed that Edward Millington had found, prefixed to a copy of *Eikon Basilike,* a statement in Lord Anglesey's own hand which would be "sufficient to satisfy the World, how much that King was imposed upon by Dr. *Gauden* Bishop of *Exceter.*" The statement itself, or the memorandum, told a strange but plausible story. Lord Anglesey wrote that during the 1675 session of Parliament he had shown to Charles II and the Duke of York, in the House of Lords, a written copy of *Eikon Basilike* which contained some corrections and alterations in the hand of Charles I, whereupon

[26] See Francis F. Madan, *A New Bibliography of the Eikon Basilike of King Charles the First,* pp. 126–63, for the latest discussion of the authorship problem and for reproductions of both the advertisement and the Anglesey Memorandum.

both the King and the Duke assured him that the book was none of the King's compiling but had been made by Bishop Gauden. For the undeceiving of others on this point, Lord Anglesey concluded, he had inserted his Memorandum and had attested its truth by signing his name. Such a statement by so honorable a lord, on no less authority than the sons of Charles I himself, could not be brushed aside lightly; it indeed fired the opening round in a furious battle over the authorship of *Eikon Basilike*, sounds of which echo still. In this battle, as might be expected, Jacobites claimed that Charles I had written the book, not only to protect the honor of the King but also to preserve the integrity of sentiments with which they so often refuted their enemies and to which they so often returned for spiritual refreshment. Williamites, on the other hand, pressed the charge that *Eikon Basilike*, as the Memorandum revealed and as Milton had suggested, was little more than a Royalist hoax, indicative of Stuart guile and chicanery. As Jacobites never wearied repeating, their enemies struck at the hereditary throne through the vulnerable sides of Charles I; and both *Eikonoklastes* and the Anglesey Memorandum proved to be weapons of choice to accomplish this end.

Such tactics apparently nullified Jacobite attempts to arouse sentiment in favor of James II. In any event, Williamites intensified their campaign against the memory of Charles I for the purpose of reminding the people of England how tyrannical an absolute, hereditary monarchy could be. Among Williamites attracting wide attention in this campaign was Milton's new disciple, "Major General Ludlow," who drew much of his ammunition from the arsenal of *Eikonoklastes* for a series of three tracts, the first of which he entitled *A Letter From Major General Ludlow To Sir E. S.* Both the assumed name of Milton's disciple and the person to whom the tract was addressed—Sir Edward Seymour—were such as to stir significant memories. The real General Edmund Ludlow had played an important role in the Puritan Rebellion, had approved of the trial and signed the death warrant of Charles I, and had at the Restoration fled to Switzerland, where, except for a short return to England in 1689, he remained in exile until his death in 1692. As a symbol of regicide, he still inflamed old emotions and caused men to express, in accordance with their political affiliations, either bitter hatred or unstinted praise. Though not so notorious as Ludlow, Sir Edward Seymour also commanded public attention. He had held the speakership of the House in 1673 and had the qualifications for filling that position in 1689, but lost favor by opposing an offer of the Crown to Prince William, though he soon swore the oath. Moreover, he had enjoyed Ludlow's estates since the Restoration and, upon the exile's return in 1689, fearful of losing his lands, had headed a deputation praying that William III issue a proclamation for the apprehension of the old regicide. The King listened with sympathy to the importunings of the Tory turned Juror, and Ludlow, threatened with imprisonment, found it expedient once again to shake the dust of his native heath from his shoes. Such events, coupled with old memories they would naturally arouse, gave a particular timeliness to a tract supposedly written by an infamous exile and addressed to a figure important in government circles. Ludlow's stature as a regicide, Seymour's switch to the Williamite camp, and the success of the suit to have the old Puritan apprehended would make the public eager to hear what the General might say to the Juror.

The Major General Ludlow of the pamphlet frankly stated on the title page of his tract that his letter to Sir Edward Seymour had been occasioned by Edward Pelling's memorial sermons extolling the life of Charles I. But before he set about to refute the sentiments such sermons expressed, he rejoiced that England had thrown off the tyranny of the late reigns and had made a Settlement consonant with the laws of the land and in accordance with the doctrine affirmed by Sir Robert Philips in his speech before Parliament in 1628, that the people of England were "*under no other Subjection than what they did voluntarily consent unto by the* ORIGINAL CONTRACT *between the* King *and the* People."[27] He also pointed out that he and Sir Edward Seymour agreed that James II had broken this compact, that the King had become a tyrant by transgressing and annulling the laws, that for these reasons the Crown had been most rightfully placed on King William and Queen Mary. This much agreed, Ludlow then launched into his attack upon Charles I, claiming that the martyred king equaled and perhaps transcended James II in tyranny. To Edward Pelling's extravagant portrait of Charles I, which presented him as "That great *Monarch* and *Martyr*, of whom the World was not worthy, and perhaps will hardly ever see the like in him again; That *Incomparable Prince;* That Mirrour of Princes, the Noblest of Martyrs, the Won-

[27] *A Letter From Major General Ludlow To Sir E. S.* (Amsterdam, 1691), p. 1.

der of Ages, and the Honour of Men; That Innocent, Vertuous, Religious Matchless Prince, *The Lord's anointed, A Man according to God's own Heart*,"[28] Ludlow replied with a bill of particulars reminiscent of Milton's long list in *Eikonoklastes*. He recalled, among many things, that Charles I had approved of "popish" innovations, that he had abrogated civil liberties and rights, that he had thwarted the desires of Parliament. Finally, in a postscript, he carried out Milton's injunction to compare the King's prayer in *Eikon Basilike* with Pamela's prayer in Sir Philip Sidney's *Arcadia*, a comparison which revealed, as Milton had claimed it would, that the King's pious sentiments uttered in time of captivity had been stolen from an early romance.

Now Milton had made much of this theft. That Charles I should copy a prayer from a "vain amatorious Poem" without acknowledging his source was to him an affront to both man and God. Moreover, he made it a point to observe that the King, though outwardly reverencing his clergy, yet "being at a loss himself what to pray in Captivity, he consulted neither with the Liturgie, nor with the Directory, but neglecting the huge fardell of all thir honycomb devotions, went directly where he doubted not to find better praying, to his mind with *Pammela* in the Countesses *Arcadia*."[29] Such an observation inspired Ludlow to say that "Though King *Charles* the First hated nothing more than to Govern by *Precedent*, yet he would not pray without it; and none of the *Liturgies* suiting his Fancy, he had recourse to a *Romance*,"[30] after which statement Ludlow printed in parallel columns the two prayers. The evidence herein presented could not be denied; for all who would read these parallels indisputably proved that the author of *Eikon Basilike*, at least so far as the prayer was concerned, had copied from Sir Philip Sidney's *Arcadia*. And if the Anglesey Memorandum invalidated the accusation that Charles I was an arrant plagiarist, it need not be mentioned; it was enough for the present to demonstrate the perfidy of him who the Jacobites claimed was a man after the very heart of God. For the suggestion that such a demonstration could be made, Ludlow had Milton to thank.

Ludlow addressed his second attack upon the character of Charles I to Richard Hollingworth, an ardent defender of the King's

[28] *A Letter From Major General Ludlow To Sir E. S.*, p. 2.
[29] *The Works of John Milton*, V, 88.
[30] *A Letter From Major General Ludlow To Sir E. S.*, p. 29.

cause. In this tract he not only reiterated what he had said to Sir Edward Seymour but answered specifically Richard Hollingworth's *A Defence of King Charles I* and at the same time freed the Parliament of 1640 from the aspersions Jacobites had cast upon its motives and acts. In a sense, his task paralleled Milton's earlier one in *Eikonoklastes.* Even as Milton had attempted to break the idolatrous image of Charles I presented in *Eikon Basilike,* so Ludlow tried to counter Jacobite claims that the martyred monarch was a very paragon of innocence and virtue. Parallel tasks suggested parallel means. Hence it is not surprising to find that Ludlow consulted *Eikonoklastes* for methods which best could reveal the perfidy of Charles I and the integrity of the Long Parliament, particularly since Milton's attack had been so successful. Milton left no doubt as to the way he would approach his task: he would confront and lay parallel the "fair spok'n words" of Charles I to "his own farr differing deeds, manifest and visible to the whole Nation"; and this should be enough to convince anyone, Milton continued, except those "whose judgement was not rationally evinc'd and perswaded, but fatally stupifi'd and bewitch'd, into . . . a blinde and obstinate belief."[31] Now Ludlow claimed in the preface of his tract that, in view of the way Jacobites had extolled the reputation of Charles I, he had "*taken some little pains in* comparing his fair-spoken Words, with his far differing Deeds," convinced as he was that the world ever looked "more at real Actions than verbal Protestations" and that he wrote "*to Men endued with Reason.*"[32] The debt is obvious; and if Ludlow consulted *Eikonoklastes* for method it would be only natural to expect that he utilized much of its matter also.

Even a hasty glance at *Eikonoklastes* and Ludlow's answer to Richard Hollingworth fulfills such expectations. Recalling first his words to Sir Edward Seymour, he stressed his position that Charles I had trampled on the religious and civil liberties of the people of England, citing as evidence, among many instances, the intrusion of Archbishop Laud's "popish" ceremonies into the church liturgy and the proceedings of the Star Chamber and the Court of High Commission, which had dealt such heavy blows to Henry Burton, John Bastwick,

[31] *The Works of John Milton,* V, 72.

[32] *A Letter from General Ludlow to Dr. Hollingworth, Their Majesties Chaplain at St. Botolph-Aldgate* (Amsterdam, 1692), p. viii. See George W. Whiting, "A Late Seventeenth Century Milton Plagiarism," *Studies in Philology,* XXXI (1934), 37–50, for an account of Ludlow's dependence upon Milton in his second and third tracts.

and William Prynne. Mention of such particulars, many of which are reminiscent of those Milton had listed, brought Ludlow to the trial and death of the Earl of Strafford, a case which, according to Richard Hollingworth's *A Defence of King Charles I*, had disturbed the peace and quiet of the King's mind all his life. That the Earl's case should have had this effect on the King, Ludlow replied, should cause no surprise; indeed, he had a "strong fancy" that the affair was very much like an earlier one of the Duke of Buckingham, and "that it disturbed the Quiet of the King's Mind, that he could not preserve this, as he had done his other Servant, in the execution of his own Commands." No "marvel" it was, then, that it stung the King's "conscience to adjudg to death those Misdeeds whereof himself had been the chief Author."[33] This is exactly what Milton had said about the effect of Earl Strafford's case on the mind of Charles I: "No marvel then, if being as deeply criminous as the Earle himself, it stung his conscience to adjudge to death those misdeeds whereof himself had bin the chiefe Author";[34] and from this point on, in varying degrees, Ludlow took details from *Eikonoklastes* to answer Hollingworth's defense of the King. A few parallels, by way of example, will show how thoroughly he ransacked Milton's storehouse for information to deflate Jacobite efforts to restore confidence in James II by reference to the pious life of Charles I:

A LETTER	EIKONOKLASTES
The KING *had been tampering with the Army which he had raised against the Scots*, and which lay undisbanded in the North, to bring them up to curb the Parliament, and subdue them to his Will. . . . To joyn with this Army, and strengthen the Plot, *a French Army was to be landed at Portsmouth* . . . and *the Irish Army*, consisting of 8000, *almost all Papists*, was to be brought over. (p. 32.)	[The King] being soon after found to have the chief hand in a most detested conspiracy against the Parlament and Kingdom . . . to bring up the English Army out of the North, joyn'd with eight thousand Irish Papists rais'd by *Strafford*, and a French Army to be landed at *Portsmouth* against the Parlament and thir Friends. (V, 93–94.)
He had tempted the ENGLISH ARMY, *with no less Reward than*	The King . . . first tempts the English Army, with no less reward

[33] *A Letter from General Ludlow to Dr. Hollingworth*, p. 31.
[34] *The Works of John Milton*, V, 94.

the Spoil of the City of LONDON, *to come up and destroy the* PARLIAMENT; *He had, in an unexcusable and hostile manner, made a most high Invasion upon the Priviledges of* BOTH HOUSES: Hereupon many *Citizens, unarmed,* resorted to *Westminster* to present their *Petitions,* and express their stedfastness to the *Parliament,* whose Lives and Safeties, by more than slight Rumours, they doubted to be in Danger; the *King* having fortified *Whitehall,* and entertained Armed Men, not a few, planted them at the *Gate of his Palace,* where they reviled menaced, and with drawn Swords actually wounded many of the *Citizens,* as they passed by in a peaceable manner, whereof some died. Nay, they went farther, and were come to that height of Boldness, as to give out insolent and menacing Speeches against the *Parliament* it self, and to *imbrue their Hands* in the Blood of the *King's Subjects* in *Westminster-Hall,* and at the Doors of the *Parliament,* as well as at his own Gate. And when the *Parliament* and People complained, and demanded Justice for those Assaults, he justified and abetted his own Crew in what they did. (p. 41.)	then the spoil of *London,* to come up, and destroy the Parlament. . . . The Parlament moreover had intelligence, and the people could not but discern, that there was a bitter & malignant party grown up now to such a boldness, as to give out insolent and threatning speeches against the Parlament it self. . . . The people therfore, lest thir worthiest and most faithfull Patriots, who had expos'd themselves for the public, and whom they saw now left naked, should want aide, or be deserted in the midst of these dangers, came in multitudes, though unarm'd, to witness their fidelitie and readiness in case of any violence offer'd to the Parlament. . . . He had, besides all this, begun to fortifie his Court, and entertained armed Men not a few; who standing at his Palace Gate, revil'd, and with drawn Swords wounded many of the People, as they went by unarm'd, and in a peaceable manner, whereof some dy'd . . . And both the Parlament and people complain'd, and demanded Justice for those assaults . . . he . . . justifi'd and abetted them in what they did. . . . (V, 104–12.)

Ludlow thus picked from Milton's discussion of the tumults around Whitehall those particular events which reflected on the character of Charles I and which at the same time threw favorable light on the people and Parliament. No information could have served better his purpose, as the close paraphrase itself testifies; and in consequence he followed *Eikonoklastes* in much the same way through Milton's discussion of the King's attempt to seize Hull, and of the Treaty of Uxbridge.

This treaty brought Ludlow to "*The business of* Ireland," which Milton had discussed in an earlier chapter but which, Ludlow declared, Hollingworth had not seen fit to touch. So that such an important matter would not remain hidden, he further revealed to the people of England, as he had promised to do, that the King's declarations simply did not square with his deeds, particularly as they bore upon the Irish question. For this demonstration, he followed Milton's general claim, as well as his words. Milton had observed that Charles I "vowed solemnly to the Parlament with imprecations upon himself and his Posterity, if ever he consented to the abolishing of those Lawes which were in force against Papists, and at the same time, as appeard plainly by the very date of his own Letters to the Queen and *Ormond,* consented to the abolishing of all Penal Lawes against them both in *Ireland* and *England.*"[35] Ludlow also observed that the King had made "divers *solemn Protestations, with fearful Imprecations upon himself and invocation of God's Holy Name, That he intended nothing but the Peace and Welfare of his People, the maintenance of Religion, and the Laws of the Kingdom*"; but his "*underhand Transactions,*" Ludlow went on, belied "*his pretended Intentions of Peace.*" To substantiate his claim, Ludlow reproduced the substance of the letters to which Milton referred and allowed them to demonstrate that Charles I, far from desiring to carry out his public utterances, by secret negotiation flatly denied them. He wrote Queen Henrietta Maria, for example, when the Treaty of Uxbridge was pending, that Parliament was unreasonable, stubborn, and perfidious and pressed upon her to "*hasten all possible Assistance to him, particularly that of the Duke of* Lorrain." Furthermore, he wrote the Marquis of Ormond to make peace with the Irish by promising that "PENAL LAWS *against Roman Catholicks*" would not be put into execution. Such transactions demonstrated to Ludlow that Charles I had acted perfidiously and he was half-certain that they would bring Richard Hollingworth to the same opinion, unless he appeared as "*a man of resolved Prejudices, or else of profound and stupid Ignorance.*"[36] But this, of course, was only a part of Ludlow's aim; as a Williamite, he purposed to demonstrate that Parliament had been right and

[35] *The Works of John Milton,* V, 200.

[36] *A Letter from General Ludlow to Dr. Hollingworth,* pp. 61–65. For a recent discussion of this matter, see Merritt Y. Hughes, "The Historical Setting of Milton's *Observations* on the *Articles of Peace,* 1649," *PMLA,* LXIV (1949), 1049–73.

Charles I wrong, that the very king the Jacobites so extravagantly extolled had levied war on the people of England and had secretly planned the destruction of their liberties and laws. If by such a demonstration he convinced anyone that the Stuart regime should never return and that the government of William and Mary should receive the support of the people, he owed his success to Milton.

Ludlow made his third attack upon the character of Charles I in *Ludlow No Lyar;* and here, too, he utilized *Eikonoklastes.* Designed mainly to answer Richard Hollingworth's *A Second Defence of King Charles I,* this pamphlet at the same time vindicated the Parliament of 1640 and upheld Anthony Walker's *A True Account of the Author of a Book entituled Eikon Basilike,* a tract which claimed, with a wealth of detail, what the Anglesey Memorandum had so briefly stated: that Bishop Gauden, and not Charles I, had written the King's Book. In the main part of the pamphlet, Ludlow reiterated many of his earlier positions. He pointed to the King's sympathy for Catholics, his threats to Parliament, his subversion of the laws of the realm. The obvious inference from such positions, as it had been in his earlier tracts, was that the King had been rightly tried and sent to his doom, even as James II, for the same reasons, had his crown taken away and granted to William and Mary. In this repetition of how Charles I had subverted the laws of the land and of how Parliament had justly challenged his power, echoes of *Eikonoklastes* sound many times; indeed, Ludlow no doubt had this tract directly before him as he assembled his charges. But these echoes, as well as the repetitious main part of *Ludlow No Lyar,* are of less significance than his use of *Eikonoklastes* for his long introductory statement, in which he contributed something new to the Williamite-Jacobite controversy over the character of Charles I.

In this long introduction, Ludlow analyzed Anthony Walker's *A True Account of the Author of a Book entituled Eikon Basilike* and *Dr. Hollingworth's Defence of K. Charles the First's Holy and Divine Book, Called Eikon Basilike,* an obvious answer to the claim that Bishop Gauden had written the King's Book. All the details of this analysis need not be reviewed here; but it is important to know that Anthony Walker had been Bishop Gauden's curate at Bocking and that now, in his old age, he had bestirred himself to testify in the great debate over the authorship of *Eikon Basilike* that his superior in religious affairs had composed the reputed King's Book. Moreover, he had died while his testimony was still in the press and hence could not answer the immediate Jacobite outcry that greeted his work. But what Walker could not do, Ludlow could and willingly did; he countered Richard Hollingworth's attack upon Walker by comparing the claims of both and by allowing the laurels to fall upon Walker's *A True Account.* That Bishop Gauden had composed *Eikon Basilike* was indeed the burden of the introductory statement, which Ludlow addressed to Luke Milbourne, Hollingworth's assistant in the "mighty Undertakings" to exalt the King's Book and to lay Anthony Walker low.[37] But a burning passion for truth, of course, was not the only motive which inspired Ludlow to defend Walker's conclusions; he knew that a mere reiteration of his claims, judiciously compared with those of Hollingworth, would be enough to discredit *Eikon Basilike* in the eyes of the public, and this in turn he calculated would damage the Jacobite cause. He also knew that he could discredit the cause further if he could conclude his analysis with an attack upon the martyr himself; and for this task he turned to *Eikonoklastes.*

Milton, as previous analysis has shown, had satirically commented on the theft of Pamela's prayer in *Eikon Basilike.* He had begun his discussion by claiming that Charles I had never been truthful in his dealings with Parliament; and this trait of mendacity, he went on, unfortunately followed him up the very steps of the scaffold. Consider how he mocked God and fooled his best friends by repeating just before he went to his doom a prayer taken word for word from Sidney's *Arcadia!* So colorful was Milton's description of the whole Pamela affair, and so sharp was his estimate of the character of Charles I, that, rather than holding up for comparison the two prayers as he had formerly done, Ludlow lifted from *Eikonoklastes* the main lines of the portrait Milton had painted:

LUDLOW NO LYAR	EIKONOKLASTES
The King begins his Book, saying, That *he called his last Parliament, not more by others Advice, and the Necessity of his Affairs, than by his own Choice and Inclination.* This is	That which the King layes down heer as his first foundation, and as it were the head stone of his whole Structure, that *He Call'd this last Parlament not more by others ad-*

[37] *Ludlow No Lyar, Or a Detection of Dr. Hollingworth's Disingenuity in his Second Defence of King Charles I* (Amsterdam, 1692), pp. iii–xx.

to all knowing Men so apparently not true, that a more unlucky Sentence hardly could have come into his Mind. He never lov'd, never fulfilled, never promoted the true End of Parliaments: But having first tried in vain all undue Ways to procure Money; his Army beaten by the Scots, the Lords Petitioning, and the general Voice of the People, almost hissing him and his ill-acted Regality off the Stage, compelled at length both by his own Wants and Fears, upon meer Extremity he summon'd this last Parliament.

And as to what we find in the end of this Book, his *Prayer in the time of Captivity*. Who would have imagined so little fear in him of the All-seeing Deity; so little care of Truth in his Words, or Honour to himself or to his Friends, or sense of his Afflictions, as immediately before his Death to pop into the Hands of that grave Bishop, Doctor *Juxon*, who attended him, as a special Relick of his Saint-like Exercises, a Prayer stollen, word for word, from the Mouth of a Heathen Woman praying to a Heathen God, and that not in a serious, but a vain Amatorious Book, Sir *Philip Sidney's Arcadia*; a Book, how full so ever of Wit, not worthy to be named among Religious Thoughts and Duties: Not to be read at any time without good Caution, much less in time of Trouble and Affliction to be a Christian's Prayer-Book. 'Tis worthy of remark, that he who had acted over us so Tragically, should leave the World at last with such a

vice and the necessity of his affaires, then by his own chois and inclination, is to all knowing men so apparently not true, that a more unlucky and inauspicious sentence, and more betok'ning the downfall of his whole Fabric, hardly could have come into his minde. . . . Much less therfore did hee call this last Parlament by his own chois and inclination; but having first try'd in vaine all undue ways to procure Mony, his Army, of thir own accord, being beat'n in the North, the Lords Petitioning, and the general voice of the people almost hissing him and his ill-acted regality off the Stage, compell'd at length both by his wants, and by his feares, upon meer extremity he summon'd this last Parlament. . . .

Who would have imagin'd so little feare in him of the true all-seeing Deitie, so little reverence of the Holy Ghost, whose office is to dictat and present our Christian Prayers, so little care of truth in his last words, or honour to himself, or to his Friends, or sense of his afflictions, or of that sad howr which was upon him, as immediately before his death to popp into the hand of that grave Bishop who attended him, for a special Relique of his saintly exercises, a Prayer stol'n word for word from the mouth of a Heathen fiction praying to a heathen God; & that in no serious Book, but the vain amatorious Poem of Sr *Philip Sidneys Arcadia*; a Book in that kind full of worth and witt, but among religious thoughts, and duties not worthy to be nam'd; nor ridiculous *Exit*, as to bequeath, among his deifying Friends, such a piece of Mockery to be publish'd by them, as must needs cover both his and their Heads with shame and confusion. And sure it was the Hand of *God* that let them fall, and be taken in such a foolish Trap, as hath exposed them to all Derision; if for nothing else, to throw Contempt and Disgrace, in the sight of all Men, upon this his idoliz'd Book, and the whole Rosary of his Prayers. (p. xx.)

to be read at any time without good caution; much less in time of trouble and affliction to be a Christians Prayer-Book. . . . Yet hardly it can be thought upon (though how sad a thing) without som kind of laughter at the manner, and solemn transaction of so gross a cousenage: that he who had trampl'd over us so stately and so tragically should leave the world at last so ridiculously in his exit, as to bequeath among his Deifying friends that stood about him such a pretious peece of mockery to be publisht by them, as must needs cover both his and their heads with shame, if they have any left. . . . And sure it was the hand of God to let them fal & be tak'n in such a foolish trapp, as hath exposed them to all derision; if for nothing els, to throw contempt and disgrace in the sight of all men upon this his Idoliz'd Book, and the whole rosarie of his Prayers . . . (V, 75–87.)

With this devastating sketch of Charles I, Ludlow brought his discussion of the authorship of *Eikon Basilike* to an illogical but nevertheless politically astute close—illogical because he assigned the King's Book to Gauden in one place, only to assume it came from the hand of Charles I in another, but astute because he recognized the political value of an attack upon Stuart character. Nothing could have been more effective in the Williamite-Jacobite conflict than to paint the King as a moral leper—an enemy of Parliament, a stealer of prayers, a mocker of man and of God—a man who had so little respect for his friends that, in his very hour of agony, he perpetrated a hoax upon his confessor and bequeathed to the publishers of *Eikon Basilike* a legacy of laughter and shame. Such a portrait would not only nullify claims of men like Luke Milbourne and Richard Hollingworth but also arouse derision and scorn for the very sovereign through whose memory Jacobites hoped to inspire sympathy for James II and thus effect a restoration of the hereditary Stuart line. For weapons to carry out such tactics, Ludlow owed much to the arsenal of *Eikonoklastes*.

Ludlow thus drew generously from Milton in his campaign to counter Jacobite efforts to advance the cause of James II through the memory of the martyred King Charles. How many people turned away from Jacobite principles and began to favor the government of William and Mary because Ludlow convinced them with arguments taken from *Eikonoklastes* will perhaps never be known; but Jacobites considered his plagiaries of Milton important enough to reveal them, even as Ludlow had revealed the theft of Charles I. In *The Plagiary Exposed*, for example, a Jacobite pamphleteer accused Ludlow of belonging to the "*new Race of the old Republican Stamp*" and of intruding "*amongst his Friends Mr.* Milton" and John Cook, of appearing to be a copy of their malice, "*tho not their Wit.*"[38] Moreover, he continued to draw Jacobite fire and before the century closed became something of a revolutionary symbol, a man whose arguments, as later discussion will show, supposedly convinced thousands of people that the principles guiding the Settlement stemmed from ancient constitutional rights and that hence the government of William and Mary superseded that of James II. If his efforts earned such rewards, Milton indeed contributed significantly to the Williamite cause.

IV

If the Revolutionary Settlement witnessed new disciples supporting and spreading abroad through their own tracts Milton's principles of government, it also saw old ones returning to the original fount for inspiration and strength. Among the most notable of these was Charles Blount, who adapted *Areopagitica* anew under the title of *Reasons Humbly offered for the Liberty of Unlicens'd Printing* in order to convince Parliament that the Press Act, which James II had revived in 1685, should be allowed to lapse. This Act, to be sure, was renewed by a marginal vote in 1693; but it died for lack of support in 1695 and never again came to life in the form it had known through a great part of the seventeenth century. To its demise, Charles Blount made a signal contribution. For, although the old Whig battle for

[38] *The Plagiary Exposed* (London, 1691), "Preface to the Reader." The original pamphlet was probably written earlier and has been attributed to the hand of Samuel Butler; but the "Preface to the Reader" was composed after the Settlement and spoke to the issues of 1691.

freedom of thought and expression had by this time been largely won, Blount's adaptation of *Areopagitica,* to which was subjoined an attack upon Edmund Bohun, the present Surveyor of the Imprimery, brought the Press Act to the attention of Parliament and in so doing delivered it a clear coup de grâce.

Edmund Bohun himself, because of his inept activities in office, helped Blount deliver this final blow.[39] Bohun had long shown himself to be a Tory of the most definite stamp. He had, for example, been a strong champion of the doctrine of passive obedience and had upheld the theory of regal supremacy. Moreover, he had supported the principles of Sir Robert Filmer against the attack of Algernon Sidney. With the coming of William and Mary, however, he had seen fit, as indeed most Jurors had, to compromise his earlier principles and swear allegiance to the new government; and soon he found himself, through the efforts of the Bishop of Norwich, holding the surveyorship of the imprimery, an office specifically designed to prevent the dissemination of subversive doctrines. Such an office called for a clear head and a firm hand; and Bohun possessed neither. In the first place, as Blount revealed, Bohun came to the surveyorship with so many Tory prejudices that he could not recognize subversive thought when he saw it and hence licensed numerous tracts actually dangerous to the Settlement of William and Mary. He had allowed many pamphlets on the side of the suspended bishops, for example, to be printed, as well as others "highly favouring the *Jacobite Interest.*" Furthermore, he had licensed a speech made by the Earl of Warrington, in which the Earl had criticized Tory tactics, upheld the election of kings, and presented the "Opinion that it would never go well with *England,* till every Man might worship *God* in his own way"; but when the publisher desired to advertise it in *The City Mercury,* "this *Press-Superintendent* disliking his *Lordship*'s excellent Positions, struck out the Advertisement, and forbad it to be printed."[40] In addition to this, he had expunged from the same paper Samuel Johnson's *An Argument Proving that the Abrogation of King James Was According to the Constitution of the English Government,* a book which,

[39] *Reasons Humbly offered for the Liberty of Unlicens'd Printing. To Which is Subjoin'd, The Just and True Character of Edmund Bohun, The Licenser of the Press* (London, 1693). This adaptation, together with Blount's earlier one, also appeared in *The Miscellaneous Works of Charles Blount, Esq.* ([London], 1695). See *The Works of Lord Macaulay* (London, 1866), III, 636 ff., for a dramatic account of this coup de grâce.

[40] *Reasons Humbly offered*, pp. 25–26.

in Blount's opinion, set the government upon its true basis. These and other practices so unfriendly to those who supported the Settlement compelled Blount to call Bohun an avowed enemy of the government of William and Mary; and he marveled that such a man, in view of the Revolution, should be allowed to hold a position of such responsibility and profit.

Blount not only marveled; he laid a trap which he rightly anticipated would catch and expose Bohun in his true light: a menace to the government of William and Mary. In pursuit of his plan, he anonymously composed and presented for licensing *King William and Queen Mary Conquerors*, a tract which claimed, among other things, that these sovereigns came to the throne by right of conquest and that subjects, in accordance with the doctrine of passive obedience, owed allegiance to any person who thus or otherwise wore the crown. Such positions, of course, threatened the whole Settlement, and at the same time abrogated the theory of compact; but Bohun was so delighted with the sentiments the tract expressed that he immediately licensed it, no doubt believing that it would go far in healing party divisions over the rights of the crown. But he awoke to find that by licensing a tract expressing such sentiments he had pleased no one; indeed, it aroused such animosity that the House of Commons brought Bohun in for questioning, after which it was resolved that the tract should be burned by the hangman and that the King should be requested to remove Bohun from office. No other man than Blount himself gleefully reported that Bohun had come under the displeasure of Parliament; and with considerable malice he suggested that Bohun must have been the author of *King William and Queen Mary Conquerors*, since the positions herein laid down smelled so strongly of his old Tory principles. Such unseemly crowing over a man whose defeat he had planned hardly redounds to Blount's credit; but the nation profited by the whole affair, for Blount's trick called attention to the stupidities of licensing the press at the very time when Parliament was considering a renewal of the old act. That a licenser could, as Bohun had revealed, allow the publication of tracts subversive to the very government he was supposed to protect no doubt convinced many that the office itself served little purpose and hence should be done away with.

As an additional argument that the Licensing Act should be allowed to lapse, Blount presented to "a Member of Parliament" *Rea-*

sons Humbly offered for the Liberty of Unlicens'd Printing, his adaptation of *Areopagitica*. He had made use of this essay before in 1679, when he thought it might convince Parliament at that time that the existing Licensing Act should not be renewed; and now, in 1693, he turned to Milton again. This new adaptation, as might be expected, was directed to the inadequacies of Bohun and the menace he presented to the government of William and Mary; but it nevertheless followed, though in greatly condensed form, the movement of the original essay. Blount began, for example, with a discussion of how the concept of licensing came into being. With Milton, he claimed that the whole notion had crept out of the Inquisition, that before that time the primitive councils and bishops had been "wont only to declare what Books were not commendable, passing no further, but leaving it to each one's Conscience to read or lay by."[41] After the year 800, Blount continued, though the popes of Rome extended their dominion over men's eyes, burning and prohibiting to be read what they fancied not, yet they were sparing in their censure, it not being until the time of Pope Martin V that men were excommunicated for reading heretical books, a course which Pope Leo X and his successors followed, "until the Council of *Trent*, and the *Spanish Inquisition*, engendring together, brought forth, or perfected those Catalogues and *Expurging Indexes*, that rake through the Entrails of many an old good Author, with a Violation worse than any could be offered to his Tomb." "Nor did they stay," Blount went on from Milton, "in Matters Heretical, but any Subject that was not to their Palat, they either condemned, or had it streight into the *New Purgatory* of an *Index*. To fill up the Measure of Encroachment, their last Invention was to ordain, That *no Book*, *Pamphlet or Paper* should be printed, (as if St. *Peter* had bequeath'd them the Keys of the Press also out of Paradise) unless it were approv'd and licens'd under the Hands of two or three Glutton-Friars."

Such a genealogy, of course, argued against the Licensing Act in 1693 as effectively as it had in 1644, when Milton first had presented it. The people of England still shuddered at the attempts of James II to make his religion prevail, and they recognized the threat of Catholic Louis XIV from abroad. Blount thus shrewdly allowed a good part of Milton's historical account of the Catholic origin of licensing to remain

[41] *Reasons Humbly offered*, pp. 3–4.

with scarcely a change of a word, knowing that antipapal feeling would prejudice people against anything with such a hated paternity. But he utilized *Areopagitica* most effectively in his attack upon the futility of licensing acts and upon the inadequacies of Edmund Bohun. What was the use of a law if it conduced nothing to the end for which it was framed? Blount asked with Milton. If the regulation of the press was meant to rectify manners, then all recreations and pastimes must come under the law: no music must be heard, no song sung, except that which was grave. And with this beginning, Blount pointed out with examples taken from Milton how ridiculous it would be to attempt a rectification of manners through the regulation of singing, dancing, and other customs delightful to man. But grant, he finally said, also with Milton, that the things to be prohibited were books only; even so "it appears that the Law is far insufficient to the End which it intends"; and with this he pointed an accusing finger directly at Bohun and his office, changing Milton's words here and there to make his charge more appropriate:

REASONS HUMBLY OFFERED	AREOPAGITICA
Do we not see, not once or oftner, but weekly, nay daily, that continued *Jacobite Libels* against our present happy Establishment, are printed and dispersed amongst us, for all that *Licensing* can do? Yet this is the prime Service a Man would think, wherein this Law should give proof of it self. If it were executed you'l say. But certain, if Execution be remiss or blindfold now, and in this Particular, what will it be hereafter? (pp. 5–6.)	Do we not see, not once or oftner, but weekly that continu'd Court-libell against the Parlament and City, Printed, as the wet sheets can witnes, and dispers't among us, for all that licencing can doe? yet this is the prime service a man would think, wherein this order should give proof of it self. If it were executed, you'l say. But certain, if execution be remisse or blindfold now, and in this particular, what will it be hereafter . . . (IV, 320–21.)

In view of the fact that Bohun had licensed books such as *King William and Queen Mary Conquerors* and had refused advertisements for the Earl of Warrington's speech and for Samuel Johnson's *An Argument Proving that the Abrogation of King James Was According to the Constitution of the English Government*, Blount's accusations could not be misunderstood.

Bohun had indeed failed in his office by suppressing books friendly to the rationale of the Settlement and by licensing those inimical to it; and the future held little hope for improvement for the very reason, Blount continued from Milton, that few men possess the high qualities of judiciousness and learning necessary to discharge the duties of Licenser and that those who do would be soon wearied by the tedious and unpleasing journeywork such an office entailed. Such a difficulty in itself offered another argument for discontinuing the Act. And with this observation, Blount focused attention upon "*the present Licencer*, Mr. Bohun," a man whose actions in office revealed clearly that he had already become weary. Seeing then, Blount concluded in Milton's words, that "he who now possesses the Imployment, by all evident Signs, wishes himself well rid of it; and that no Man of Worth, none that is not a plain Unthrift of his own Hours, is ever likely to succeed him, except he mean to put himself to the Salary of *a Press-Corrector*," the people of England might anticipate what kind of Licenser would follow in Bohun's place: a man "either Ignorant, Imperious and Remiss, or basely Mercenary."[42] Blount himself perhaps anticipated a return of Roger L'Estrange, whom he mentioned in his remarks subjoined to his adaptation of *Areopagitica;* but whoever came to his mind it is clear that he turned Milton's general arguments into specific reasons for allowing the Press Act to lapse in 1693. A simple shift of a word, a cut here and an additional phrase there, made Milton's powerful rhetoric speak directly against the stupidities and misjudgments of Edmund Bohun and revealed, as eloquently as his term in office, the futility of licensing books. If people had been only dimly aware of how woefully Bohun had failed to serve the cause of his government, after Blount's revelation they could no longer plead ignorance.

From the failure of Edmund Bohun in his office, Blount turned to the more philosophical consideration of the manifest hurt a Press Act could cause a nation; and here, too, he turned to Milton for strength. He pointed out that such an act was the greatest affront and discouragement which could be offered to learning and learned men, that it was an undervaluing and vilifying of the whole nation, that it was a let and hindrance to the discovery of truth. Discussion of such general and philosophical matters allowed him to follow Milton almost verbatim; indeed, the ringing words of the original could bear little change and, furthermore, spoke to any age with equal power and

[42] *Reasons Humbly offered*, p. 6.

convincement. When Milton paused from his philosophic discussion, however, to eye the defection of Presbyterians, who before the Puritan Rebellion had helped break restraints on the press but who, once in power, had enacted a Licensing Act, Blount saw a chance to make a thrust at the Jacobites. A few changes turned Milton's admonition into a plea that Jacobites, who before the Revolution had written against popery and arbitrary power but who now, delivered from these threats, continued their old ways, desist from persuading the people of England to return to their earlier bondage:

Reasons Humbly offered	Areopagitica
There were not a few Men of Note about the time of the late happy Revolution, who by their *unlicensed Books*, to the Contempt of an *Imprimatur*; first cured that *Cataract* that blinded our Eyes, and inabled the People to see Day. It may be reasonably hoped that none of those will be the Perswaders to renew upon us the Bondage which they themselves have wrought so much Good by contemning, and execute the most *Dominican* Part of the *Inquisition* over us: Should they be guilty in this Respect, I conclude that the Change of their Condition hath puffed them up more than their late Experience of *Tyrannous Practices* hath made them wise. (p. 8.)	There have bin not a few since the beginning of this Parliament, both of the Presbytery and others who by their unlicenc't books to the contempt of an *Imprimatur* first broke that triple ice clung about our hearts, and taught the people to see day: I hope that none of those were the perswaders to renew upon us this bondage which they themselves have wrought so much good by contemning . . . and execute the most *Dominican* part of the Inquisition over us, and are already with one foot in the stirrup so active at suppressing, it would be no unequall distribution in the first place to suppresse the suppressors themselves; whom the change of their condition hath puft up, more then their late experience of harder times hath made wise. (IV, 352.)

Such an appeal to men in high place—all Tory Jurors, for example, who had turned against James II but who also still clung to their old Tory beliefs—probably had little effect; but it served to reveal to the people of England the inconsistencies of those who would support the Government of William and Mary and still wish to maintain a Press Act. And with this, followed by a few comments upon Archbishop Laud and Richard Baxter, Blount presented his concluding recommendation, also taken from Milton: "as for regulating the Press, surely no better Advice can be given, than that no Book be printed, unless the *Publisher* and the *Author*'s Name, or at least the *Publisher's* be registred."[43] Blount thus found his main philosophical arguments, as well as his recommendation to Parliament, in *Areopagitica;* and, though much of the original never appeared—the great vision of an awakening nation, mewing her strength and searching for truth, for example—enough of it remained to make *Reasons Humbly offered for the Liberty of Unlicens'd Printing* a creditable and an effective document.

Surprisingly, however, neither the adaptation itself nor Edmund Bohun's poor judgment in office stirred up a great pamphlet war.[44] Unlike the vexed period following the Popish Plot, when a lapse of the Act precipitated a battle royal between Tories and Whigs, the struggle now aroused little comment. Perhaps the people of England had already come to believe in the iniquity of licensing acts and in the desirability of a free press, even as they had come to accept toleration along with the Settlement. But the Press Act still stood on the statutes in 1693, and public inertia might have retained it beyond 1695 had it not been for Blount's efforts to reveal the stupidities of Edmund Bohun and the futility of the office he held. Whatever effectiveness Blount had in overcoming this inertia, he owed directly to Milton.

V

Jacobites openly recognized Milton's contribution to the Williamite cause but made no special effort at this time, as they had in the attempted Whig Revolution, to counter his influence with a concerted campaign of obvious falsehood. They heaped upon him many choice epithets, to be sure, and considered him a prime enemy. Even biographers of the time took delight in besmirching his name. William Winstanley, for example, though cognizant of Milton's abilities, nevertheless claimed that his "Fame" had gone out "like a Candle in a Snuff" and predicted that his "Memory" would "always stink, which might have ever lived in honourable Repute, had not he been a notorious Traytor, and most impiously and villanously bely'd that blessed

[43] *Reasons Humbly offered*, p. 8.

[44] Blount's *King William and Queen Mary Conquerors*, of course, aroused considerable discussion.

Martyr King *Charles* the First."[45] Moreover, Gerard Langbaine recorded that "Had his Principles been as good as his Parts, he had been an Excellent Person; but his demerits towards his Sovereign . . . [had] very much sullied his Reputation";[46] and Anthony Wood, in *Athenæ Oxonienses*, saw fit to say, among other things, that Milton "at length arrived to that monstrous and unparallel'd height of profligate impudence, as in print to justifie the most execrable Murder of him the best of Kings," and in his account of George Morley, Wood felt compelled to call Milton an "impudent lyer."[47] But such vituperation was often accompanied, particularly in the controversies over passive obedience and the character of Charles I, with sober appraisals of Milton's power and influence; Jacobites recognized and at the same time deplored that he had significantly contributed to the decline of old Tory doctrines and had prepared the people of England to accept the terms of the Settlement.

Jurors and Nonjurors alike joined hands in this recognition during the controversy engendered by the oath of allegiance to William and Mary. In this last significant attempt to save the old Tory doctrines from utter destruction, Nonjurors particularly made heroic efforts to re-establish confidence in divine right and passive obedience, a task which led them to examine the origin and growth of these unique Anglican beliefs, as well as the reason that so many had defaulted from them during the Glorious Revolution. Among those most seriously devoted to this task was Abednego Seller, who, as has already been seen, dedicated *The History of Passive Obedience Since the Reformation* and *A Continuation of the History of Passive Obedience* to a defense of the old positions. In the first tract, which appeared in the year of the Settlement, Seller attempted to show by reference to the Thirty-nine Articles, various constitutions and canons ecclesiastical (particularly those of 1640), the homilies against disobedience and willful rebellion, the doctrine of the liturgy, the orders of bishops,

45 *The Lives of the Most Famous English Poets, Or the Honour of Parnassus* (London, 1687), p. 195. Commendatory accounts by John Aubrey and the anonymous biographer remained in manuscript.

46 *An Account of the English Dramatick Poets* (Oxford, 1691), p. 375.

47 *Athenæ Oxonienses* (London, 1691), I, 880–84; II (London, 1692), 582. Moreover, in his account of Edward Phillips, Wood spoke of John Phillips as "having early imbib'd in a most plentiful manner the rankest antimonarchical principles, from that villanous leading incendiary Joh. Milton his uncle" (*Athenæ Oxonienses*, IV, 764, ed. Philip Bliss, London, 1820). See also J. G. G., *Some Observations Upon The Keeping The Thirtieth of January. And Twenty ninth of May* (London, 1694, p. 10) for doubt of Milton's veracity.

the censures of universities, and the opinions of learned men that passive obedience and nonresistance stood at the very center of Anglican belief; and in pursuit of this task he had occasion to name enemies of this position, among whom Milton appeared several times. He recalled the Oxford proclamation of 1683, for example, which condemned "the Books of *Milton, Baxter, Goodwin, Owen, Johnson, &c*";[48] and asked John Moore to testify, as he had in an earlier sermon, that "Knox, Milton, Rutherford, *&c. could not have spit ranker venom at Kings, or spoke with greater contempt of their Authority, than* Hildebrand."[49] Such references indicate Seller's realization that Milton had played a significant role in opposing doctrines so important to the Church.

But he spoke more to the point, so far as Milton's significance is concerned, in his Preface, a brief statement in which he explained his method and purpose and ventured at the same time an explanation for defection within the Anglican communion. Here he deplored that the one position distinguishing the Church of England from Geneva and Rome had been ridiculed, "*and the Assertors and Practisers of it exploded*" by those who should give assent to it. The assaults of enemies he could understand, but defection within the Church of England amazed him beyond words. Yet he consoled himself that it was the portion of the Church never to do evil, no matter what good might be procured, that its members should never rebel against the authority which God had established, however worthy their aims. In view of this, shame more than a desire to upbraid forced him to observe that many clergymen of late had turned away from the distinctive positions of the Church and had received the doctrines of Thomas Hobbes, whose "*Authority*" and "*Reasons*" had been derived "*from* Milton, *and both from* Doleman, *i.e.*, Parsons *the Jesuite*," as if they "*were Apostolical, and ought to be preached in all the World.*" The doctrines thus received and preached, Seller described in detail: "That Power is originally in the Body of the People, that the Foundation of all Government is laid in compact, and that the breach of Conditions by one Party dispenses with the Duty of the other, tho confirmed by Sacraments, Oaths, and reiterated Promises; that a Prince may be opposed in his Politick, tho not in his personal Capacity, that when Re-

48 *The History of Passive Obedience Since the Reformation*, p. 18.

49 *Ibid.*, p. 99.

ligion is a part of our Property it may be defended." Such principles, of course, had animated the Glorious Revolution and had allowed many Anglican clergymen to turn against James II. Finally, with a deep expression of shame, Seller pointed at those who had accepted the Machiavellian positions "that the Determinations of Providence are to be followed, or that the Prosperity of a Cause is a Mark of its goodness"—equivocations which William Sherlock presented to the people of England in such eloquent detail to support his defection from hereditary monarchy and his loyalty for the government of William and Mary. Now "*the owning and complying with such Principles,*" Seller declared, had encouraged "*many weak and ignorant Persons*" who could not "*distinguish between the steady Doctrines of a Church, and the Opinions and Practices of some of her Members*" to embrace the Roman communion, and had led to the accusation that the Church had complied with its central beliefs only so long as it had proved expedient to do so.[50] Adherence to such doctrines perhaps had such results; but of significance to the present discussion is Seller's recognition of Milton as one of the main enemies of passive obedience, as one whose principles, accepted and preached by numerous clergymen, helped "explode" both the asserters and practicers of that doctrine unique to the Anglican Church. The growing roster of Milton's disciples and the continued activity of Samuel Johnson, whose name appeared several times in *The History*, give Seller's analysis an accuracy of which perhaps even he was not fully aware.

Seller's position that the principles of Hobbes, Milton, and Parsons had turned many clergymen away from the doctrine of passive obedience, however, failed to secure unanimous assent, though no Jacobite disagreed with his observation that the doctrines of these men stood squarely opposed to the Church. Indeed, Jurors who before the Revolution had preached passive obedience flatly denied that they had sworn allegiance to William and Mary because they had favorably received the theory of compact, and resented the inference that their adherence to the new government made them traitors to their earlier beliefs. Thomas Long, for example, an old Tory now turned Juror, thought Seller's tract important enough to answer it fully in *The Historian Unmask'd*, a pamphlet in which he not only attempted to show that as a believer in neither divine right nor government by

[50] *Ibid.*, sigs. [A3-A4].

compact he could take the oath of allegiance and never contradict the doctrine of passive obedience, but also to disclose, in a section devoted to Seller's prefatory analysis, that he and other clergymen, far from accepting the principles of their foes, still exploded "the wild Opinions of *Hobs*, *Milton*, and *Cressey*" and had "acted in a direct Opposition to them."[51] With such a vehement but illogical position Thomas Bainbrigg fully agreed. In his *Seasonable Reflections, On a Late Pamphlet, Entituled, A History of Passive Obedience Since the Reformation*, he found that he "could willingly chime in" with Seller and "fault *Hobbs*, and *Milton*, and *Doleman*, or *Parsons;* and with him declare against those Doctrines, *That Power is originally in the Body of the People, and that the Foundation of all Government is laid in compact*, as he says in his Preface." Bainbrigg could also agree with Seller's conclusion, "*That Power is only from God*." But this hardly meant, Bainbrigg went on to say, that law, religion, and common sense should be laid aside; and he concluded with an exhortation that men put away anger and heat and say "*That Power is only from God; That Resistance is a dangerous thing, and in most Cases very ill; That Passive Obedience (well explained) is a Duty*."[52] Thus both Thomas Long and Bainbrigg, as Jurors, denied that the principles of their foes had turned them away from passive obedience and allowed them to take the oath of allegiance; but if *they* had not been so affected, Nonjuring George Hickes supported Seller to say that some had. He admitted, to be sure, that many had justified their taking the oath by the expedients of "*Possession, Abdication* and *Conquest*," and that those so explaining their repudiation of James II and their acceptance of the Settlement had not necessarily turned against the doctrine of passive obedience. But there were "others again" who had justified "the taking of the Oath upon such Principles, as seem indeed to overthrow the Doctrine of Non-resistance"; and Seller was "very angry" at such men, Hickes continued, "for embracing the doctrine of *Hobbs, Milton*, and *Parsons*." If Seller had blackened "any in his Book with the imputation of *Apostacy*," it was only these few.[53]

Seller had indeed revealed, and Hickes had confirmed his opinion, that some within the Anglican fold had repudiated the doctrine of

[51] *The Historian Unmask'd: Or, Some Reflections on the Late History of Passive-Obedience* (London, 1689), p. 29.

[52] (London, 1689/90), pp. 54, 66.

[53] *A Letter to the Author of a Late Paper, Entituled, A Vindication of the Divines of the Church of England, &c. In Defence of the History of Passive Obedience* (1689), p. 5.

passive obedience and had favorably received the principles of the primary foes of the church. Perhaps both had in mind men like Gilbert Burnet and Samuel Johnson, who even before the Revolution had moved far away from doctrines expressed by old Tories and Nonjurors—men who had, in fact, indirectly come under the influence of Milton's program for man and society. Perhaps they had in mind simply the fact that the Convention Parliament had openly settled the crown on William and Mary in accordance with the theory of compact, and hence for this reason believed that any who supported the new government tacitly accepted the principles upon which it had been erected. Such a conclusion at least possessed a semblance of logic, whereas Jurors who still claimed to revere passive obedience ransacked their brains to find plausible reasons to make their actions square with their professions of faith.

To show the illogic of the Juror's position, as well as to press further Nonjuror claims, Seller returned to his former task in *A Continuation of the History of Passive Obedience Since theReformation*, to some copies of which was attached a discussion of the oath of allegiance. As before, in the course of his argument he designated Milton as one of the main foes of passive obedience and implied that his principles had turned many against this central doctrine of the Anglican Church. He paraphrased from Joseph Jane's *Eikon Aklastos*, for example, to show how impious Milton had been and how rebellion had been dearer to him than religion. Indeed, Jane had so fully revealed Milton's character in his answer to *Eikonoklastes* that Seller realized he could do little better than cite liberally from him, making changes only as present circumstances demanded. He pointed out that Milton had commended the superstitious actions of a blind age and the very dregs of popery, that he had called obedience and suffering "servility and wretchedness," mere "*Pulpit stuff of the Prelates.*" Moreover, he called on Robert Hancock, whose work has already been seen, to testify that Milton had held popish principles of government, that he and other regicides had drawn from Jesuits like Bellarmine and Parsons for precedents and arguments to war against the king and finally to bring his head to the block.[54]

But, as in his first tract, Seller made his most significant observations concerning Milton's importance in his introductory analysis.

[54] *A Continuation of the History of Passive Obedience Since the Reformation*, pp. 131–32, 187–88.

Here he spoke of the specific foes of passive obedience, among whom was John Milton—that miscreant Milton, who had designated the first reformers "*as the genuine assertors of the Doctrin of Resistance*," who had, in answer to Salmasius' true allegation "*that the Doctrin of the Sacred, and Inviolable Authority of Princes was preserved pure, and uncorrupt in the Church; till the Bishops of* Rome *attempted to set up a Kingdom in this World Paramount to all kings and Emperors*," replied "that *Salmasius* strove in vain to transfer the guilt upon the Pope, which all free Nations, every Religion, all the Orthodox take upon themselves, and that he had as many Adversaries in this point, as there were most excellent Doctors of the Reformed Church."[55] Milton had indeed argued in this wise and had, furthermore, undermined the Anglican story of the primitive Christians, upon which clergymen rested so much of their case for passive obedience. It is thus little wonder that Seller, in his concern over the declining power of the old Tory party, should blame Milton for helping turn some of the Anglican clergy away from the central teachings of the Church to an acceptance of the rationale of the Settlement, or that even those who denied being so influenced should deem him as a prime foe of the principles they avowedly followed.

Comment on Milton in the controversy attending the celebrated conversion of William Sherlock to taking the oath of allegiance tells much the same story. Even as Abednego Seller shamed Juring clergymen in general for repudiating the doctrine of passive obedience and receiving the principles of Hobbes, Milton, and Parsons, so Thomas Wagstaffe, as an ardent Nonjuror, challenged Sherlock in particular for his declaration that Bishop Overall's Convocation Book had furnished him with reasons for swearing obedience to William and Mary, and at the same time, because of Sherlock's conversion, placed him among those who would, if they had a mind to it, "defend *Hugh Peters*, *Bradshaw*, and the *High Court of Justice*," or among those who might, if they would, "applaud the Practices of *Nye*, *Marshall* and *Milton*, and dislike those of the Glorious Sufferers for their King and their Consciences." To bring principles to the Church of England which would allow men to do such, as indeed Sherlock had, was to Wagstaffe as "ridiculous" as it was "shameless and impudent."[56]

[55] *A Continuation of the History of Passive Obedience*, sig. [A3]. The "Prefatory Epistle," though addressed to Seller himself, expresses his sentiments and apparently came from his hand.

[56] *An Answer to a Late Pamphlet, Entituled Obedience and Submission to the Present Government, Demonstrated from Bp. Overall's Convocation-Book* [London, 1690], p. 23.

Moreover, George Hickes, in a series of bitter reflections upon Sherlock's continued defense of his taking the oath, accused him of apostasy from the true beliefs of the church and, to vindicate Nonjurors, placed him where he logically belonged—among those who approved resistance to kings. All Sherlock's "malicious Speeches and Slanders" against James II had been "filed up in Heaven," George Hickes declared; and he went ahead to prophesy that they would be brought in as "Evidence" against him at the great day of Judgment when, "without publick and bitter Repentance," he would "appear at the left Hand, with *Cromwell*, *Bradshaw*, *Cook*, *Milton*, and *Thom. Goodwin*, and be sent with those Worthies of the Old Cause into" his own place.[57]

But Sherlock himself, like Thomas Long, contended that swearing the oath had not meant a repudiation of the doctrine of passive obedience; and to Samuel Johnson's accusation that he had perjured himself by turning away from James II and supporting the government of William and Mary—a point upon which both Whigs and Nonjurors agreed—Sherlock replied that not he, but Samuel Johnson, should be deemed an apostate, that were the canonization office divided between Johnson and Richard Baxter, the Church would have to reform the calendar of saints and "in the room of the twelve Apostles, (those Church of *England* Preachers of Passive Obedience,) Insert the Names of *Cromwell*, *Bradshaw*, *Ravilliack*, and *Milton*, in the Company of some now alive."[58] Samuel Johnson had indeed, since the attempted Whig revolution, invoked his patron saint Milton and should have been glad to admit how much strength he had found at his shrine; but to Sherlock, as to many other old Tory Jurors, the thought that swearing the oath meant a tacit acceptance of the rationale of the Settlement and hence an association with rebels of an earlier day was wholly repugnant. Sherlock therefore went out of his way to disclaim any connections with Milton by refuting his principles, though in the same breath, with perhaps more vigor than logic, he made a case for resistance against the supreme powers. "The *Patrons* of *Resistance*," Sherlock claimed, had employed all manner of arts to evade the force of St. Paul's significant words to the Romans: *For there is no power but of God; the powers that be, are ordained of God.*

[57] *A Vindication of Some Among Our Selves Against the False Principles of Dr. Sherlock* (London, 1692), p. 45.

[58] *Observations Upon Mr. Johnson's Remarks, Upon Dr. Sherlock's Book of Non-Resistance* (London, 1689), p. 16.

Whosoever therefore resisteth the power, resisteth the ordinance of God. They had, Sherlock continued, attempted to make the apostle's argument signify nothing; and for this reason he believed it important to consider briefly what they had said. With these prefatory remarks, he turned specific attention to *Pro Populo Anglicano Defensio*, where Milton had agreed, with St. Paul, that sovereign princes came into their thrones by the power of God; but Sherlock pointed out that Milton had gone on to say that even as princes came from God, so did all other things, such as pestilence, and famine, and all manner of evils and calamities which might befall any nation. Did this mean that such evils should not be resisted? Such would not logically follow; and by the same token, Sherlock went on from Milton, the patrons of resistance defended the legitimacy of endeavoring to break the yoke of a tyrant. "That is, in plain English," Sherlock concluded, "that when the *Apostle* proves, that we must not resist *Princes*, because they are set up by God, he does not reason truly; for notwithstanding this, we may resist *Tyrannical Princes*, as we would do the *Plague*, though they are both sent by God."[59]

Now Sherlock claimed that he agreed with St. Paul, and not Milton; but in actuality, as Whigs and Nonjurors never ceased to remind him, his swearing the oath of allegiance to William and Mary repudiated the sense of the Apostle's injunction as it had been embodied in the doctrines of the Anglican Church and placed him in the company of Milton and other old rebels. Being associated with such a company before the eyes of the public no doubt caused him considerable anguish; but such logical affiliations, as well as his specific attack upon a significant argument in *Pro Populo Anglicano Defensio*, indicate that Sherlock *had* accepted the view he professed to abhor and that Jacobites considered Milton responsible for turning him and others against Anglican beliefs. Had they cared at this time to recall how much Samuel Johnson owed to *Pro Populo* for his argument against passive obedience or to mention his quantitatively unknown but admittedly great influence both before and after the Glorious Revolution, they could have shown in even more detail that Milton's principles indeed turned the clergy away from the old doctrines of the church and shaped their minds in accordance with Whig views.

If in the controversy over the oath of allegiance Jacobites indi-

[59] *The Case of Resistance of the Supreme Powers Stated and Resolved, According to the Doctrine of the Holy Scriptures* (2d ed., London, 1690), pp. 117–19.

cated in some measure the extent of Milton's influence upon the minds of the clergy, in the conflict over the character of Charles I they pointed to his effect upon the general public. This should be only expected. The fine points of passive obedience concerned chiefly the sons of the church; the person of Charles I and his dramatic struggle with Parliament encircled national emotions and loyalties and hence reference to them could affect a much wider audience. This is undoubtedly the reason that Williamites, in their effort to discredit the concept of hereditary monarchy and to secure the terms of the Settlement, so vigorously vilified him who stood in Jacobite eyes as the best of all kings and so openly justified the activities of the Long Parliament of 1640. Such an emotional campaign, conducted in great measure with ammunition stolen from Milton, apparently succeeded beyond expectations. At any rate, Major General Ludlow, as prior analysis has shown, repeated his tactics again and again, and to counter his influence Jacobites arose in their fury to vilify both him and his master. The very fury of their counter campaign, as well as several open admissions, reveals that Williamite thrusts at hereditary monarchy through the sides of Charles I turned many away from the old Tory doctrines of Church and State and made them look with favor upon the rationale of the Settlement.

Not all counterattacks, to be sure, explicitly recorded this signal Williamite victory. In their attempts to discredit Williamite claims, some Jacobites purposed simply to vindicate the name of Charles I and to blacken all his detractors. *Our Modern Demagogue's Modesty and Honesty in its True Light*, for example, a pamphlet devoted solely to "A VINDICATION OF THE Royal Martyr's Sacred Memory, FROM The Antiquated Calumnies, and Fictions, of the Villain MILTON," as they had been "lately reviv'd with Additions, by the same Bellowing Relicts of the *Old Bulls of* Basan,"[60] brought forward witnesses, both living and dead, to explain the appearance of Pamela's prayer in *Eikon Basilike* and to testify that no one but Charles I could have written so holy a book. Even as the tract lifted from Charles I the accusation of dishonesty and plagiarism, so it accused Williamites of these very crimes. It was pointed out, for instance, that "that Grand Reformer *J. Milton*" had been "Reform'd" into "A Scandalous Pamphl[et] called, *Pro Populo adversus Tyrannos*," and that the

[60] [London, 1691], p. 1.

postscript to *A Letter From Major General Ludlow To Sir E. S.*, which had charged the Royal Martyr "with using a Prayer in Sir *P. Sydney's Arcadia*," had been "stolen from *Milton's Eikonoklastes*."[61] The tract assailed *Eikonoklastes* itself, moreover, as a "wicked Burlesque upon Christianity," a "Leud Book" which, together with the Anglesey Memorandum, had attempted at one stroke to brand as "vile Imposters" the "Martyr-father, and his two Royal Sons."[62] Furthermore, it attacked Milton for his slander and Ludlow for his republicanism and both for their Jesuitical doctrines, and deemed the period of the Puritan Rebellion one of the worst in the history of England. In short, the author of *Our Modern Demagogue's Modesty and Honesty in its True Light* fought fire with fire; and he had good reason, he believed, for employing such tactics. For with the Settlement, he explained in the first part of his tract, a "whole Gang" of "inveterate Republicans" had begun, like body lice, to frisk freely about; nor did they now, as of late, "confine their Venome to their own Religious Assemblies, the Coffee houses, &c." but impudently dispersed their "Persons, and their Politicks on the *Change*," particularly through the agency of the press, which labored with "their montanous Malice, and monstrous Lyes," to give the country "at one Clap, by wholesale, the Catalogue of that Knight-Errantry, which they" had exercised on the nation from 1636 to 1648. Indeed, he went on, this "Gang" so crowded their tracts upon the people of England that he could only suspect that something more than ordinary must be in the wind when they so openly and with such bare faces revived "those Damnable Calumnies, which Hell and they so long since most injuriously cast on the most *spotless Soul* that ever sway'd *English* Scepter."[63] But if he hoped that by vindicating the memory of Charles I, tarring Williamites with their own brush, and revealing their aims and his fears he could revive credit in the Jacobite cause, he apparently had little faith in his efforts. At any rate, as a concluding remark, he expressed a wish that some one "would be as zealous to Re-print" Joseph Jane's *Eikon Aklastos* as the Faction had "been in sending *Milton* abroad."[64] Such a statement was an admission not only of his own weakness but also of Milton's strength.

[61] *Our Modern Demagogue's Modesty*, pp. 3, 8.

[62] *Ibid.*, p. 4.

[63] *Ibid.*, pp. 1–2.

[64] *Ibid.*, p. 8.

No Jacobite, apparently, followed the suggestion that *Eikon Aklastos* be reprinted and sent out in the world, but Richard Hollingworth arose to do battle with the detractors of Charles I in a series of pamphlets, one of which he entitled *Vindiciæ Carolinæ*, a specific answer to the 1690 edition of *Eikonoklastes*. This tract, advertised in the Postscript of *A Second Defence of King Charles I* as "*an Answer to* Milton's *scurrilous Book against K.* Charles, *which came out the last Year, worthy to be in every good and true* English-man's *hand*,"[65] analyzed *Eikonoklastes* chapter by chapter even as Milton had examined *Eikon Basilike*; and, as might be expected, it lifted from Charles I and placed on the shoulders of Long Parliament most of the blame for the troubles of the Puritan Rebellion. Hollingworth's intent to restore confidence in hereditary monarchy and to throw doubt on Parliament was clear; but lest any one misunderstand his tactics, he explained in his prefatory matter exactly why he felt compelled to answer the 1690 reprint of *Eikonoklastes*. Milton had, Hollingworth began, held notions directly contrary to the constitutions of England, which recognized "no Superiour under God but only the King" and knew "nothing but an Hereditary, Imperial Monarchy"; Milton had, furthermore, justified the villainies of his age, that is, the deposition of Charles I and the recognition of Parliamentary supremacy. Moreover, Milton was a man of "large thought" and never wanted words to express his conceptions, however twisted by a depraved temper, as "Witness his *Paradise Lost*; where he makes the Devil,—*Who, though fallen, had not given Heaven for lost*,—speak at that rate himself would have done of the Son of this Royal Martyr (upon his Restauration) had he thought it convenient; when, in his *Paradise regain'd*, he is so indifferent, poor, and starvling, as if he never expected any benefit by it."[66] In brief, Hollingworth saw Milton as a depraved genius, arguing powerfully against doctrines which Jacobites still held and deemed sacrosanct; and when he heard him speaking again, in accordance with Williamite plans, "to re-mind the People of the days of old, and hint to them, how the same Cards may be play'd over again, as God shall enable them, *i.e.* as oppor-

[65] London, 1692, p. [54]. Several tracts other than those analyzed mentioned the reprint of *Eikonoklastes* and the Anglesey Memorandum. See, for example, *Restitution to the Royal Author* (London, 1691), pp. 3, 7–8.

[66] *Vindiciæ Carolinæ: Or, A Defence of Eikon Basilike, The Portraicture of his Sacred Majesty in his Solitudes and Sufferings* (London, 1692), sig. A4v, pp. 1–3.

tunity shall offer,"[67] he could do no other than make a complete and detailed answer to positions so inimical to the Jacobite cause. Hollingworth feared indeed that the new impression of *Eikonoklastes*, seconded by *A Letter from Major General Ludlow To Sir E. S.* and the Anglesey Memorandum, would make people wary of "Hereditary, Imperial Monarchy" and incline them toward the rationale of the Settlement, would convince them of the iniquities of hereditary succession and of the desirability of government by compact. If Hollingworth failed to state that his fears had been realized, his detailed answer to Milton testifies that they haunted his mind.

What Richard Hollingworth expressed as a fear, Thomas Long, in the Preface to *Dr. Walker's True, Modest, and Faithful Account of the Author of Eikon Basilike*, stated as an accomplished fact. The person writing "*under the name of that Impious Regicide* Ludlow," he declared, had gained "*the Assistance and Applause of too many, who suck up his venomous Poyson, and become professed Enemies to Episcopacy in the Church, and Monarchy in the State.*" Moreover, Long continued, "*because their Predecessors prevailed so far against the most Pious and Innocent of Kings, and the best of the Reformed Churches, as to kill and take possession of their Inheritances; having now, as* Milton *says, lost their Paradise, they attempt to regain it, by the same Methods as were used in* 1640."[68] What Thomas Long meant was that Ludlow, and of course Anthony Walker, against whom he directed the main part of his tract, had turned many against old Tory principles, which he, as an old Tory now become Juror, still illogically believed supported the government of William and Mary; and he intimated that they had succeeded in doing so because they had followed the tactics of their predecessors in crime, one of whom was Milton himself.

Indeed, Long made it a special point to reveal that Ludlow had drawn from Milton, and that he and his like, because they frankly accepted the rationale of the Settlement, embodied the very spirit of those who, in earlier days, had in accordance with the theory of compact brought the best of all kings to his doom. He disclosed, for example, with particular reference to *Ludlow No Lyar*, that the author of this pamphlet, whoever he was, had justified murder in the

[67] *Vindiciæ Carolinæ*, p. 4. See also Hollingworth's *The Death of King Charles I* (London, 1693), sig. a2, for a further vindication of the King in connection with Milton.

[68] London, 1693; "The Preface," p. 1.

very words of Milton and had, furthermore, not only defamed *Eikon Basilike* by affirming "*That it begins with Falshood, and ends with fraud*" but also had blasphemed the person of Charles I "in the same words of that profligate Person, p. 4. of his *Iconoclastes*, viz. *That the King never loved, never fulfilled, never promoted the true Ends of Parliament*"—a debt which led Long to observe that if there were such a thing as "a Metempsychosis," then surely "the Souls of *Bradshaw*, *Milton*, and other Regicides" had migrated into the souls of "this Juncto of Republicans," that is, into Ludlow and his followers, who accepted the Settlement as a triumph of the theory of compact.[69]

So great was Long's concern over the migration of Milton's soul that, though he loathed to "defile" his hands by meddling with the old regicide, he nevertheless felt it incumbent upon himself to "stop the foul Mouths of some People whom he hath taught to object, that his Majesty made use of a Prayer made by a Heathen to a false God or Goddess in time of Captivity." In pursuit of this difficult task, he made no attempt to deny that the King had employed in his rubric of prayers the devotions of Pamela in Sidney's *Arcadia*, but he saw no reason why Milton should account such usage blasphemous. Had not St. Paul himself employed for religious purposes the words of a heathen philosopher and poet? For Long, the prayer in its new form possessed a certain beauty and holiness and hence he saw no reason why anyone should object to either it or its author.[70] In contrast to such sanctity, as Long had observed at the outset, Milton was "a Compendium of all the Villanies and Impieties of the Age," "a profest Enemy to Monarchy," "a Pleader for Divorces on Trivial Occasions, and against Tithes and the Clergy," an "Infamous" man "whom the Regicides hired by the Price of three hundred Pounds" to deface the memory of Charles I.[71] From such a man, Long believed, no good could come; but he was forced to admit that Milton and his disciples, through *Eikonoklastes* and its various Williamite adaptations, had subverted many to favor the doctrines which in reality underlay the Settlement of William and Mary but which Tory Jurors still feared would dissolve the very foundations of Church and State.

69 *Dr. Walker's True, Modest, and Faithful Account*, pp. 4–5.

70 *Ibid.*, pp. 59 ff.

71 *Ibid.*, p. 2. See *The Royal Martyr* (London, 1693), pp. 226–27, for a repetition of Perrinchief's earlier vituperation; and John Hacket, *Scrinia Reserata* (Savoy, 1693), II, 161–62, for choice epithets probably written about 1655 but not printed until 1693. The 1693 issue of *The Royal Martyr*, it should be noted, may exist by title page only.

To such tacit and expressed testimony of Milton's influence in the years immediately following the Glorious Revolution, Thomas Rogers, an avowed enemy of Whig doctrines, added an estimate that Milton and Ludlow together had guided thousands of people to accept the principles which legally placed William and Mary on the English throne. An early supporter of the Settlement but now, in 1694, suddenly frightened by the inroads of revolutionary thought, Rogers offered this estimate to the people of England in answer to William Stephens, who, in a sermon preached before the Mayor and Aldermen of London, had denied that the Settlement meant the supremacy of Parliament. Stephens had admitted, it is true, that "Princes may be said to be accountable to their People," but he had hastened to add that "it would be very false reasoning from hence to conclude, That because God is pleased in such a manner to submit his Sovereign Administrations to the Judgment of Men, (and Men will in the like manner judge of the Actions of Princes) that therefore a People may assume to themselves a Judicial Power over their Sovereign Lord." He had indeed dismissed the "Pretence of the High Court of Justice to judge of their King" as "an upstart monstrous Opinion, hatch'd by the heat of War," "an Insect of a Days Duration," "never own'd by the Body of the People."[72] With such an appraisal of the ideological conflict in 1694, Thomas Rogers could hardly agree. In a direct but heavy-humored answer to Stephens, he pointed out that the concept of popular supremacy, or the right of a people to judge of their king, stretched back to Knox and Buchanan, and some "*English* Apers" of Mariana and Suarez, and that with the aid of Milton and Ludlow this principle had become favored of many:

It was so far from being an *Insect of a Days duration*, That, as it was the most Prodigious Monster on this side Hell (and never Equall'd by any Poet's Invention, Enthusiastical Draughts of Antichrist, or Melancholy Vision of a Pining and Despairing Lover) so was it also Nurst with all Imaginable Tenderness and Care, Christen'd by *Milton* and other Famous Apologists, and borne about with great Ostentation and Triumph. And whosoever shall peruse the *Secret History* (propagated throughout the Nation) the Works of *Milton* (of ever Blessed Memory) the Letters of *Ludlow* (that pretious Orator in Christ Jesus) I say, whosoever shall peruse the Writings of these Legendary

[72] *A Sermon Preached before the Right Honourable the Lord Mayor, And Aldermen of the City of London, At St. Mary-Le-Bow, Jan. 30th. 1693/4* (London, 1694), pp. 14–16. By the turn of the century, Stephens had become an ardent supporter of Whig principles.

Scriblers, and observe withal what kind Entertainment they have met with in the World, amongst the *well-affected, the harmless, and the hidden ones*; will readily conclude, That there are Thousands among us who are so far from *disowning*, that they secretly Applaud, the Glorious and Triumphant Villany.[73]

Rogers not only estimated here that thousands of persons had favorably received the doctrine of Parliamentary supremacy through Ludlow and Milton but also recognized that with the Revolutionary Settlement it had actually triumphed. Why, then, had Stephens equivocated? Why had he given allegiance to a government whose actual principles he both denied and claimed were ephemeral? Why had he not, Rogers concluded in a mock sermon, flatly declared that he could "no more Digest the Fulsom and Crude Tenets of *Milton* and *Ludloe*," together with "the Black and Dirty Divinity" of the "New *Mechanick* Apostles," than he could "the Dreams of a *Bridget* or *Juliana*, or the whole *Council* of *Trent*."[74] This, at least, would have been honest.

Out of the mouths of Jurors and Nonjurors themselves thus came testimony that Milton's program for man and society had prepared the people of England to accept the rationale of the Settlement. Though Thomas Wagstaffe might report that the venerable William Sancroft had resisted encroachments upon the doctrines of divine right and passive obedience and hence had refused to swear allegiance to William and Mary, and that he had been as little satisfied with rebellious principles "when baited with modern Names" as "when they came immediately from the Pens and Persons of the first Authors themselves, from *Regicide Cook*, and *Milton*, from *John Goodwin*, and *Hugh Peters*,"[75] many others apparently succumbed to the barrage of Williamite tracts. Indeed, Jacobites apparently agreed that the "disciples and followers of Buchanan, Hobbs, and Milton" had, through their activity, sown discord through the world, "the influence of evil principles" having no bounds but, like "infectious air," spreading over the whole earth.[76] But to this recognized triumph even

[73] *A True Protestant Bridle: Or Some Cursory Remarks Upon A Sermon Preached before the Lord Mayor, At St. Mary-Le-Bow, Jan. 30th 1693/4* (London, 1694), pp. 7–8.

[74] *Ibid.*, p. 24. In *The Common-Wealths-Man Unmasqu'd* (London, 1694), pp. 67–68, Rogers spoke of Milton as a man who "durst say any thing in the perillous Times of Darkness and Usurpation."

[75] *A Letter out of Suffolk to A Friend in London* (London, 1694), p. 18.

[76] Sir Philip Warwick, *A Discourse of Government* (London, 1694), sig. A4. Written 1678, this book appeared in 1694 with prefatory matter appropriate to the times.

Milton's disciples scarcely nodded their heads to give their master his due. Charles Blount, to be sure, signed the initials J. M. to his *Reasons Humbly offered for the Liberty of Unlicens'd Printing*; and Ludlow, in his conflict with Richard Hollingworth, once gave Milton acclaim for his having first discovered the forgery of Pamela's prayer.[77] Furthermore, Sir P. Georgeson openly referred to Milton in *The Defence of the Parliament of England in the Case of James the II*;[78] and the publisher of Joseph Washington's translation of *Pro Populo Anglicano Defensio* went so far as to state that Milton and his book were "*sufficiently*" known both at home and abroad, and that in it he had, with "*great Freedom of Language, and Strength of Reason,*" detected "*the Fallacy of all the Cobweb Arguments made use of by the Flatterers of Princes, to prove their Power to be derived immediately from God, and to be superior to that of the Law, whether deduced from Scripture, Reason, or Authority.*"[79] Whigs signally failed, however, to proclaim to the people of England what Tories had long known and publicly disclosed: that Whigs had employed Milton's tracts and by so doing had made many favor the principles underlying the Settlement. Discipleship as successful as this could not go much longer unclaimed; sooner or later, in the fullness of political time, Whigs would find it expedient to acknowledge their master and to acclaim his power and genius.

[77] *Truth Brought to Light* (London, 1693), p. 31.
[78] London, 1692; p. 21.
[79] 1692, sigs. A3-A3v. The translation also appeared in 1695.

Chapter Five

WHIG THEORY TRIUMPHANT

THE TURN OF the seventeenth century witnessed almost a complete realignment of the principal parties which had dominated the political scene in England since the attempted Whig revolution. After the deposition of James II and the settling of the Crown upon William and Mary, fewer and fewer, either in the Church or without, could accept Jacobite claims that the absconded king still legally ruled by divine right and by laws of inheritance, though loyalties flared in 1715 with the Old Pretender and in 1745 with Bonnie Prince Charlie, both of whom symbolized the rights of primogeniture. In the main, however, Englishmen began to turn away from the concept of a hereditary, absolute throne. At the death of Queen Mary in 1694, for example, those who had approved the new government because they could see through her an unbroken hereditary link now had to find other reasons for their support of the Settlement. Moreover, with the attempt on William's life in 1696, Whigs forced on many Tories the admission that if the sovereign were not the "rightful and lawful" king, he at least held "the right by law."[1] Furthermore, Robert Harley,[2] one of the most notable Tories of the time, strove to turn his party away from Jacobitism and attempted to change it into a party of constitutionalism. In addition to this, the Act of Settlement in 1701, which secured a Hanoverian succession, received the fervid approval of both Tories and Whigs. When Queen Anne ascended the throne in 1702, the old parties, which, before the Glorious Revolution, could be distinguished by their sharp differences on the nature of kingship, no longer existed, and new alignments, at least on ideological grounds, had not yet become clearly distinguishable. Indeed, both parties now accepted principles of government for which Whigs had long argued. Continued support of the Revolution, wide acceptance of the Bill of Rights, the lapse of the Licensing Act, and the Settlement of 1701 all testify that, except for a diminishing number of Jacobites, Whig doctrines had at last triumphed in Englishmen's minds.

[1] See Keith Feiling, *A History of the Tory Party* (Oxford, 1924), p. 319.

[2] Early in life a Whig, Harley turned toward the Tory party in the last decade of the seventeenth century.

With this victory of Whig principles the party which owed Milton so much at long last gave him proper acclaim. His nephew, Edward Phillips, began the parade of adulation in 1694 with a short account of his life prefixed to an edition of Milton's *Letters of State.* In 1697 a collection of *Poems on Affairs of State,* obviously Whig inspired, saw Milton as a great defender of liberty; and in the same year John Toland, one of the most articulate Whigs at the turn of the century, gave to the people of England the first collection of Milton's tracts, which he followed in the next year by *A Complete Collection of the Historical, Political, and Miscellaneous Works of John Milton, both English and Latin; with some Papers never before Published,* and a commendatory biographical account. Moreover, in the next year, he published a defense of Milton's life under the title of *Amyntor;* and in the same year Charles Gildon, a defender of Whig views, seconded Toland's adulation in a shorter sketch of his life. Such sudden acclaim, after years of Whig silence, naturally attracted the attention of Jacobites, who created new myths to tarnish his name; but despite expressions of hatred for the man and his doctrines,[3] some of which still color critical comment, the new century opened with Milton firmly established as a great spokesman of the Whig party and a great defender of the rights and liberties of the English people.

I

The debate over liberty of conscience and the power of kings which began early in the seventeenth century came to a close, in so far as its issues affected high government policy, during the reign of King William. This is not to say that the issues of toleration, divine right, and passive obedience ceased to be topics of interest or of heated discussion. The doctrine of passive obedience particularly continued to arouse strong emotions well into the following century, though it took on a new meaning; but with the opening of the Age of Reason so many Englishmen had come to accept Whig principles that, in times of crisis, like the attempt on William's life in 1696 and his demise in 1702, public discussion revealed no acrimonious cleavage on matters

[3] See particularly John Robert Moore, "Milton Among the Augustans: The Infernal Council," *Studies in Philology,* XLVIII (1951), 15–25, for a discussion of how considerations of Church and State affected comment on Milton early in the eighteenth century. For a political interpretation of *Paradise Lost* in the eighteenth century, see George W. Whiting, "The Politics of Milton's Apostate Angels," *Notes & Queries,* CLXIII (1932), 384–86.

which split the country at the time of the Popish Plot and the Rye House conspiracy but rather disclosed a general agreement that the government of England, though monarchical, stood squarely on the theory of compact and that the law as enacted in Parliament, not the king, was supreme. Such conclusions to the great debate found acceptance even among clergymen who before the Glorious Revolution would have shied away from such doctrines as they would have from the plague. Once enough men could be brought to see that the principles which allowed them to support the government of William and Mary matched many which had animated the Puritan Rebellion, acclaim for Milton could only logically follow.

Jacobites themselves, through sermons and pamphlets, inadvertently brought some to this understanding. Charles Leslie, for example, a Nonjuror to the end, while searching into the reasons for Tories having been "shifted out apace" and, openly and aboveboard, members of "the *Fanatical* and *Whiggish* Tribe" having been placed in positions of "*Trust* and *Profit*," and for men having forsaken and neglected the Church, concluded that, for one thing, Tories had lost out because the Dissenters had caught them in "a very *fatal Dilemma*" and had "Improv'd it amongst the *People*."[4] The dilemma was fatal indeed. For if, Leslie continued, Tories stuck to "*Passive Obedience* in the High Sense," as it had been expressed in the Homily against Willful Rebellion, then they, if Jurors, must condemn what they had done and still continued to do. But if, on the other hand, they called the doctrine an error, then they must admit that the Church had been "all along, before this Revolution, a false Guide," and that the Dissenters had "taught the Truth, in this point of Doctrine." People would therefore conclude, Leslie went on, that it would be safer to trust the Dissent than the Church; they would say that the Dissent had never gone over to the Church "in any of their *Doctrines*" but that the Church had gone over to the Dissent in that very belief which it had "Formerly pressed as Positively and Zealously as any other *Doctrine* of the *Gospel*; nay, more than most others, and as Indispensibly necessary to Salvation." Would a people thus prejudiced against the Church be zealous for it? Would they passionately oppose

[4] *Querela Temporum: Or the Danger of the Church of England* [London, 1695], p. 21. It is interesting to note that Leslie, in his Preface to *The History of Sin and Heresy* (1698), questioned some unorthodoxies in *Paradise Lost*. See *The Theological Works of the Reverend Mr. Charles Leslie* (London, 1721), I, 777–78.

the Dissent, to whom the Church had at last submitted in the "so long boasted *Characteristical Discrimination* of *Passive Obedience*"? How could the Church retract "all the hard Words" given the Dissent for opposing the doctrine the Church now professed?[5] Leslie failed to answer these rhetorical questions; but he held up, without fear or favor, the dilemma which had caught Jurors like William Sherlock; and, furthermore, he pointed out that the death of Queen Mary had broken the last hereditary link with the throne, an event which, he observed, would force King William to turn more than ever to Whig theory for support of his government.[6] The dilemma itself, as well as the death of the Queen, offered good reasons why Jacobites continued to lose the support of the people; and by the same token both must have driven many to accept the Whig rationale of the Settlement.

Nevertheless, voices still rose to defend the Settlement by the dubious device of accepting the new government *de facto* and at the same time of recognizing James II as the sovereign of England *de jure*. In *A Letter to Mr. Secretary Trenchard* in 1694, it was estimated that among Jurors two out of every three recognized King William "by *Exercise*, but not by *Right*," that in this matter Sherlock had "many more Followers than *Johnson*," the "Rich, Great, Learned being of the *Sentiments* of the former, whereas few but your unthinking *Mob*, and downright *Republicans* . . . [were] of the belief of the latter."[7] The accuracy of this estimate would be hard to determine, but it is certain that a number of clergymen still openly held to their old beliefs in divine right and passive obedience and refused, as yet, to admit that acceptance of King William meant, as Charles Leslie made clear, a repudiation as false of what the Church had long taught and an agreement with doctrines of the Dissent. Peter Birch, for example, in a sermon preached before the House of Commons on the anniversary of the martyred Charles I, uttered many of the old sentiments, yet as a Juror he gave allegiance to the government under whose sufferance he officially spoke. But if Birch himself failed to see his own intellectual dilemma, a member of Commons, who presumably heard the sermon, arose to castigate him for his stupidity. The trouble with clergymen, this member declared in *A Birchen Rod for Dr. Birch*, is that they "are never *aware of the Consequences of*

[5] *Querela Temporum*, p. 21. [6] *Ibid.*, pp. 30–31.

[7] *A Letter to Mr. Secretary Trenchard, Discovering a Conspiracy against the Laws and Ancient Constitution of England* ([London], 1694), p. 6.

their own Doctrine," as "witness that unhappy one of *Passive Obedience,* which was good, nay superlatively good, and the *Characteristick* of the Church, so long as the Court and Church did agree together; but whenever the Court came to touch the Church in her own Property, then *this Characteristick* was *laid aside, and Passive Obedience turn'd to actual Resistance.*" To make his rod sting the more, this wroth member of Commons recalled that the Church had considered it "horrid, nay damnable Doctrine" in Lord Russell and others "to Associate for the defence of their Lives, Liberties and Religion, and Mutinous for them to Petition their Prince on that Head; but it gave the Seven Petitioning Bishops a Right to the Title of Confessors, to Address and Cabal against King *James,* for giving Liberty to Dissenters."[8]

Such flagrant inconsistency made no sense, and hence neither did Birch's adherence to the old doctrine and concurrent acceptance of the Settlement; nor could this member of Commons find that Birch had resolved any more satisfactorily the Juror dilemma of divine right. To him, the Settlement stood as testimony that the King held his title by compact, that, if some still wished to call him chosen of God, "*The Choice of the People*" was all the "Evidence" that could now be advanced to claim his divine appointment.[9] *Vox Populi, Vox Dei.* "And though this doctrine," this member of Commons concluded with a final thrust at Birch, "was in the late Reigns cried down as Rebellious, yet most thinking-Men are sufficiently convinced, that it was without any shadow of Justice: and if it be otherwise, as the Doctor would seem to hint by the tenor of his Discourse, it shews how well he deserves to eat Their Majesties Bread, who would go about to shake Their Title."[10] The title to the throne, legally invested in William and Mary by the Convention Parliament, derived indeed not from the doctrine of divine right but from the theory of compact; and if in 1694 two-thirds of the Jurors still considered James II their sovereign *de jure,* many "thinking men" apparently held other opinions.

With the attempt on King William's life in 1696, which was to serve as a prelude to a French invasion, opinion veered sharply in favor of Whig views and in opposition to passive obedience. By this time relentless attacks upon equivocators of William Sherlock's stamp by both Whigs and Nonjurors made it exceedingly difficult for men to hold

[8] [London], 1694, pp. 5–6. [9] *A Birchen Rod for Dr. Birch,* p. 8. [10] *Idem.*

to their old Tory beliefs and to have their new king, too. What man of right mind, for example, could answer the logic of George Hickes, who unkindly, at least from a Tory Juror point of view, recalled in print that Gilbert Burnet and John Tillotson had, in the celebrated case of Lord Russell, informed that unfortunate lord even as he went to the block that the doctrine of passive obedience commanded absolute loyalty to the Crown and allowed no resistance under any circumstance whatever?[11] How could their advice to a doomed man square with their open rebellion against James II? Support of the Settlement by reference to the theory of compact might wrench many an old Tory conscience, but it could hardly violate the canons of logic. At any rate, the attempt on King William's life forced many clergymen to search into and lay open reasons for their lending support to the government; and in their thanksgiving sermons for the sovereign's happy deliverance, in sharp contrast to those which followed the discovery of the Rye House conspiracy, the balance of opinion fell noticeably upon the Whig side. William Wake, for example, consecrated Archbishop of Canterbury in 1716, made an especial point of demonstrating the rationality of the revolt against James II. Before he came to this conclusion, he first discussed, among many things, the concept of a limited monarchy, which he defined as a government of mutual trust between subject and king, both of whom recognized laws of the people's approval. Such a concept of constitutional government, he explained, if it "be not a *Meer Notion*, that has neither *Meaning*, nor *Priviledge* in it," allowed people to provide lawfully for their own safety. "In short," he declared in summarizing his case, "if it be Absurd to say, that a whole *Kingdom* may have a *right* to its *Laws* and *Liberties*, and yet have *no right* to *defend* them, tho' they should never so *Apparently*, or in such *considerable Instances*, be *Broken* in upon; tho' such things should be enterprized, as all Men must see were *design'd*, and if not prevented, must *End* in a total *Dissolution* of the *Constitution:* Then had *This Kingdom* also Reason to stand up in Defence of its *Laws*, and its *Religion*, establish'd by Those *Laws:* And to lay hold on the Happy Opportunity of the *Desertion* of a *King*, who was resolved rather not to *Rule* at all, than not to *Rule* in his *Own Way*."[12]

[11] *Some Discourses Upon Dr. Burnet and Dr. Tillotson* (London, 1695), pp. 35–36.

[12] *A Sermon Preached in the Parish Church of St. James Westminster, April XVI th. 1696* (London, 1696), pp. 9–10.

With such Whig theories of resistance Francis Gregory, the Rector of Hambleden, fully agreed, though he too, with William Wake, displayed a deference to Tory opinion by stating that the Revolution came with the desertion of James II. As a clergyman, he spoke of kings as the anointed of God, referring specifically to David, who through the seventeenth century had allowed the Anglican Church to make claims for divine right. David was "God's anointed by his own immediate and *special Command*," Gregory maintained; but he went on to say that in modern times no such king could "be found in all the World; none *named* from *Heaven*, none anointed or *crowned* by *God*'s own immediate Institution." Perhaps it could be said, he continued, that Providence guided Prince William through the hazards of arriving in England; perhaps God moved the "*Nobility* and *Gentry* to place this Prince upon that *Throne*, which the late King had *deserted*."[13] But only in this sense could King William be viewed as the Lord's special vicegerent on earth. And with this repudiation of the doctrine of divine right in the old Tory sense he declared that if it were "put to the general Vote" of the nation "whether the *late King* should be restored, or the *present King* be continued" he was sure that, "aside the *Roman Catholicks* and the debauched *Ruffians*" of the age, "of twenty Religious and sober *Protestants*, nineteen would vote for *King William*." His opinion was that the attempt on the King's life had "given him a *greater* Share in the Affections of his loyal Subjects; and thereby settled him the more *firmly* upon his Throne."[14]

William Stephens, now an open exponent of Whig doctrines, confirmed this conclusion. Deploring the Jacobite equivocation of accepting James II *de jure* but William *de facto*, a piece of reasoning which he believed inspired the attempt on the King's life and the plan for a French invasion, Stephens recalled that Jacobites had with "wonderful Zeal and Industry" defended the "weak Title (if it be any)" of possession and conquest not by "Address" but by "meer Noise and Effrontery," and had confronted with enmity those who had "asserted His Majesty's Right to the Crown, from the Peoples Grant in Parliament." But, though the King's dutiful subjects had "been discouraged, because they own'd themselves bound in Conscience to support his Rightful Title, whilst the Right of King *James* was sacredly pre-

[13] *A Thanksgiving Sermon For the Deliverance of Our King From the Late Intended Assassination of his Sacred Person* (London, 1696), pp. 9–10.

[14] *Ibid.*, pp. 10–11.

served and warmly defended by the *De Facto* Subjects of King *William*," Stephens implied that Jacobites of this kind had not been successful. Did "these Apostates think to impose their Passive Doctrine of blind Obedience upon the Protestant Church and Kingdom of *England?*" Did "they think" that the King's true subjects could not "rightly distinguish this matter? as for instance, Passive Obedience to the Law of the Land, is the Doctrine of *Jesus;* Passive Obedience to the will of the Prince, is the Doctrine of *Judas;* a false and trayterous Doctrine, whereby all civil Governments and legal Rights are betray'd to arbitrary Power."[15] Such a definition of passive obedience, coupled with Francis Gregory's Whiggish definition of the Lord's anointed, gave George Hickes good reason to rise up and condemn many in the Church as traitors to the old Tory cause. By 1696 a majority in the Church had indeed accepted William as their king by reference to Whig principles of government.

The death of King William and the ascent of Queen Anne to the throne inspired the same Whiggish sentiments. Thus John Piggott, in *The Natural Frailty of Princes Consider'd*, declared flatly that the principles which had governed the Glorious Revolution also gave to Queen Anne the scepter and crown, though he hastened to add that she also derived her right "by a long Succession of Royal Ancestors." These principles, clarified by reference to William Wake's thanksgiving sermon of 1696, he stated succinctly: that no pretense of allegiance or duty could justify trust in a prince whose visible conduct declared his defiance to Heaven and whose arts of government were leveled "against the Laws of God, and those of the Realm over which he presides"; that, though magistry must be conceived of as an ordinance of God, "if a Prince once break his Coronation Oath, and invade the Liberties of his People, he is no longer a Prince but a Tyrant; for certainly the People have as just a Right to the legal Government of the Prince, as the Prince has to the legal Obedience of the People."[16]

Such sentiments could hardly be distinguished from those which animated Whigs, either in 1702 or in earlier times; and this was, in fact, the point of Daniel Defoe's *A New Test of the Church of Eng-*

[15] *A Thanksgiving Sermon Preach'd before the Right Honourable The Lord Mayor, Court of Aldermen, Sheriffs and Companies of the City of London, At St. Mary-le-Bow, April 16, 1696* (London, 1696), the Dedication and p. 24.

[16] *The Natural Frailty of Princes Consider'd; In a Sermon Preach'd the 29th of March, 1702* (London, 1702), pp. 6–7.

land's Loyalty, one of the clearest expositions of divine right and passive obedience in all their absurdities to appear at the turn of the century. Defoe stressed that neither Church nor the Dissent adhered to such doctrines, that they both rebelled against royal prerogatives whenever kings invaded the liberties and properties of the people, as history, he maintained, could easily demonstrate. The Puritans, he recalled, joined with Parliament and rebelled against the tyrannies of Charles I in 1640; in 1688, "the *Faithful, Passively Obedient, Unshakenly Loyal* Church, return'd to the Original Nature of their Neighbours, and did the same thing exactly which the Whigs, *the Factious Rebellious Whigs*, had done before." And to the followers of William Sherlock, who might claim that in the Glorious Revolution the Church did not dip its "Hands in Royal Blood, nor hurt the Lord's Anointed," Defoe replied that the only difference was that "the Whigs in 41. to 48. took up Arms against their King; and having conquer'd him, and taken him Prisoner, cut off his Head, *because they had him:* The Church of *England* took Arms against their King in 88. and did not cut off his Head, *because they had him not.*"[17] Yet, though both Church and the Dissent *acted* the same in times of stress, Defoe made it clear that, of the two, the Whigs had been the more honest. For Whigs had "never profest any such blind, absolute and undisputed Obedience to Princes" as the other party had done; it had always been their opinion "That Government was originally contrived by the Consent, and for the mutual Benefit of the Parties Govern'd, that the People have an Original Native Right to their Property, the Liberty of their Persons and Possessions, *unless forefaulted to the Laws*, that they cannot be divested of this Right but by their own Consent, and that all Invasion of this Right is destructive of the Constitution, and dissolves the Compact of Government and Obedience."[18] Though Defoe mentioned that some in the Church still adhered to doctrines their actions so patently denied, his clear analysis showing that the two parties actually stood together on many positions, together with testimony from some in the Church, indicates that, by the end of King William's reign, Whig theories had gone far in conquering men's minds.[19]

[17] *A New Test of the Church of England's Loyalty: Or, Whiggish Loyalty and Church Loyalty Compar'd* ([London], 1702), p. 13.

[18] *Ibid.*, pp. 14–15.

[19] See W. K. Jordan, *The Development of Religious Toleration in England* (4 vols; London, 1932–40) for earlier phases of this battle.

Subsequent political history in England testifies to the validity of this conclusion. After the reign of William III, no party of any significance argued again for the concept of divine right or the doctrine of passive obedience as Tories had reasoned during the times of Charles II. In truth, the principles of constitutional government, embodied in the Revolutionary Settlement and in the Bill of Rights, inspired Whigs and Tories alike through the next two centuries and a half, however much they might have differed on other issues, both foreign and domestic. The triumph of Whig theory in Englishmen's minds was not to suffer a reversal.

II

Milton came into his own as an organ voice of the party which owed him so much shortly after the triumph of Whig theory. Though the party never officially admitted that for years its members had employed, without acknowledgment, pertinent parts of his program for man and society and had made his arguments their own, exponents of Whig principles now answered aspersions that Tories had cast upon his motives and character and raised him to heights of political wisdom and literary fame. Disciples could do no less for a master who had served them and their party so well.

Edward Phillips, Milton's nephew and pupil, opened the way for such exoneration and praise in a biographical sketch prefacing his edition of Milton's *Letters of State*. Not an avowed Whig and supposedly unaffected, as John Evelyn had claimed, by his uncle's political principles, Phillips nevertheless displayed sympathy for the Puritan Rebellion and for the role Milton had enacted in that dramatic event. As a student, he had sat at Milton's feet and learned Latin and Greek; as an author of sorts, he had presumably expressed many of his tutor's opinions on lexicography and poetry. And now, in 1694, he thought the time ripe to translate Milton's letters of state and to answer Tory attacks of long standing. To the Tory sneer that Milton had been a mere pedagogue, and a needy one at that, Phillips answered that it was "well known he never set up for a Publick School to teach all the young Fry of a Parish, but only was willing to impart his Learning and Knowledge to Relations, and the Sons of some Gentlemen that were his intimate Friends."[20] To the Tory accusation that Milton had ac-

[20] *Letters of State* (London, 1694), p. xxviii. In 1694 Sir Thomas Pope Blount in *De Re Poetica* (pp. 135–38 in "Characters and Censures") gave an account of Milton as a poet, but also

cepted the secretaryship of foreign tongues out of mercenary motives to advance his estate, Phillips replied that "he was courted into the Service of this new Commonwealth, and at last prevail'd with (for he never hunted after Preferment, nor affected the Tintamar and Hurry of Publick business) to take upon him the Office of *Latin* Secretary to the Counsel of State for all their Letters to Foreign Princes and States."[21] To the exultant Tory chant that Milton's blindness had come as a judgment of God for his having answered *Eikon Basilike*, Phillips felt constrained to say that it was "most certainly known, that his Sight, what with his continual Study, his being subject to the Head-ake, and his perpetual tampering with Physick to preserve it, had been decaying for above a dozen years before, and the sight of one for a long time clearly lost."[22] Indeed, through the whole of his account Phillips relieved Milton from the calumny that had clustered about his name since the Puritan Rebellion and presented him as a man of high motive and genuine excellence. He unhesitatingly and, he believed, safely and justly affirmed that Milton, taken in all his respects, was "for Acumen of Wit, Quickness of Apprehension, Sagacity of Judgement, Depth of Argument, and Elegancy of Style, as well in *Latin* as *English*, as well in Verse as Prose . . . scarce to be parallel'd by any the best of Writers . . . [the] Nation hath in any Age brought forth."[23] Now Tories, of course, had allowed Milton such powers of expression and largeness of mind, but Phillips' praise for both the man and his talents struck a new note and in a very real sense opened up the era of great Whig acclaim.

At any rate, Charles Gildon, an author reputedly dependent upon Whigs for his livelihood, took occasion once in 1694 and again in 1699 to acknowledge Milton's greatness both as a poet and as a political writer. Though undistinguished for either his person or talents, Gildon wrote extensively on poetry and politics and in a series of letters and essays, one of which he addressed "*To Mr.* T. S. *in Vindication of Mr.* Milton'*s Paradist lost*," indirectly replied to the Tory legend that Milton had lost his sight because of the judgment of God. As a

said, following Edward Phillips' earlier comment, that he was sufficiently known to all the learned of Europe by "his other Works, both in *Latin* and *English*." Joseph Addison also commented at this time, in verse, on Milton as a poet and as a writer of prose.

21 *Ibid.*, p. xxx.

22 *Ibid.*, p. xxxiv.

23 *Ibid.*, p. iii. See *The Present State of Europe*, V, No. 11 (November 1694), p. 378, for a reference to Milton's *Letters of State*, printings of which had appeared earlier, in 1676, 1682, and 1690. Phillips' edition and that appearing in 1682 were translations.

matter of course, he praised "Mr. *Milton*'s admirable Dexterity in this his *Matchless Performance*," confessing that all he could say would fall short of giving Milton his due merits; and then, with Milton's greatness duly averred, he ventured to say further that Milton could not have sung of unrevealed Heavenly mysteries "had he not been altogether depriv'd of his *Outward Sight*, and thereby made capable of such *continued Strenuous, Inward Speculations.*" The "*bountiful Powers* above" indeed, Gildon continued, "did more than make him amends for their taking away his Sight, by so *Illumining* his Mind, as to enable him *most compleatly* to sing of *Matchless Beings, Matchless Things*, before *unknown* to, and even *unthought* of by the whole race of Men; thus rewarding him for a *Temporary Loss*, with an *Eternal Fame*, of which *Envy* it self shall not be able ever to deprive this *best of Poems*, or its most *Judicious Author.*"[24] What Tories had seen as a punishment, Gildon interpreted as a reward; and in contrast to Winstanley's contention that Milton's fame had gone out like a snuffed candle, Gildon claimed that despite the onslaughts of envy it would live always. Furthermore, in his revision of *The Lives and Characters of the English Dramatick Poets*, Gildon changed Langbaine's derogation of Milton's principles and person into unqualified praise. To Gildon, Milton was "An Author of that Excellence of Genius and Learning, that none of any Age or Nation," in his opinion, had excelled him; he had been, moreover, "advanced to considerable Posts in the Government, as Under Secretary of State, *&c.* and he was a strenuous Defender of the Power and Liberty of the People, upon which that Government immediately stood."[25] Gildon here not only exonerated Milton and praised his achievements but also looked with some favor upon the Commonwealth government itself, which he declared had been based upon liberty. With the triumph of Whig theory, even the Puritan Rebellion, the remembrance of whose chaos had long made members of both parties uneasy, began to take on the appearance of an event ultimately fortunate for the people of England.

Milton's greatest champion at the turn of the century, however, was neither Edward Phillips nor Charles Gildon but John Toland, the celebrated deist whose freethinking, as well as his politics, brought him in conflict with the established Church. Too independent of mind,

[24] *Miscellaneous Letters and Essays, On Several Subjects* (London, 1694), pp. 41–44.
[25] London, 1699, p. 100.

perhaps, to attach himself officially to any definite party, he nevertheless sought and found patronage among Whigs in both city and court and wrote in behalf of their political principles. Such affiliations led him to publish, in 1697, *The Works of John Milton*,[26] which he followed in the next year with a complete edition of Milton's prose, both Latin and English, and an extended account of his life, the latter appearing separately as well as a part of the three-volume edition. Moreover, he followed these publications in 1699 with *Amyntor*, a defense of his interpretation of Milton's life and works, together with a history of *Eikon Basilike*. And even as Toland completed the first part of this generous program, another voice united with his to proclaim Milton a great exponent of freedom. In the Preface to *Poems on Affairs of State*, whose declared design was "to remove those pernicious Principles" which lead "directly to Slavery" and "to promote a Publick and Generous Spirit," Milton appeared, along with Andrew Marvell, as an illustration "that there is nowhere a greater Spirit of Liberty to be found, than in those who are Poets."[27] Unfortunately for the design of this collection, no poem by Milton actually appeared; the inclusion of his name both in the Preface and in the Table of Contents was apparently meant to make the volume more vendible. But Toland played no such game; he presented to the people of England for the first time the collected prose works of Milton and simultaneously, in his biographical accounts, revealed him as a great exponent of individual and political freedom.

Toland stated at the outset of his first biographical account that he intended to present Milton, without favor or fear, exactly as his subject had disclosed himself in his works. For the most part, he remained faithful to his intentions, listing Milton's faults as well as his virtues. But the picture he painted differed radically from that which Tories had conjured up during the last several decades of the seventeenth century. He stressed, for example, as Edward Phillips had also, that Milton's blindness came not as a judgment of God but as a result of long and diligent application to books. Moreover, he made

[26] The politically important *History of Britain* appeared in 1695 without comment.

[27] *Poems on Affairs of State: From The Time of Oliver Cromwell, to the Abdication of K. James the Second* ([London], 1697), "The Preface." Editions of this volume appeared from time to time at the turn of the century. See also *The Athenian Mercury* (January 16, 1691), Vol. V, No. 14, for an evaluation of Milton and Waller as poets. Jacob Tonson's promotion of Milton's poetry and Patrick Hume's full annotations on *Paradise Lost* in 1695, however, clearly gave Milton the palm.

a special point to answer Tory insinuations that Milton, as a needy pedagogue, had been inspired by mercenary motives to accept the secretaryship of foreign tongues in the Commonwealth government. By what right, he pointedly asked, had his adversaries opprobriously termed him a schoolmaster, who themselves had been but "mean Tutors in the University, and the greatest of 'em only a Professor?"[28] Such a "laborious occupation" should in no way tend to Milton's dishonor, particularly if he discharged it with due honesty and care. It was indeed, Toland maintained, the "greatest sign of a good Man in him, and the highest Obligation he could lay on his Friends," that "without any sordid or mercenary purposes" Milton had taken upon himself the hard work of teaching his pupils the principles of knowledge and virtue. But not only this. Before the advent of the Commonwealth government, he had "gratuitously lent his Country the aid of his Pen, content with the esteem of good Men, and the internal Satisfaction of having perform'd his Duty; while others that deserv'd it not so well, were variously rewarded, som with Riches, som with Honors, and all with Liberty." So generously had Milton given of his time and talents, Toland continued, that, with the publication of *The Tenure of Kings and Magistrates*, the new government, recognizing the excellency of Milton's style and his affection for the Good Old Cause, made him Latin Secretary of State, a position in which he "gain'd no less Reputation to himself than Credit to the State that imploy'd so able a Person."[29] While holding this office, he wrote his masterpiece in prose, *Pro Populo Anglicano Defensio*—a work "for Argument the noblest, as being the Defence of a whole free Nation, the People of *England;* for stile and disposition the most eloquent and elaborat, equalling the old *Romans* in the purity of their own Language, and their highest Notions of Liberty; as universally spread over the learned World as any of their Compositions; and certain to endure while Oratory, Politics, or History bear any esteem among Men."[30] This great and good man, Toland concluded, this man who had done so much for the people of England, far from being mercenary and low in his motives, "look'd upon true and absolute Freedom to be the greatest Happiness of this Life, whether to Societies or single Persons," "thought Constraint of any sort to be the utmost Misery: for which Reason he us'd to tell those about him the intire Satisfaction

[28] *The Life of John Milton* (London, 1699), pp. 26–27.
[29] *Ibid.*, pp. 80–81. [30] *Ibid.*, p. 95.

of his Mind, that he had constantly imploy'd his Strength and Faculties in the defence of Liberty, and in a direct opposition to Slavery."[31] If, to Tories, Milton had been a compendium of villainies, to Toland he was a repository of genius and virtue. After all, only good men could love freedom; and Toland left the impression, despite his final reference to Anthony Wood's portrait, that Milton's virtues far outweighed any frailties common to man.

In *Amyntor* Toland defended the portrait he had painted.[32] To Tory complaints that he should never have meddled with Milton's works or revived the quarrels of the past, he replied that his methods had revealed the true Milton and reiterated a willingness to let the chips fall where they might. In the course of this defense, which encompassed a discussion of apocryphal books of the Bible and an account of *Eikon Basilike* ,Toland indicated that his interpretation of Milton, as well as the edited works, had made inroads on the Jacobite cause by attacking "the sacred Majesty of Kings, the venerable Order of Bishops, the best constituted Church in the World," and hundreds of other things still held sacred. If this *had* been the effect, as Jacobites themselves appeared to admit, Toland could only advise them to betake themselves "for Reparation" to Milton himself, and if Milton could not be brought to easy terms, then to defend their "Castles and Territories" against him with all the vigor they possessed, for Toland claimed that he himself had writ in behalf of no party. Such a claim, of course, was only partially true; for toward the end of *Amyntor* Toland attacked Thomas Wagstaffe, Offspring Blackall, and Thomas Long—all rabid defenders of Charles I and among the most bitter of Milton's enemies; and at the same time he reviewed, by way of contrast, the tyrannies of Charles I and James II and the liberties enjoyed under the reign of King William. Through Milton, as well as in his own right, Toland spoke in behalf of the Whig cause.

Nor was he alone. In the last years of the century someone again, in the manner of Major General Ludlow, employed Milton to defend the Parliament of 1640 and the people of England against the tyrannies of Charles I;[33] and a good but anonymous Whig arose to strike down a Juror who, like William Sherlock, opposed the rationale of

[31] *Ibid.*, pp. 150–51.

[32] *Amyntor: Or, A Defence of Milton's Life* (London, 1699). See particularly pp. 1–19, 82–172.

[33] *A Defence of the Parliament of 1640* (London, 1698). See particularly pp. 15–17.

the Settlement and therefore viewed the editors of "Mr. *Harrington's Common-Wealth of Oceana*, and all Mr. *Milton*'s Antimonarchical Treatises, and that too, which justifies the *Murder* of *Charles* the First, and many Discourses of other Authors, as *Ludlow*'s Letters, and Mr. *Sidney*'s Discourse of Government" as enemies of their king and country, as men who, like the rankest Jacobites in England, employed methods of lying and slander to weaken and destroy the government of King William.[34] Only a servile drudge at court, this good Whig maintained, could take such a stand and make this comparison; only an exponent of absolute authority could revile "the Works of the Honourable Mr. *Sidney*, the judicious Mr. *Ludlow*, and the unanswerable Mr. *Harrington* and Mr. *Milton*"; and he expressed a hope that, for his attack upon the principles of these men and for his associating true supporters of the government with Jacobites, the masters of this servile drudge would "Condemn him to the Punishment of answering those Elaborate Discourses of Government, and the Liberties and Priviledges of the Subject, for then he'l undergo the Fate of *Salmasius*, and the Government will save the charge of keeping up his Coach, there being enough of Mr. *Milton*'s Scholars left to Vindicate that Noble cause, till they have Writ him to Death, as their Tutor did *Salmasius*."[35]

A sufficient number of Milton's scholars still lived indeed—men like Samuel Johnson, the architect of "the Bridg on which the *Prince of Orange* came over,"[36] and Charles Gildon and John Toland, who, in their labors to write the enemies of the Settlement to death, not only employed Milton but also advertised his works[37] and publicly proclaimed him a great and good man, a mighty champion of religious, domestic, and civil liberty. Such accolade, coupled with public approval of his political principles, opened the way for disciples in the Age of Reason to take up his banner—for Whigs like Thomas Birch, Richard Baron, Francis Blackburne, and Thomas Hollis to accept Milton as their master, to set him up before the world as an oracle of political wisdom, and to work out his principles through their own activities and writings.

34 *Cursory Remarks Upon Some Late Disloyal Proceedings* (London, 1699), pp. 6–7.

35 *A Just Rebuke Of a Late Unmannerly Libel* (London, 1699), p. 4.

36 John Toland, *Vindicius Liberius* (London, 1702), p. 73. See p. 8 for a reference to Milton.

37 See, for example, *The Post Boy*, Nos. 590 and 656 (1699); and *The Post Man*, Nos. 553, 559, 610, 628, 631 (1698, 1699).

III

Whig appraisals of Milton as a compendium of virtue and the new editions of his tracts naturally met opposition and inspired bitter reprisals. In these reprisals Tories expressed regret that the times would allow accolade to fall on him whom they considered their most inveterate foe; and, to destroy the portrait Whigs had so lavishly painted, they smeared him with stories designed to blacken his name. That Whigs had at last openly proclaimed Milton as their brother-in-arms and had now recognized before the people of England his effectiveness in party disputes made Tories more bitter than ever.

Offspring Blackall, early a Nonjuror and even after the ascent of Queen Anne suspected of Jacobite leanings, led the counterattack in a thirtieth-of-January sermon preached before the House of Commons in 1699. Though mainly concerned with the martyrdom of Charles I, he nevertheless found time to refer specifically to Toland's biography of Milton and to answer the assertion, found in that account, that *Eikon Basilike* was little more than a forgery.[38] In his sermon Blackall maintained, in accordance with Jacobite tactics, that none but the King could have written so holy a book—a position he continued to support in his answer to Toland's reply to him in *Amyntor*. Here, furthermore, in a discussion of the Apocrypha, Blackall turned Toland's arguments back on himself by reference to Milton. If Toland had questioned the authenticity of some writings about Jesus Christ because the record revealed that the Saviour had written only in sand, might it not, then, be proved that, because of his blindness, Milton could not have written *Paradise Lost* and other late pieces?[39] Common sense, of course, kept Blackall from pressing such an analogy, though he no doubt would have been glad, had he any evidence whatever, to point out that many tracts which Toland attributed to Milton had not been by his hand.

But if Offspring Blackall aimed his guns more at Toland than at Milton in his commemoration of Charles I, the same cannot be said of John Gilbert, the Vicar of St. Andrew's Plymouth and Canon of Exeter, who, in the Preface to his memorial sermon preached on January 30, 1699, directly attacked Milton and his disciples. Deploring

[38] *A Sermon Preached before the Honourable House of Commons, At St. Margaret's Westminster, January 30th, 1698/9* (London, 1699), p. 16.

[39] *Mr. Blackall's Reasons For Not Replying to a Book Lately Published, Entituled,* Amyntor (London, 1699), pp. 7–8. Milton's name appears several times in this pamphlet.

that, contrary to the liturgy commemorating the death of the martyr, men reproached the character of the King not only in private cabals but also "in Swarms of Libels, openly sold in *Westminster-Hall*, and Cry'd by the Hawkers at the *King*'s *Palace* Gate, in the Face of the Supream Authority, and Highest Judicature of the Nation," Gilbert reminded his audience that these same men just as openly, and in print, extolled and applauded "*as Protestant Heroes, English Patriots, Men full of Grace, the Knowledg of God, and true Religion; Men of Honour, Prudence,* &c. Those execrable Traytors, and proscribed Regicides, who in divers Statutes, stand Branded for horrid Murtherers, *Parricides, Miscreants, Sons of* Belial, *neither true Subjects, nor true Protestants, but Authors of the greatest Reproach and Infamy, it was possible for the greatest Enemies of God and the King, to bring on the Protestant Religion, and the Nation.*" In order that no one could possibly fail to recognize those responsible for blackening the name of the martyr and washing away the sins of Commonwealth villains, Gilbert specifically mentioned a few, among whom was Edward Phillips for his biographical sketch preceding his edition of Milton's *Letters of State*.[40] And as Gilbert developed the theme of his Preface—that Parliament itself had condemned the old regicides and had set aside, by law, a day to worship the memory of Charles I—he asked all sober men of sense to decide which would likely be in the right, "the Law, or the Libels? Parliament, or Pamphlets? Surely, all unprejudiced Men," Gilbert went on, would "believe the former, before *Cook, Milton, Goodwin, Ludlow, Jones, Oates,* and all the rest of these scandalous Traytors."[41] But apparently many remained prejudiced and believed otherwise than Gilbert had hoped that they would. At any rate, pamphlets "vindicating the whole Scene of Violence, transacted in that Bloody War against the *King*, and stigmatizing the great Instruments of the *Restoration*," among which was Milton's *Eikonoklastes*, so turned people's minds against the Church and toward the secular theories of Whigs that a loyal old Anglican presented a letter to a member of Parliament "Shewing the Necessity of Regulating the Press."[42]

Such thoughts of suppressing undesirable tracts and consequently

[40] *A Sermon Preached at St. Andrew's Plymouth, January 30th, 1698/9* (London, 1699), sig. [B2]. Gilbert did not mention Phillips by name, but simply referred to the "Pref. to *Milton*'s Letters."

[41] *Ibid.*, sig. C2v.

[42] *A Letter to a Member of Parliament, Shewing the Necessity of Regulating the Press* (Oxford, 1699), p. 37.

of preventing their influence no doubt entered the minds of many old Tories; but since public opinion at the close of the century would hardly support another Press Act, they turned to the tactics of reviling those whom Whigs had of late invoked in support of their cause. Thus William Baron, in a detailed answer to the real General Ludlow's recently published *Memoirs,* after discussing in his Preface what he called a design of the Commonwealth party to get into the "Steerage" through reprints of old regicide tracts, pointed a finger directly at John Toland as one of the main plotters, a man, according to Baron, who dared "*to recommend an* Author, *that once occasion'd several hours Debate in the* House of Commons, *whether he should not be Hang'd, and had some of his now admired* Books *order'd, and actually Burnt by the Hands of the* Common Hangman."[43] What a blessed turn of affairs, Baron went on, what a commentary on the times, "*that this Fellow*'s Works *should be all Reprinted, and for fear of too little Mischief that way, have an Abridgment of the most poisonous Passages put all together in an Account of his* Life, *with many high* Elogiums *of his* Personal Qualities, *which so far as true, might as well have been said of the* Devil, *for so they equally abus'd, according to their several* Capacities, Great Parts, Extraordinary Endowments, *to the* Dishonor *of that* God *which gave them, and the* Destruction *of* Mankind." Baron somewhat admired, to be sure, the frankness with which Toland expressly declared that the government needed reform, a project which, Baron assumed, the "*new* Club" would undertake "*according to some old* Draughts *of* Milton";[44] but it is evident that he feared, with a sort of deadly fascination, both Toland and Milton and believed he could best help his party by revealing enemy plans and by recalling to the national memory that the man whom Whigs painted in such glowing colors had once been, in the eyes of Commons, a recognized criminal. He was aware—as, of course, Whigs were, too—that character assassination often proved more effective than a sober analysis of principles. Indeed, as the theory of compact and the concept of parliamentary supremacy made inroads on men's minds, an attack upon Milton's positions might only have disclosed, as Whigs claimed, how cogently their newly avowed champion had argued for

[43] *A Just Defence of the Royal Martyr K. Charles I* (London, 1699), sig. A3v.

[44] *Ibid.*, sig. A4. For other references to Milton see pp. 10, 13; Part II, pp. 209–10, 216. See John Walter Good, *op. cit.*, p. 59, for Thomas Yalden's comment, in verse, upon the reprinting of Milton's prose.

notions now receiving widespread approval; and this was the last thing Jacobites wanted to do.

Realizing that they could best forward their cause not so much by analysis of principles as by vilification, Jacobites intensified their campaign against the character of Milton and turned him, as Whigs had Charles I, into a person without integrity or shame, a sort of moral leper to be shunned by the rest of mankind. Among those most active in this campaign was Thomas Wagstaffe, who, for his loyalty to James II, was, in 1694, secretly consecrated by other Nonjurors the Bishop of Ipswich. In the year before his consecration, he had, in the controversy over *Eikon Basilike,* questioned the authenticity of the Anglesey Memorandum and the testimony of Anthony Walker, and had produced, to his own mystification, a list of impressions of the King's Book, only half of which contained Pamela's prayer. In 1697 he returned to his task of vindicating Charles I with additional information "concerning the Mystery of this *Prayer.*" On the testimony of Thomas Gill and Francis Bernard, physicians to Henry Hills, who was Oliver Cromwell's printer, Wagstaffe announced to the people of England that Pamela's prayer was simply "an Artifice of *Bradshaw,* or *Milton* or Both, and by them surreptitiously thrust into the King's Works, to discredit the whole." To substantiate his claim, Wagstaffe reproduced, verbatim, letters written by both physicians early in May of 1694. Thomas Gill testified that Henry Hills had told him many years ago how "*Mr.* Dugard, *who was* Milton'*s intimate Friend, happen'd to be taken printing an Edition of the King's Book,* Milton *used his interest to bring him off, which he effected by the means of* Bradshaw, *but upon this Condition that* Dugard *should add* Pamela'*s Prayer to the aforesaid Books he was printing, as an attonement for his fault, they designing thereby to bring a scandall upon the Book, and blast the Reputation of its Author, pursuant to which design they industriously took care afterwards as soon as published to have it taken notice of.*" Francis Bernard's testimony was briefer but more devastating. Henry Hills had told him, he wrote, that "*he had heard* Bradshaw *and* Milton *laugh at their inserting a Prayer out of Sir* Philip Sidney'*s* Arcadia *at the end of King* Charles'*s his book and then* Milton *had jeer'd it in his answer, adding withall that they were men would stick at nothing that might gain their point . . .*"[45] Fortified with

[45] *A Vindication of King Charles the Martyr* (London, 1697), pp. 50–51.

such information, Wagstaffe could claim that Milton, not Charles I, had cheated and lied, that Milton, indeed, was a reprehensible political schemer, capable of employing any device to achieve the ends of his party.

Such accusations apparently proved so effective that Wagstaffe returned to them again in his answer to John Toland's *Amyntor*. Irked that Toland had presented Milton so favorably, Wagstaffe felt compelled, in order to discredit the Whig portrait, to review again the whole case of *Eikon Basilike* from the correspondence of Bishop Gauden in 1661 through the Anglesey Memorandum down to the testimony of many new witnesses, both living and dead; and toward the end of his review he quoted from the physicians of Henry Hills, knowing that no better evidence could be presented to make Milton appear to the public as a blackguardly villain.[46] Such information was so choice, from a Jacobite point of view, that William Baron repeated it toward the end of his vindication of Charles I, together with a story of his own, heard from his relations when he was a boy, that the printer Dugard also published George Bate's *Elenchus Motuum*, "which gave a due, that is, severe Character of many Rebels, more especially the *Regicides*, upon Detection whereof they had got the School-Master under their Lash, and would not take the Rod from over him, till gratified in this abominable *Foregery*."[47] Jacobites left no story untold that might reflect on Milton's integrity, left no tale unturned that might help destroy the picture Whigs had so sympathetically painted.

But the most imaginative story of all came neither from Thomas Wagstaffe nor from William Baron but from Edward Ward, a Jacobite pamphleteer popular known as "Ned." Giving embodiment to a legend which had developed in the latter part of the seventeenth century, Ward, in *The Secret History of the Calves-Head Clubb*, made Milton the founder of what rumor claimed was the most blasphemous political organization of the day. Ward began his history by deploring recent attacks upon the memory of Charles I, such as Toland's *Life of Milton*, for example, though he rejoiced at Thomas Wagstaffe's replies. He also revealed reports of indignities cast upon the martyred king by Ludlow, while that doughty old regicide resided in Switzerland. But such indignities, either in print or report, Ward continued,

[46] *A Defence of the Vindication of K. Charles the Martyr* (London, 1699), pp. 93–94. Milton's name, of course, appears often in this *Defence*, as well as in the second edition of *A Vindication*.

[47] Baron, *op. cit.*, pp. 209–10.

could scarcely match those officially endorsed by members of the Calves-Head Club; in fact, this strange organization appeared to him so inhuman and profane that he at first believed it existed only in fiction "contriv'd on purpose to render the *Republicans* more odious than they deserv'd."[48] An "active Whigg" in the reign of William III, however, assured him of its reality. This Whig further told him "that *Milton*, and some other Creatures of the Commonwealth, had instituted this Clubb, as he was inform'd, in Opposition to Bp. *Juxon*, Dr. *Sanderson*, Dr. *Hammond*, and other Divines of the Church of *England*," who even during the "Time of Usurpation" had compiled a service for January 30 not differing much from the official liturgy composed after the Restoration. Naturally enough, Ward went on through his informant, during the times of the Stuarts the Calves-Head Club met "with a great deal of Precaution"; but within the second year of the reign of William and Mary it convened "almost in a Publick Manner, and apprehend[ed] nothing." And what blasphemy it perpetrated! Meeting in a blind alley about Moorfields, Ward continued through still another informant, members of the Club, consisting wholly of Independents and Anabaptists, opened their sessions with a prayer, after which "the Table-Cloth was removed, the Anniversary *Anthem*, as they impiously call'd it, was sung, and a Calves-Skull fill'd with Wine or other Liquor, and then a Brimmer went about to the Pious Memory of those worthy Patriots that had kill'd the Tyrant, and deliver'd their Country from his Arbitrary Sway; and lastly, a Collection made for the Mercenary Scribler, to which every Man contributed according to his Zeal for the Cause, or the Ability of his Purse."[49] To top off this account of its ritual, Ward reproduced the anthems supposedly sung at meetings of the club from 1693 through 1697—all of them ribald or derogatory to the memory of Charles I. If Ward believed, before his friends told him otherwise, that the Calves-Head Club was merely a story contrived to render republicans more odious than they deserved, he did little to change his party's design and much to make the fiction take on the appearance of truth. By so doing, he hoped to make a rumor even more damaging to the Whig cause.

[48] *The Secret History of the Calves-Head Clubb, or, The Republican Unmasqu'd* (London, 1703), p. 8. See also *An Answer to an Infamous Libel* ([London], 1701), p. 15, for a reference to Milton in connection with a character of a "Modern Whig."

[49] *Ibid.*, pp. 9–10.

The Jacobite campaign to destroy the Whig portrait of Milton and to discredit the principles for which he stood, however imaginative, could only fail. Jacobites might cry, with Edmund Elys, "Monstrum Impudentiæ horrendum!"[50] But Jacobitism weakened as the new century unrolled, Whig principles continued to triumph in men's minds, and more and more disciples flocked to Milton's poetical and political standard. Nevertheless, stories of Milton's chicanery, some of which high churchmen sincerely believed,[51] brought fears to Queen Anne, prompted political interpretations of *Paradise Lost*, and colored criticism of Milton for more than two centuries. The legend of the Calves-Head Club perhaps never gained general credence, but the testimony of Henry Hills, which Thomas Wagstaffe accepted without question, bobbed up from time to time to serve Milton's enemies and only recently has been placed in the realms of political fiction.[52] The very vigor of the Jacobite campaign to discredit the biographies of John Toland and other disciples stands as evidence of how much Milton had contributed to the strength of the Whig party.

IV

The triumph of Whig theory, which appropriately concluded the century of debate over liberty of conscience and the power of kings, brought England to the Age of Reason with a government pretty firmly established upon constitutional grounds. After the turn of the century, few would be inclined to argue for an Erastian concept of Church and State or for an absolute monarch appointed directly by God to whom subjects owed absolute passive obedience. Rather, the majority of Englishmen seemed to approve toleration within limits, the Whig theory of compact, and the concept of parliamentary supremacy, all of which now began to take on the appearance of rational, self-evident truths; and to this shift in public opinion Puritan and Whig pamphleteers contributed much. As one of those pamphleteers, first during the Puritan Rebellion and later revived by disciples during the Whig-Tory struggle for power, Milton spoke in organlike tones

50 *Joannis Miltoni Sententiæ Potestati Regiæ Adversantis Refutatio* (Londini, 1699), p. 1. Though Elys attacked Milton's character, he spent most of his time refuting his positions. Curiously, he possessed Quaker leanings.

51 Thomas Milles, for example, in his dedication to *The Happiness of those that Suffer for Righteousness Sake* (Oxford, 1701), cast aspersions on Milton's honesty and questioned his reading of history.

52 See Francis F. Madan, *op. cit.*, pp. 119–21.

and many increasingly gave heed to his voice. But the story of Milton's contribution to the struggle that ended with the triumph of Whig theory would not be complete without an epilogue relating the debate of the century to a much older conflict.

For the struggle over liberty of conscience and the power of kings in seventeenth-century England simply localized, very dramatically and for the first time with public opinion recognized as a main stake, a conflict in political theory stretching back through the medieval period to classical times. The Roman Jurists, for example, whom Sir Robert Filmer invoked, argued, as James I contended late in the sixteenth century, that the king was the sole *legis lator;* and among the early Church fathers St. Optatus recommended that good Christians, according to the injunction of St. Paul, offer up prayers for those in authority and conceived of the Church as an agent of empire with the king as the supreme head. Moreover, Gregory the Great, with David's obeisance to Saul as an example, argued that proper behavior for subjects was unquestioned submission and that to resist even an evil ruler was to resist God himself, Who had made the regal appointment. Such positions, it is true, failed to develop into a rounded political theory during the medieval period; but in the sixteenth century Jean Bodin in France developed a theory of state in the tradition of the Roman Jurists, and Martin Luther in Germany and William Tyndale in England expanded the reasoning of fathers like Gregory the Great. The seventeenth century inherited, as revealed in the political works of James I, the *Constitutions and Canons Ecclesiasticall* of 1640, secular writers like Sir Robert Filmer, and Tory divines, this tradition of long standing; and events logically shaped it into the doctrines of divine right and of passive obedience, into a concept of government which recognized the Church as an instrument of State and the king supreme over both.[53] Royalists of the Puritan Rebellion and of the Restoration, and Tories of the attempted Whig revolution and of the early days of the Settlement quite rightly contended, in view of the tradition they invoked, that the testimony of God, of nature, and of man upheld their theories of state.

But Puritans and Whigs also invoked a long political tradition—one even more venerable and more widely accepted in the West than

[53] For these and the subsequent generalities see R. W. Carlyle and A. J. Carlyle, *A History of Mediæval Political Theory in the West* (London, 1936), VI, 503–26. For details, see the earlier volumes.

that of their enemies. Beginning with Plato and Aristotle and continuing through Cicero, St. Thomas Aquinas, and Richard Hooker, to name but a few major witnesses, this tradition proclaimed the great principle of justice under the law—justice working itself out through the adherence of all men, kings and subjects alike, to the laws of the land, which reflected in part the laws of nature and of God. Through the medieval period this concept developed into a great rational scheme. Church and State, in theory at least, became two separate spheres, each with its own sovereignty but both harmoniously wedded to cover the whole life of man. In matters religious, the pope stood supreme; in affairs of state, the king ruled. But the king himself, either by written compact or by tacit agreement ratified by custom reaching beyond the memory of man, held his position by the consent of the people and could be relieved of his tenure if he failed to govern by law. *Lex facit regem.* The law makes the king; and the law itself sprang from community custom which received either open or silent assent of the people. Such concepts of government, made familiar to the seventeenth century by Puritans and Whigs, represented the main stream of political thought in the West, beside which the doctrines of absolutism, as expressed in the *Constitutions and Canons Ecclesiasticall* of 1640 and by Tory divines, appeared as alien intrusions. Both the Earl of Shaftesbury and Algernon Sidney recognized this when they referred to the novelty of divine right in comparison with the concept of justice under the law; and Milton himself, less than midway through his program for man and society, claimed that he had simply argued by the known rules of ancient liberty.

The Revolutionary Settlement and the Bill of Rights, then, based as they were upon the theory of compact and upon a separation of religious and secular powers, marked a return to principles of government which had animated European political thought from Plato to Hooker. The alien doctrine of absolute regal supremacy, which Henry VIII had initiated as a weapon to challenge the authority of Rome and which his successors had sharpened with official pronouncements, after serving to secure for England a national church and an independent state, so affected Englishmen's minds and hearts that it seriously threatened, for more than a century, the main European tradition. Neither Puritan arms nor polemics could dislodge it, and the Commonwealth failed. Only after the struggles over the succession of York and after James II had turned the weapon of regal supremacy against the Anglican Church did the irrationality of this doctrine, and its associated one of passive obedience, became painfully evident; only after bitter experience with a Catholic king did the desirability of government based on the great rational scheme inherited from classical and medieval times impress a majority in England. But the Revolutionary Settlement and the Bill of Rights, of course, signified more than a return to the main stream of European political thought. Pamphleteers of the Puritan Rebellion had stressed Christian liberty as vouchsafed by St. Paul—that is, the liberty of each individual to attain his own salvation—and had sharpened the old conflict over the power of kings by emphasizing the supremacy of the people in Commons. Furthermore, they had conceived of a dynamic state, rather than one of unified worship or belief, a state to which God would reveal more and more truth as men strove, through controversy and debate, to attain it. To such thought, modified by a half-century of discussion, the Revolutionary Settlement and the Bill of Rights gave recognition by proclaiming the supremacy of Parliament, toleration for the Dissent, and, by 1695, a free press; but even these achievements, as Puritans and Whigs knew, stood solidly upon the immemorial theory of compact and upon the medieval separation of Church and State. This return of the English government to classical[54] and medieval foundations, like the return of literature at this time to the forms and thought of the ancients, helped usher in the great Age of Reason.

To this return, to this triumph of the main European tradition modified by Puritan and Whig thought, Milton made a notable contribution through his revolutionary program for man and society. Recognized as a man of genius and learning even in his days of comparative neglect, he arose later in spirit to become through the efforts of an increasing number of disciples one of the most powerful spokesman for the Whig cause and a main source of party polemics. Not in vain had he doffed his singing robes and plunged into a sea of hoarse disputes; not in vain had he hoped that men would listen to the voice of reason and convincement and tread to the measure of his thought. So eloquent was his message of freedom and justice that people would

[54] Zera S. Fink, in *The Classical Republicans*, points out that Milton incorporated into his tracts the ancient theory of a mixed state and that this theory shaped thought at the time of the Settlement.

not willingly let his sentiments die; and if Whigs, for tactical reasons, sometimes revived his purely temporal arguments to answer Tory contentions, they knew, as their adaptations revealed, that he had contributed most significantly to the political life of England through his universal propositions on individual liberty and the nature of government—propositions which, because of his powerful rhetoric, echoed in the hearts of his countrymen until they became, as Royalists had feared, a part of the popular consciousness and an expression of the national mind. Perhaps not even John Locke, the traditional spokesman of Whig theory, more effectively shaped public opinion into eighteenth-century molds of self-evident political truth. For long before Locke famously justified the Glorious Revolution, Milton had earned the right to be called "that grand Whig."

INDEX

Chiefly names of authors, and shortened titles of primary works.